on track ...
Depeche Mode

every album, every song

Brian J Robb

sonicbondpublishing.com

Sonicbond Publishing Limited
www.sonicbondpublishing.co.uk
Email: info@sonicbondpublishing.co.uk

First Published in the United Kingdom 2023
First Published in the United States 2023

British Library Cataloguing in Publication Data:
A Catalogue record for this book is available from the British Library

Copyright Brian J Robb 2023

ISBN 978-1-78952-277-8

Typeset in ITC Garamond & ITC Avant Garde
Printed and bound in England

Graphic design and typesetting: Full Moon Media

Follow us on social media:
Twitter: https://twitter.com/SonicbondP
Instagram: https://www.instagram.com/sonicbondpublishing_/
Facebook: https://www.facebook.com/SonicbondPublishing/

Linktree QR code:

on track ...
Depeche Mode

every album, every song

Brian J Robb

sonicbondpublishing.com

on track ...

Depeche Mode

Contents

Introduction

It took less than a year for Depeche Mode to become properly famous. From the point where singer Dave Gahan joined Vince Clarke, Martin Gore and Andy Fletcher in spring 1980 and then chose the name 'Depeche Mode' from the title of a French fashion magazine (literally meaning 'fast fashion' or 'fashion dispatch') in September 1980, to their triumphant debut on *Top of the Pops* on 25 June 1981 with their second single 'New Life', their lives had changed immeasurably.

Depeche Mode had its origins in the dying days of punk and the musical aspirations of Vince Clarke – born in 1960, he was the oldest of the Mode men. After finishing high school, Clarke was an attendee at the Youth Fellowship meetings run in Basildon by Kevin Walker, who was three years older. Gospel songs had been part of the meetings, and Walker and Clarke formed a 'Simon and Garfunkel kind of duo' in 1976. They scored a handful of gigs, playing a 30–40-minute set of songs, but split up in 1979 when Clarke expressed an interest in moving into electronic music.

In May 1979, Clarke formed No Romance in China, with Pete Hobbs from Martin Gore's group Norman & the Worms and The Vandals' guitarist Sue Paget. At this point, Clarke was heavily influenced by The Cure. Clarke's Boys' Brigade pal Andy Fletcher – who was on the fringes of No Romance in China – admitted to being a reluctant musician, mainly involved for the social aspect. No Romance in China never progressed beyond playing in bedrooms and occasionally using Woodlands Youth Club in Basildon as a rehearsal space.

Clarke was constantly experimenting and was part of another loose group at this time, known as The Plan. Clarke and Robert Marlow got together just as enthusiasm for No Romance in China was petering out at the end of 1979 into early 1980, and Marlow's The Vandals (which included future Yazoo singer Alison Moyet) had wound up. Marlow was heavily influenced by John Foxx-era Ultravox and had got his hands on a Korg 700 synthesiser. In Jonathan Miller's Depeche Mode biography *Stripped*, Clarke remembered: 'Gary Numan did "Are 'Friends' Electric?", so suddenly we were all turned on to synthesisers. That was what sparked off The Plan.' Another musical inspiration for Clarke and Marlow was Orchestral Manoeuvres in the Dark.

Having worked any number of crappy jobs, Clarke finally saved up enough to buy a Kawai 100F portable synthesiser with a 37-note keyboard, which he described as 'cheap and cheerful'. Growing ever more serious about his musical interests, Clarke was developing his songwriting skills while most of the others were involved just for the fun of it, especially Fletcher. As the 1980s began, Clarke and Marlow went their separate ways, Clarke to Composition of Sound and Marlow to French Look (with Martin Gore, who'd picked up his own synthesiser, a Yamaha CS5).

Composition of Sound was the true forerunner to Depeche Mode, initially consisting of Clarke and Fletcher, with Gore joining later. In April 1980, both

French Look and Composition of Sound were rehearsing in adjoining rooms at Woodlands (Gore being the connection between both groups; Fletcher and Gore had also been in the same class at school). Marlow's group, including Gore, had been temporarily joined by aspiring singer Dave Gahan, who sang on an impromptu jam cover of David Bowie's 'Heroes', which captured the attention of the curious Composition of Sound duo.

According to Marlow, Clarke immediately recognised the potential in Gahan, later phoning him up to enlist him into Composition of Sound as a vocalist. Now a foursome (with Gore), Composition of Sound began regular rehearsals from spring 1980, with Clarke writing various songs that would form the backbone of early Depeche Mode material, among them 'Photographic'. The seriousness of intent and musical skill displayed by both Clarke and Gore quickly drove Composition of Sound to become a much more dedicated and near-professional outfit compared to the various earlier bands both had been involved in.

They finally graduated from playing in bedrooms, living rooms and rehearsal spaces to performing gigs in front of actual paying customers. The first gig Composition of Sound played with Dave Gahan on vocals, took place on 14 June 1980 at the Nicholas School discotheque; among the tracks performed were 'Ice Machine', 'Photographic' and the Gore composition 'Tora! Tora! Tora!', with Roxy Music and The Beach Boys covers mixed in.

In the summer of 1980, Clarke encouraged the other band members to produce a demo tape that he could take out to record companies, consisting of the songs 'Ice Machine', 'Photographic' and 'Radio News' (a Numan-like track played during early concerts, but unreleased commercially), all written by Clarke. Also, a favourite of early gigs was 'Television Set', which never made any Depeche Mode recording as it had been written by Jason Knott rather than Clarke. The Human League-like 'Tomorrow's Dance' was another early live favourite, penned by Clarke, that also remained unreleased. Similarly, 'Reason Man' was another live track (with an opening uncannily like the *Doctor Who* theme) that didn't make their first album, as was 'Addiction' (aka 'Closer All the Time' or 'Ghost of Modern Time') which had something of Clarke's later Yazoo about it.

The resulting demo tape was taken to Beggars Banquet, Rough Trade and – finally – Mute Records. Mute's Daniel Miller first dismissed Composition of Sound as 'fake New Romantics', according to a 2005 issue of *Mojo* magazine. Miller re-encountered the band – by now called Depeche Mode – at their pivotal gig on 12 November 1980 (supporting Mute's own Fad Gadget) at The Bridge House in London's Canning Town, where he was much more impressed by their live sound and immediately signed the band. Almost as impressive to Miller was the crowd's reaction: '[The band] clicked immediately. The people were dancing and didn't even look at the band. Dave was still very shy. He stood very still, sang the lyrics and didn't move an inch, and yet, the spark flew over.' Miller later recalled that the band seemed musically mature from the start. 'They were great pop songs,' he told *Electronic Beats*. 'They were really well structured and really well arranged, based on just a drum machine and three monophonic synthesizers. The melodies, the counter-melodies to the vocals were great. It was kind of perfect, almost.'

Speaking of the handshake deal with Mute many years later, Andy Fletcher wryly reflected (in the 2006 *Speak & Spell* 'making of' video): 'We were working-class kids from Basildon. We didn't have much money, so we went for the guy who was offering us no money just because we trusted him and we liked the music on his label.'

Depeche Mode's first formal studio recording was 'Photographic' for the Some Bizzare [sic] compilation album (which also included tracks from The The, Soft Cell and Blancmange, among others) released in December 1980. Around the same time, the band were in the studio with Daniel Miller starting work on what would ultimately become their debut album, *Speak & Spell*.

From small acorns...

Little could anyone involved in 1980 have known that Depeche Mode would become a world-bestriding behemoth, a stadium-playing band inducted into the Rock and Roll Hall of Fame 40 years later. Track by track, this is the five-decade story of Depeche Mode...

Speak & Spell (1981)

Personnel:
Dave Gahan: lead vocals
Martin Gore: keyboards, backing vocals, lead vocals on 'Any Second Now
(Voices)'
Andy Fletcher: keyboards, backing vocals
Vince Clarke: keyboards, programming, backing vocals
Recorded at Blackwing Studios, London, December 1980 to August 1981
Producer: Depeche Mode, Daniel Miller
All tracks written by Vince Clarke, except 'Tora! Tora! Tora' and 'Big Muff',
written by Martin Gore
UK release date: 6 November 1981 (delayed from 5 October 1981). US release
date: 11 November 1981. Label: Mute
Running time: 44:58
Highest chart places: UK: 10; US: 192; Germany: 49; New Zealand: 45; Sweden: 21.

Depeche Mode – most of whom still looked like the schoolkids they'd been
until very recently – gathered at Tape One Studios in London's East End with
Mute's Daniel Miller in December 1980 to embark upon the first in a series of
professional recording sessions. The band had no formal contract with Miller,
but he'd agreed to release their debut single and all concerned would see
where things went from there. There was also interest from DJ and promoter
Stephen 'Stevo' Pearce, who was compiling a 'futurist' sampler album entitled
Some Bizzare [sic]. Miller agreed to record 'Photographic' (a very different
version to that on *Speak & Spell*) for Stevo's release, selecting 'Dreaming Of
Me' to be the first official Depeche Mode single. The group picked their live
standard 'Ice Machine' for the B-side.

   As an electronic band, Depeche Mode travelled light, which had been
incredibly useful when gigging around venues in Southend and London. They
turned up at the studio, carting their three cheap synths and a drum machine.
Miller supplied his own ARP 6000 synth, which immediately captured Vince
Clarke's attention when he discovered that it was programmable, meaning
not every note had to be played live. Miller had a musical model he wanted
Depeche Mode to follow, and Vince Clarke seemed to be in tune with this.
Earlier, Miller had created a non-existent electronic group called The Silicon
Teens with Fad Gadget frontman Frank Tovey. They performed electronic
cover versions of old rock and pop staples. It was Miller's belief that all an
early 1980s electronic-driven band needed to succeed were a handful of
catchy pop tunes. Vince Clarke looked like the man to supply them, and
Depeche Mode could have been the Silicon Teens made flesh.

   Recording sessions for what would become Depeche Mode's debut album
Speak & Spell were scheduled around the day jobs that several band members
continued to hold. Martin Gore worked as a cashier at the NatWest Bank
branch in Fenchurch Street, while Andy Fletcher also worked in finance at

Sun Life Insurance in the City of London. Eighteen-year-old Dave Gahan was still a student at Southend Technical College with occasional work as a window dresser in London stores. Only odd-job man Vince Clarke was free – and, more importantly, driven – to work on the band's music more or less full-time, writing the majority of the songs – music and lyrics.

Across a two-day session, this time at Blackwing Studios (housed in a former church in Southwark), the band recorded 'Dreaming Of Me' and 'Ice Machine'. Clarke was like a sponge, soaking up studio and musical know-how and 'electrickery' from the decade-older Miller. Gahan, Gore and Fletcher only joined these sessions in the evenings. After a day spent hanging clothes on showroom dummies, Gahan belted out the vocals for both tracks having sung them many times during the early live gigs of Composition of Sound and Depeche Mode. These initial recordings would lead to Seymour Stein of America's Sire Records signing them for distribution in the US.

The band were back in the same studio in the summer of 1981 following the initial chart success of 'Dreaming Of Me', which had won them some Radio 1 airplay and music press attention. Still gigging on occasional weekends and with two-thirds of the band still working during the day, the structure of the December 1980 recordings was replicated. Miller continued to instruct Clarke in getting the most out of the band's futuristic instruments and the studio equipment; Clarke had the run of Blackwing's 16-track studio. No vocals could be laid down until Gahan made his way from Southend Technical College to London and then down to Southwark.

With Clarke, Miller had serendipitously stumbled across a nascent songwriter who could effectively combine catchy pop tunes with electronic instruments. Breakthrough track 'New Life' and third single 'Just Can't Get Enough' were simply good songs with audience-pleasing hooks. Elsewhere on *Speak & Spell*, 'What's Your Name?' and 'I Sometimes Wish I Was Dead' (despite its ominous title) sounded like pop songs from the 1960s in the style of The Beatles reconfigured for the new electronic instruments of the 1980s. They had straightforward storytelling lyrics, but much of Clarke's lyrical output was lexical nonsense that simply sounded good alongside the tune. Gore said of Clarke's songwriting: 'He looks for a melody, then finds words that rhyme,' while Clarke admitted, 'There were no messages in the songs at all. They were very stupid lyrics...'

Having reached number 11 in the UK Singles charts with 'New Life' and played *Top of the Pops* repeatedly, Fletcher and Gore finally felt secure enough with their new 'pop star' status to quit their day jobs. Gahan joined them, walking out on his art course – pop stardom awaited and Depeche Mode were ready. Then songwriter Vince Clarke decided to quit the band ...

'New Life' 3:43
Although not the band's first single release (that was 'Dreaming Of Me'), it was 'New Life' that effectively launched Depeche Mode into the public

consciousness. It, therefore, made perfect sense for this widely-heard track to be the opener for the band's debut album. It has the perfect mix of the contemporary synth sounds of 1981 with the nonsensical lyrics that were a big part of the New Romantic movement, which Depeche Mode would reluctantly find themselves on the fringes of.

It's clear from the lyrics that songwriter Vince Clarke was more concerned with the sounds of the words than their inherent meaning. A perfect three (or so) minute pop song, the track starts slowly, almost in a stately manner, with gently tapped keyboards. It's 23 seconds before the pace picks up and the drum machine kicks in, followed by Gahan's vocals at the 35-second mark. Within just half a minute or so, Depeche Mode had arrived.

The song is unconventionally structured, with the vocals against backbeat break coming at just under the two-minute mark and running longer than most listeners probably expected, followed by the chanting ('Aaahhhh') climax starting at three minutes, in which all four members participate. It's a song that reeks of youth and the excitement of being in a band in the early 1980s.

Released on 13 June 1981, 'New Life' enjoyed a full 15 weeks on the UK charts, debuting at number 55 (their first single, 'Dreaming Of Me', had peaked at number 57, so this was progress). It climbed steadily over the weeks as the song won more airplay, hitting the high point of number 11. 'New Life' couldn't crack the Top 10, but it did sell in excess of 500,000 copies and led to the new-to-fame band performing three times on *Top of the Pops* (25 June, 15 July and 29 July, with the new pop stars miming for all they were worth).

Mute hadn't bothered paying for a music video, and the immediate impact of 'New Life' came as a surprise to all involved. The band also won their first *Smash Hits* cover, the fresh-faced, clean-cut quartet appearing on the 9–22 July 1981 edition. *Hot Press* dubbed the track 'honest synthpop', while *Sounds* hailed it as a 'tinkly bonk excursion'. 'New Life' was a staple of the live set for a good few years, right up to 1985. In the US, 'New Life' peaked at number 29 on the *Billboard* Dance Club Songs Chart at the end of August 1981, and stayed around for 12 weeks. As a calling card, it'd be hard to beat 'New Life', both thematically and musically, to mark the arrival of Depeche Mode.

'I Sometimes Wish I Was Dead' 2:16

The shortest track on *Speak & Spell*, this strangely titled song is one of several early Mode tracks that sound like 1960s pop songs, bubblegum pop for the electronic era. Like several of the tracks on *Speak & Spell*, this opens with an almost twee synth riff which kicks off into something deeper when the rhythms hit. Vocal harmonies abound, a style that runs through much of the album. It was tracks like this that led *Record Mirror* to dub the album as 'bubbly and brief, like the best pop should be'. Self-aware – the lyrics reference the 'New sounds all around' – Clarke appears to be exploring dancing and teen relationships, just the kind of things going on in the band's lives. Ultimately, this is a form of 'modern love' and the music of Depeche Mode is central to it. 'I Sometimes Wish I Was Dead' was released as a flexi-single with *Flexipop!* magazine #11, which had Dave Gahan smiling while lying in a coffin (curiously prefiguring his later on-tour antics). The track on the flexi-disc release was slightly mistitled as 'Sometimes I Wish I Was Dead' and it ran for 2:12. The intro is very different, but the rest is much as on the album, with slight changes to the middle harmonies and the lengthy outro.

'Puppets' 3:55

Sometimes referred to by Gahan during early live performances as 'Operator', 'Puppets' is the first track on *Speak & Spell* to hint at the darkness that Depeche Mode would later specialise in. From the start it's edgy and slower than the two opening numbers, taking a turn for the melancholic. The lyrics fulfil the promise of the title, suggesting a relationship of dominance: 'You think you're in control... I'll be your operator, baby/I'm in control'. It's not Clarke's usual lightweight poppy material, a move away from bubblegum electronica and a dive into Kraftwerk territory. Lyrically, 'Puppets' prefigures some of the later Mode tracks written by Martin Gore in his perverse pomp.

The synths on 'Puppets' may be light, but the lyrics are heavy-duty, backed by a tension-inducing synth-violin crescendo that wouldn't be out of place on the soundtrack of a VHS rental horror flick of the time. The song is in the voice of a controlling partner in a relationship, with Gahan's near-whispering delivery of the subversive lyrics adding to its edginess. Alternatively, it could be about something totally different. According to Clarke's one-time girlfriend Deb Danahay: '['Puppets'] sounded like a love song, but was written about drugs.' It's a stark track, steeped in a sinister ambience offset against the upbeat lead synth line. The insistent rhythm propels the track to its downbeat drawn-out conclusion.

'Boys Say Go!' 3:03

Vince Clarke wrote perfect pop songs for Depeche Mode's early output, many of them straightforward love songs, often reflecting the teenage longings of the not long out of school band members themselves and those of their record-buying audience. 'Just Can't Get Enough' is the pre-eminent example. Clarke was not only the most musically and lyrically sophisticated member of the group's original line-up, he was also the most commercially minded. He learned from Daniel Miller how to 'produce' music, but he was also learning how to 'sell' music to the widest audience.

It's clear that early synth-pop in 1980–81 had a big gay appeal. Ambiguous sexuality was everywhere, from Gary Numan (was he a robot?) to Annie Lennox (was she a he?), and Clarke used two songs on *Speak & Spell* to appeal to that community: 'Boys Say Go!' and 'What's Your Name?' The ambiguous sexuality inherent in so much pop music was much more to the fore in the 1980s than it had ever been (with an exception in the 1970s for the unique David Bowie). It was in this atmosphere that 'Boys Say Go!' landed, a blast of disco-infused homoerotic tunefulness launched by a football terrace chant. Lyrics like 'Take me for a ride' would recur in later post-Clarke songs (as in 'Never Let Me Down Again'), but it is the 'Boys meet, boys get together/Boys meet, boys live forever' refrain that seems to mark out the song's sexual territory and energy. Or maybe, as the band once claimed, it's simply a song about going out for a few beers with the lads.

'Nodisco' 4:11
Despite all the evidence to the contrary, notably 'Big Muff' and 'Boys Say Go!', Depeche Mode claimed not to be inspired by 1970s disco music. 'Nodisco' goes out of its way, musically and lyrically, not to emulate 1970s Donna Summer ('I Feel Love', 1977). It's Kraftwerk and Gary Numan through and through, which makes it all the funnier that the track seems to be about someone indulging in 1970s John Travolta *Saturday Night Fever*-style 'disco dancing' at a new wave club like The Blitz: 'Sometimes when I wonder if you're taking a chance/This ain't no disco/And you know how to dance'. Dancing to synth-pop often meant making out like a robot. Dave Gahan was a reticent dancer during Depeche Mode's earliest performances, often simply swaying from side to side, unlike his later 'Iggy Pop meets Mick Jagger' rock god persona.

'Nodisco' is easily the prime offender in Vince Clarke's 'nonsense' approach to lyrics. It's doubtful even he knows what he meant at the time, but it sounded good. The driving, electronic beat is present, but over the top is a neat synth line that leads into the kind of darker, heavier tone of the likes of 'Photographic' or 'Puppets' but without the lyrical support needed. The middle instrumental section suggests where the track could have gone, but in the end, it's let down by lyrics like 'Baby don't you let go' and 'There's a thousand watts in you'.

'What's Your Name?' 2:41
Another fine example of 1960s pop filtered through 1980s electronica, 'What's Your Name?' is a trifling track that Martin Gore would go on to emulate on Depeche Mode's second album *A Broken Frame*. Originally titled 'Pretty Boy', this is the second gay-sounding track on *Speak & Spell*, a simple (musically and lyrically) love song with a boy seemingly singing about another boy. 'All the boys, we got to get together/All the boys together we can stand' sound like rejected lines from 'Boys Say Go!', while the harmonic chants are back. Even the spelling out of the word 'pretty' by Gore sounds straight out of a 1960s bubblegum track, while the climactic cheer is a second-hand lift from 'New Life'. Mode legend has it that Vince Clarke wrote the song in response to him being misquoted in a newspaper, suggesting that 'good-looking' bands tended to prosper. There's a reason

that both Gore and Andy Fletcher singled out 'What's Your Name?' as their least favourite song on an instalment of Channel 4 show *Popworld* in 2005. Accordingly, it is one of the band's least performed live songs, last heard on a stage back in 1982 as part of the See You Tour.

'Photographic' 4:44

Side Two opens with one of early Depeche Mode's strongest cuts. It's longer, with a nice rhythmic build before the vocals begin. The simple chorus – 'I take pictures/photographic pictures' and the chant-like 'Bright light/Dark room' – is perfect and works on repetition to give the song structure. Varying interpretations have been given to Clarke's (as usual) impenetrable lyrics. The song could be about a stalker, relentlessly photographing his object of sexual interest, or (as one interpretation has it) it could be about a crime scene photographer, photographing a murder victim who is also his girlfriend. The opening lyrics are very Numan-like, focusing on synth-pop obsessions such as lights, eyes, maps and 'programs'. More simply, 'The years I spend thinking/ of a moment we both knew' might simply be of a nostalgic nature, as a man studies a photograph of a former girlfriend.

The song was subject to multiple revisions during its evolution and it is one of the few early songs for which the evidence of this evolution is available. Written by Clarke, he first prepared a 'bedroom' demo in early summer 1980 when the band went by Composition of Sound (the other demos were 'Television Set' and two unidentified tracks, one John Foxx-like possibly called 'Sunday Morning' and an instrumental that sounds like the theme tune for a 1970s sci-fi show). The 'Photographic' demo is a faster take, more propulsive and almost punk-like. The Clarke vocal is more declarative, while the synthesiser instrumentation is rougher. Later that summer, another demo was recorded, this time with Dave Gahan on vocals. The tempo slowed down, much more in keeping with the final track, while Gahan nails the vocal delivery he'd later use. There is, however, an annoying click-like drum sound used throughout (wisely later abandoned). The first professional recording of the song (in November 1980) was the even darker version released on the *Some Bizzare* [sic] album, which featured a mid-point tempo between the fast first demo and the slower finished track. It's a more haunting take on the track that opens Side Two of *Speak & Spell*.

'Tora! Tora! Tora!' 4:34

The title comes from the code signal used by the Japanese bombers that attacked Pearl Harbor on 7 December 1942, bringing the United States into the Second World War. It was also the title of the 1970s movie that chronicled the events surrounding the attack, directed by Richard Fleischer and featuring a mix of American and Japanese actors. In Japanese, the two-syllable word 'tora' means 'tiger' and was used to signify that complete surprise had been achieved in the attack on America.

As the first of two tracks on *Speak & Spell* written by Martin Gore, 'Tora! Tora! Tora!' is an outlier. It's much slower and deliberate than many of the others, with a ponderous keyboard section leading up to the tune proper kicking in, along with faster rhythm backing. Gahan's vocals are equally ponderous, dragging out the final syllable of each line. Despite that, there is an urgency to the later moments, bringing some life to proceedings. So is the song about the events of Pearl Harbor or about the making of the film? The line 'I played an American' suggests the latter, but there is also an analogy between love and war: 'They were raining from the sky/exploding in my heart' could be read as being about bombs, or about the process of falling in love. Continuing in that vein, 'you took my love then died that day' could suggest the end of an affair, or the death of a loved one. There is a fan theory that the theme of suicide runs through many of the songs on *Speak & Spell*, which just goes to prove you can interpret these early lyrics any way that takes your fancy!

'Big Muff' 4:20
Gore's second song is an instrumental, something featured on many early synth-pop albums, but Depeche Mode stuck with the tradition longer than most. The title, while sounding rude, is actually named after a popular American-made distortion effects pedal. Despite being a take on a form of electro-disco, 'Big Muff' is curiously engaging, especially to anyone whose musical tastes were shaped in the late 1970s or early 1980s. It's the band playing around with what can be done with the new technology, Geoff Love style, aping an older form of music using their new instruments. The track was used as introduction music for several of the band's earliest concerts in 1980 and it remained a part of their live set right through to the *Construction Time Again* era of 1983–84. Early on, the live version was far rougher than the polished recording on *Speak & Spell*.

'Any Second Now (Voices)' 2:35
Another movie-inspired song (*Any Second Now* was a 1969 film starring Stewart Granger, about a photographer who plots to kill his wife – hey, maybe that's what 'Photographic' was about!). It's a touching track, with the first example of Martin Gore on vocals. The lyrics are film-related – 'the same film' and 'vivid pictures' – but the song appears to be about the fear and doubts involved in early intimacy at the beginning of a relationship: 'she remembered all the shadows and the doubts'. There are 'warnings' and 'messages', and a moment that 'almost slips away', but everything ends well 'as you touch my hand'. It feels like a song that has been enhanced by Gore's lighter vocal, and it'd be a trick the band would continue to deploy, adding some more whimsical, wistful and alternative vocal takes to those generally offered by Gahan, especially as Gore's Depeche Mode songs became darker over time.

'Just Can't Get Enough' 3:40

Speak & Spell concludes with the band's triumphant third single release of 1981: 'Just Can't Get Enough'. While 'Dreaming Of Me' had only reached a few listeners, 'New Life' had essentially functioned as the launch pad for Depeche Mode in the pop consciousness. This track was laid down as part of the summer 1981 recordings at Blackwing that produced *Speak & Spell*. It was the final track written by Vince Clarke, and it was the first track that had a music video made to promote it. As a result, 'Just Can't Get Enough' became Depeche Mode's first Top 10 hit single upon release in September 1981, reaching a high point of number eight on the UK Singles Chart. This track was also the band's first single release in the US, hitting number 26 on the Hot Dance Club Play section of the *Billboard* US chart.

'Just Can't Get Enough' is one of a handful of Depeche Mode tracks to have stood the test of time as part of their live sets, surviving right through to the Memento Mori Tour of 2023–24.

The lyrics are catchy, with Clarke very much in 1960s pop romance mode. It has all the vital elements of early Depeche Mode – an earworm synth line, a chanting chorus that demands you sing along and a structure that is very easy to catch on to. The meaning of the lyrics is never in doubt either, unlike much of the rest of Clarke's lyrical efforts.

The video, directed by Clive Richardson and clearly shot on the cheap, featured the band – all clad in leather, including Fletch sporting an ill-advised leather cap – performing, while a handful of very 1980s-looking models dance around. A reluctant-looking Clarke is featured, while there is a great emphasis on fingers on keyboards, as if that was the key to this weird new future sound. Intercut with the performance footage were shots of the boys and girls horsing around London's South Bank and sitting in a cafe, pretending (badly) to sing the chorus.

Hugely popular, 'Just Can't Get Enough' marked the true arrival of Depeche Mode as the avatars of electro-pop (even more than the new wave 'New Life' had). It was simply a great pop song realised with new instrumentation. It also enjoyed a huge afterlife, being sampled in all sorts of movies, television episodes and adverts. As early as 1982, the track was used on the romantic comedy film *Summer Lovers*, and it went on from there taking in 1998 romantic comedy *The Wedding Singer* and 2007 British comedy *Son Of Rambow* along the way, among many others. Multiple television episodes featured the track, including instalments of *American Horror Story* and Philip K. Dick's *Electric Dreams*, as well as episodes of *Masters Of Sex*, *Gossip Girl* and *The Comeback*. Commercials for Samsung, Churchill Insurance, American retail stores Target, Walmart and Staples, and several others have used 'Just Can't Get Enough', relying upon its instant recognition for effect. It's also the track from *Speak & Spell* performed live the most often, a total of 625 times from 1980 through to the first leg of 2023's Memento Mori Tour.

Related Tracks
'Dreaming Of Me' 3:42
The first track ever released (on 20 February 1981) by Depeche Mode as a single didn't even make it on to *Speak & Spell*, largely due to its poor performance on the UK Singles Chart, reaching number 57 (it bizarrely performed better in the US on import, reaching number 47 and staying in the *Billboard* Dance Club Songs Chart for 17 weeks). There are lyrical pre-echoes of 'New Life', with its concerns with films and filming, as well as faces fusing, while the harmonies also feel like a dry run for the end of 'New Life'. Gahan's vocals are less polished and overall, the track is less commercially catchy than 'New Life', but it's basically fine early synth-pop. The song had been retired from the band's live set by 1983. Reviewing a 16 February 1981 gig at Cabaret Futura, *Smash Hits* dubbed 'Dreaming Of Me' as 'simply wonderful... tasteful and tuneful, danceable and intelligent. It deserves to be utterly huge.' It wasn't, but it is well-liked by Mode fans who attempted to get the song back in the UK charts for its 30th anniversary. That didn't work in the UK, but it did hit number 45 in Germany.

'Ice Machine' 3:53
Released as the B-side to 'Dreaming Of Me', 'Ice Machine' hints at the darker side of Depeche Mode, beyond the usual synth-pop of Vince Clarke. Like 'Dreaming Of Me', this early track didn't find a slot on *Speak & Spell*, although it was a signpost to the future direction the band would take after Clarke's departure. There's more than a hint of Kraftwerk in 'Ice Machine', but the lyrics are the usual New Romantic hints at meaning that might not actually be there at all. As a package, the 'Dreaming Of Me'/'Ice Machine' single gave early adopters a taste of the sound of the future.

'Shout!' 3:46
Released as the B-side to debut single 'New Life', 'Shout' is a rather enigmatic track. It's the perfect mix of Clarke's dual lyrical modes. There's cod-Beatles lines like 'I wanna hold your hand/We've got to get it right' and his trademark film and image-obsessed obscurantism like 'She was silent trying to be/like the girl who acted on the TV' or 'Dangerous and beautiful the/Radio transmissions that I have to know'. Musically, 'Shout' is more interesting, as it prioritises its air raid siren sounds over the vocal which is kicked into the background. It's a song that plays surprisingly well live, as revealed in Gahan's performances during the Hamburg dates of 1984. By then, Alan Wilder had joined and their musical style had matured, but 'Shout' seemed to fit right in, with the vocal much higher in the mix as required in a live performance. There's plenty of echo and verve given to the live version and it plays well with the audience, with a few trademark 1984-era Depeche Mode metal clangs thrown in for good measure. It just shows how, when approached right, the weakest recorded material can be reimagined as a live performance banger.

'Any Second Now' 3:08

Instrumental version of the song featured on the album that was released as the B-side to 'Just Can't Get Enough', making it the first instrumental ever released by the band.

A Broken Frame (1982)

Personnel:
Dave Gahan: lead vocals
Martin Gore: keyboards, backing vocals, additional vocals on 'The Meaning Of Love' and 'Shouldn't Have Done That'
Andy Fletcher: keyboards, backing vocals
Recorded at Blackwing Studios, London, December 1981 to July 1982
Producer: Daniel Miller, Depeche Mode
All tracks written by Martin Gore
Released: 27 September 1982. Label: Mute
Running time: 40:55
Highest chart placings: UK: 8; US: 177; Germany: 56; New Zealand: 43; Sweden: 22.

Just as Depeche Mode – a band mostly consisting of teenagers – hit the big time in 1981 with two hit singles and a strong debut album with *Speak & Spell*, they lost their main creative figure. Of all four band members, Vince Clarke was the most advanced, musically speaking. He was slightly older and had written the bulk of the songs on *Speak & Spell* (Martin Gore had contributed two, one of which was an instrumental). Just as their success had been achieved, it seemed to the remaining three members that it was about to be all over already.

Clarke had quit as he felt out of step with the rest of the group. He didn't enjoy being in the spotlight the way Gahan did, and he felt he was carrying too much of the creative weight of Depeche Mode while still being considered as just one-quarter of the overall set-up. It was the need to promote Depeche Mode's music as 'product' that was the cumulative 'final straw' for Clarke. He hated all the television appearances, especially on kids' television shows (and the band did a lot of those in the early days, as they were one of the few outlets on UK television for pop music). Clarke didn't particularly want to be on the cover of *Smash Hits*. The withdrawal of Clarke became clear to Mute's Daniel Miller during their mini-tour in advance of the release of *Speak & Spell*, and when they got back to Britain, Clarke made it official: he was quitting Depeche Mode. He'd continue to participate in the UK tour to support the album, but after that, he'd officially announce his departure.

For a synth-pop outfit, Depeche Mode had always been a strong live band. Although early on, they were four guys standing shyly behind keyboards, and Dave Gahan was a million miles from the rock god persona he'd later adopt, they nonetheless made an impression. It was their live performance and their effect on the audience that had caught the interest of both Mute's Miller and Sire Record's Seymour Stein. In between the release of the first singles, they continued to be a strong presence on the live circuit across the UK and began to make inroads in Europe. Gahan would gradually overcome any early reticence to become the frontman the band needed, a very human touch delivering the vocals that brought their unique brand of synth-pop to life. As Barney Hoskins noted in *NME*, on tour, the band were 'received with nothing short of rapture'.

Another problem for Clarke was the lack of interest from his band colleagues in the nuts and bolts of the technology that brought their sound to fruition. None of the rest of the band seemed interested in new developments in synthesiser technology or in how that influenced their developing sound. When they began discussing the always tricky second album, the consensus seemed to be to just do another *Speak & Spell*, and this didn't satisfy Clarke's musical ambitions. At the age of 21, he walked out on a band that was just starting to make an impression, eventually to pursue his own musical destiny in Yazoo (with Basildon's Alison Moyet; Clarke had offered Yazoo's debut track 'Only You' to Depeche Mode, but the band turned it down) and The Assembly, before landing as part of the two-man Erasure with Andy Bell.

The departure of Clarke from Depeche Mode – not exactly a shock, but not entirely expected either – saw the other members forced to take the prospect of turning what might have seemed like a teenage lark into a more lasting proposition. As a result, the division of responsibilities between Gahan, Gore and Fletcher became more organised and professional. The largely non-musical Fletcher stepped up to work closely with Daniel Miller on the management of the band, financially and creatively (a role Clarke had previously shouldered), while Gore stepped in as the main (and, at this point, only) songwriter – switching from Clarke's major (upbeat) key to his (mostly) minor – with Gahan continuing as the vocalist and frontman. Miller noted that the possibility of calling it a day and Depeche Mode splitting up was never even entertained: the lads had begun to enjoy their new pop star lifestyle too much (something Clarke certainly didn't share). Gahan, speaking to *Sounds* in 1982, said: 'I think Vince was maybe a bit surprised at how we reacted, but we were fairly prepared.'

For touring purposes, Clarke was quickly replaced. The band needed a fourth member for their two nights playing in New York in January 1982. A small ad placed in *Melody Maker* that read 'Name band require synthesizer player, must be under 21' attracted a good number of responses (it appeared in the same issue of *Melody Maker* that reported on Clarke's departure, so anyone could figure out who the 'name band' were). Out of those auditioned, one applicant stood above the rest: Alan Wilder. He wasn't 'under 21' being over 22 (born in 1959, unlike the other 1960s kids), but he had the performing chops they needed. Wilder was very different to the other Depeche Mode members, being older, middle class, and not only musically gifted but professionally trained.

Joining a 'pop group' had long been Wilder's ambition since his days in the 1970s as a fan of Marc Bolan and David Bowie. He'd enjoyed a short time in a briefly lived group, The Dragons, and a couple of other groups that went nowhere fast. Although he found Mode's early efforts 'naive-sounding', he nonetheless felt there was 'something interesting' in what the group were trying to achieve. He was initially hired as a tour-only support musician, and the other Mode men made it clear they weren't looking for a permanent fourth member. Wilder felt he had something to contribute, but he'd have to bide his time.

Going into the studio in November 1981 to begin recording their second album, *A Broken Frame*, Depeche Mode were a threesome. Initially, they simply set out to create a new single, thereby giving Gore time to work up enough material for a full album. The result was 'See You', an old Gore song that predated Depeche Mode, previously performed by Gore's Norman & the Worms. The original was a bit basic and needed working up by Gore and Miller into something more Mode-like.

Gore's developing songwriting was heavily influenced by his split from girlfriend Anne Swindell. She had accompanied the band on tour and had been part of the formation of the Depeche Mode Information Service with Gahan's girlfriend (and later wife) Jo Fox and Clarke's girlfriend, Deb Danahay. The relationship between Gore and Swindell had been troubled for a while, with Gore defining Swindell as a 'devout Christian', while he'd moved on from his earlier religious convictions and was using the new freedom provided by Depeche Mode to explore other areas of his personality. This would all feed into his songwriting, both on *A Broken Frame* and beyond.

That always tricky second album was made more so due to the absence of Clarke. Critical response saw the result as decent enough, if a little bland (certainly in comparison to Yazoo's output). *Record Mirror* dubbed the band's sophomore effort 'predictable, safe, and a trifle trying... perhaps they need to stop being so consistently nice', while *Sounds* criticised the 'use of synthesised sounds to the exclusion of almost everything else'. Over time, Depeche Mode would address both those criticisms, changing the nature of their sound and of their selves.

In the studio, Depeche Mode were a three-piece outfit, while on the road, they were a quartet with Alan Wilder. This was not a situation that could last long, and the next drama in the nascent band would come when Wilder demanded more input into the group's creative future.

'Leave In Silence', 4:51
The third single from *A Broken Frame* (16 August 1982), 'Leave In Silence' (originally titled 'The Big Drop') was seen as such a strong marker of their future direction that it became the opening track on their second album. The song is the culmination of Martin Gore's emotional break-up with Anne Swindell that informed several tracks as it deals quite expressly with the end of a romance. Gore's lyrics chronicled repeated arguments: 'We've been running around in circles all year/Doing this and that and getting nowhere... This will be the last time/I think I said that last time'.

The music video by Julien Temple took a literal approach, featuring the band smashing household items on a *Generation Game*-style moving conveyor belt. As with 'The Meaning Of Love', it was so disliked by the band that it was left off the 1985 VHS video collection *Some Great Videos*. Wilder described Temple's trio of videos as 'a collective disaster'. Their more relaxed performance on *Top of the Pops* on 2 September 1982 propelled the single to number 21 before it reached its high point of number 18.

Although the track was the band's fifth Top 20 hit in a row, it suggested diminishing returns as it peaked lower than any single (apart from 'Dreaming Of Me'). Despite that, in 2017, *Billboard* listed 'Leave In Silence' as the number one 'most underrated' Depeche Mode single. Describing it as 'a shimmering and simmering synth-pop mini-epic whose brilliance comes in its relative restraint', critic Andrew Unterberger noted that 'keys sparkle and then dissipate, built up tension dissolves into negative space, the title is practically whispered at the chorus climax'. Dubbing the track a 'break-up ballad' that sneaks out the back door rather than storming out the front, *Billboard* recognised in 'Leave In Silence' the 'instrumental and emotional complexity' the band would later become better known for. The use of a breaking glass sound on the track hints at the 'found sounds' that the band would later use. Their future is here, buried in this track, waiting to be born.

'My Secret Garden' 4:46

The first of several slower, contemplative and emotional tracks, 'My Secret Garden' is open to a variety of interpretations. From the nursery rhyme, lullaby-like, chiming opening, the track kicks into a faster, more insistent sound yet retains some of that sonic naivety. It's obviously about the discovery of a 'secret', but the exact nature of that secret is up to the listener. There's a sense of adult disapproval ('She'll catch me if she can'), but also children playing 'in among the flowers', suggesting an adolescent romance. The second half of the track looks forward musically to *Construction Time Again*, while retaining the childish sound it began with. The melancholic lyrics are juxtaposed against the upbeat sound, exploring a lost innocence, or (in light of Gore's romantic troubles) the end of an intimate relationship, destroyed by someone keeping a secret: 'Play the fool/Act so cruel'. In its simplicity, 'My Secret Garden' fits with the rest of *A Broken Frame*, but in its lyrical concerns, it seems to point towards some of Gore's later concerns expressed in tracks like 'A Question Of Lust', 'Waiting For The Night' and 'When The Body Speaks'. In the course of 1981 and into 1982, the members of Depeche Mode had lost their own innocence, their own 'secret garden'. They would fight in future to preserve both their individual identities and their privacy.

'Monument' 3:15

An oddly naive song, 'Monument' echoes 'My Secret Garden' in its simplicity (of lyrics and musically), while also looking forward to the sounds and themes that would be explored on the more mature *Construction Time Again*. It's a very short track driven by its rhythm, and while it appears to be about building an actual monument, perhaps Gore was actually thinking of the work required to sustain a relationship: 'We laid the foundations down/It didn't take long before/They came back tumbling down'. This and the previous track showed the ambition of Gore's songwriting even if, at this stage the group weren't quite able to realise the sound or lyrical complexity they were beginning to reach for. Mode-focused website Almost Predictable Almost described 'Monument' as 'a terrific song, despite the occasional lyrical oddity'.

'Nothing To Fear' 4:18
It was an interesting move to put an instrumental on Side One of the new album. While early live shows opened with a version of 'Oberkorn (It's A Small Town)', Dave Gahan was provided with a short break in the middle of the set when the others performed 'Nothing To Fear'. It would be the last instrumental featured as an album track for a while (the Wilder-Gore instrumental composition 'The Great Outdoors' formed the B-side to the *Construction Time Again* single 'Get The Balance Right!'). In 2013, speaking to *Electronic Beats*, Daniel Miller recalled the origin of the title: 'I remember Martin [Gore] was reading some weird book during the making of the record, a book of prophecies or something and he looked up his birth date and it said, "Nothing to fear." So that actually ended up being a track title, and it made him very optimistic about the future.'

'See You' 4:34
This was the first single released by Depeche Mode as a trio, on 29 January 1982. It had been recorded prior to *A Broken Frame* to give the band a post-Vince Clarke single and to establish they intended to carry on. 'See You' was one of the earliest songs Gore had ever written and it shows in its naive charm. Simple lyrics combine with an upbeat melody to produce a perfect pop song about longing and a desire to rekindle a lost romance. According to Gore's girlfriend, Anne Swindell, 'See You' was written after a foreign exchange trip to Germany in 1977 when Gore was still at school. 'He met somebody there,' she said, while according to a report on MTV Germany, Birgit Biehl claimed to be the one who'd 'had a fling' with Gore when he was just 16. In 1982, Gore insisted in *New Sounds, New Styles* magazine: 'I can't tell the story behind it. It's private.'

In 2001, Gore looked back upon his first songwriting efforts in *Kingsize* magazine: 'Do I feel any affection for things like "See You"? Not really, no. I was just trying to copy [Vince's] style.' Gore composed lyrics that made sense and even told a story, unlike the bulk of Clarke's output. The lyrics may have been simple, but the emotions underpinning them were anything but. Unrequited longing was an interesting area for a set of lads just out of their teens to be exploring. There are hints here of the later darker turn that

Gore's songwriting would take, especially in lines like: 'You can keep me at a distance if you don't trust my resistance/But I swear I won't touch you'.

The single proved that there was life beyond Clarke for Depeche Mode, peaking at number six on the UK Singles Chart. It was helped into the Top 10 by Depeche Mode's second video, directed by Julien Temple. Opening on Hounslow station, Gahan longs to meet again with the girl in a strip of photo-booth images (the girl in the pictures and at the checkout at the end was Gore's then-girlfriend Anne Swindell). Gahan's later seen wandering around a department store, while the others play various items (tills, phones, remote controls) as if they were keyboards. Wilder is featured and appeared on *Top of the Pops*, recorded on 21 January (broadcast on 25 January), the night before they flew to New York to perform two concerts; Wilder seems very at home as part of the quartet. Performed over 200 times, 'See You' was a central track in Depeche Mode's early live sets through to 1985.

'Satellite' 4:44

Is 'Satellite' another break-up song from a heart-sick Gore? It would fit the overall theme of *A Broken Frame* (even that title is telling). The lyrics suggest a tale of woe, someone suffering a great setback that has put them in a foul mood or deep depression, which in turn has turned them into a 'satellite of hate' transmitting their unhappiness to others: 'Gonna send my message through to you/And you'll receive the signal too'. It's depression as a transmittable state, a contagion that spreads from person to person. Musically, it progresses at a stately pace, slow to build and consistent throughout. It's a hidden gem of early Depeche Mode and a pointer to the future of Gore's songwriting, which would often return to this subject with more complexity.

'The Meaning Of Love' 3:06

The second single (released on 26 April 1982) from *A Broken Frame* opened Side Two of the record. Gore rose to the challenge of replacing Clarke as songwriter by channelling his synth-pop approach to perfect three-minute pop songs. Like several early Gore tracks, there's a meta aspect to this one: rather than write a simple love song, Gore instead decides to analyse what love means, questioning why anyone would want to love or be loved given all the pain it can cause.

From the very 'poppy' opening, 'The Meaning Of Love' immediately demands attention. The combination of lyrics and melody propels the song forward, with a catchy chorus that attempts to replicate the success of Clarke's 'Just Can't Get Enough'. The middle break takes a darker turn, but the song quickly recovers its light ambience. Some of Gore's old religious interests bleed through in lines like love being 'a feeling and it comes from above' and 'Tell me the answer/My Lord high above', which sounds like a hymn. Also popping up are some of Gore's darker thoughts: 'From the notes that I've made so far/Love seems something like wanting a scar'.

Julien Temple returned once more to direct another pop video for 'The Meaning Of Love', one the band came to hate (so much so that it was omitted from the *Some Great Videos* VHS compilation release of 1985). The quartet (Alan Wilder is again featured prominently) perform in front of a tinsel backdrop, while scenes of kids bashing toy drums and playing with lettered bricks are intercut. There are random guest appearances by a ballerina and Pinky and Perky, while a lab coat-wearing Gahan engages in the scientific pursuit of the meaning of love. The final scene throws a poor light on domesticity, with an argument breaking out between a young couple (Gahan being one-half) as their toddler spells out the song title with his bricks. Little wonder the band didn't like this bizarre assortment of random images. It did little to support the song, either – it was their fifth single and the first since 'New Life' not to crack the Top 10, stalling at number 12. It was all the more galling as the Mode boys watched Yazoo's 'Only You' (a song they'd rejected) slowly climb to number two by May 1982 (having been released in March), especially as Clarke's song was another take on romance and the meaning of love.

Overall, while it's a catchy enough tune, 'The Meaning Of Love' could be said to have been a 'failure' (in chart terms) and a song that 'does not work', as it failed to maintain the forward march of the band. They'd stop playing it live quite early, in 1984, and its relatively muted reception forced the band to develop a new sound for their next single, 'Leave In Silence'. Their faith in that track is indicated by its position as the opening song on *A Broken Frame*.

'A Photograph Of You' 3:04
Along with 'See You', 'A Photograph Of You' was an old track by Gore that dated back to his Norman & the Worms days, revived and revised for use on *A Broken Frame*. It encapsulates the album's mix of the melodic and the melancholic, a simple and transparent song in terms of its lyrics and meaning, helped by its upbeat presentation. Significantly faster than the likes of 'Satellite', it's another three-minute perfect synth-pop song that no doubt appealed to Depeche Mode's then teenage first fan base, drawing upon their own (and the band's recent) adolescent experiences of first love. Rhyming 'doll' with 'dull', however, shows that this was definitely one of Gore's earliest attempts at songwriting, wearing its naivety on its sleeve.

Short and to the point, it's perhaps surprising that 'A Photograph Of You' was not considered as a possible single as it may have performed better than 'The Meaning Of Love'. However, it was clear through the making of *A Broken Frame* that Depeche Mode were struggling to break away from their clean-cut 'nice boys of synth-pop' image. With the arrival of the likes of Soft Cell (Marc Almond selling himself on the basis of seedy sexuality) and Matt Johnson (of The The, just beginning to put together his more mature sound while still barely a teenager himself), the Mode boys were beginning to look a bit twee, and 'A Photograph Of You' fits right into that perception.

'Shouldn't Have Done That' 3:12

Is 'Shouldn't Have Done That' the only Depeche Mode song to feature a contribution from Blancmange? They supported the band on tour during the early 1980s, but officially never recorded together. However, according to Mute's Daniel Miller, Blancmange were recording in the studio next door, so were called upon to add some 'marching' sound effects (heard at the song's conclusion). It's a fairly straight narrative song (in that it tells a simple story) complicated by its production. The story of the rise of a repressive politician (or maybe a dictator) from the nursery to a position of power is the backbone of the nursery rhyme tale. Under the surface, though, something else is going on. Again, nursery rhymes raise their head in the presentation lyrically and musically, with a dreamy break in the song that is littered by some barely heard chatter that lasts about 40 seconds. The reason what's being said can't quite be made out is because the sound has been reversed. It's a made-up children's tale about a little bird and a fat bird vying for food, read aloud by Gore amid laughter. 'Shouldn't Have Done That' anticipates the more political tracks on *Some Great Reward*, such as 'Lie to Me' or the likes of 'New Dress' on *Black Celebration* in that it adopts a faux naive approach to tackle significant real-world issues, something the band would tackle much more often as their career progressed (and would return to strongly on 2017's *Spirit*).

'The Sun & The Rainfall' 5:02

Almost uniquely, 'The Sun & The Rainfall' is one of only two instances in which Andy Fletcher's vocal contribution is unmistakeable. The 'mystery man' of Depeche Mode can clearly be heard singing the song's last lines: 'All I'm saying, is a game's not worth playing, over and over again' (usually sung by Alan Wilder during live performances). Fletcher was always the odd man out among the Mode line-up. He'd been instrumental in bringing the various members of the band together, but he was never as musically committed as the others. Once Vince Clarke left and the band looked to be an ongoing concern, Fletcher found a niche for himself as a kind of business manager. Fletcher's other vocal contributions came on 'Interlude #2' on *Violator* in which he repeatedly sings the song's sole lyric, 'Crucified', as well as taking part in the 'choir' section on 'Condemnation' from *Songs Of Faith And Devotion* that involved every band member vocally.

The title 'The Sun & The Rainfall' sums up the entire *A Broken Frame* album, consisting as it does of upbeat, perky synth-pop tunes (the sun) like 'See You' and 'A Photograph Of You', and melancholic slow burners (the rainfall) like 'My Secret Garden', 'Monument' and 'Satellite'. It's a song that looks back and forward simultaneously. It's the final Gore 'break-up' song chronicling the fights that come before the end of a relationship and their repetitive nature (neatly echoing album opener 'Leave In Silence') while also suggesting 'Things must change'. Change was certainly coming. *A Broken*

Frame had shown that Depeche Mode could survive the departure of their original driving force (and main songwriter on *Speak & Spell*) Vince Clarke. Now the question was 'what comes next' and how the band would develop beyond their 'nice boys' synth-pop origins.

Related Tracks
'Now, This Is Fun' 3:27
Recorded as part of the *A Broken Frame* album sessions, 'Now, This Is Fun' (working title 'Reason To Be') has a strong melody and decent lyrics, and plays games with pace and structure. Gahan's vocals are de-prioritised, giving the music free rein, and the extended version (on the 'See You' 12") makes the most of this, extending the bridge. It's an uncanny mix of the upbeat with the darker sound that Depeche Mode would soon develop. A song about breaking the rules, with a 'punk' sensibility, 'Now, This Is Fun' could equally be read as Gore deconstructing his new role as the band's chief songwriter and the pressure to deliver with lyrics like: 'Here comes another sentence/It is relentless'. Andy Fletcher, speaking to *Smash Hits* in 1982, tried to suggest that this B-side was Depeche Mode trying 'to sound really mean... didn't work, though'. He suggested this was a response to the fact that 'a lot of people thought Depeche Mode were "sweet" and "cute". We wanted to show them we could be a lot of other things.'

'Oberkorn (It's A Small Town)' 4:07
An instrumental recorded during the *A Broken Frame* sessions, this was the B-side to 'The Meaning Of Love'. It's a meandering, plinky-plonky tune (a criticism thrown at much early Depeche Mode) that really goes nowhere across its four minutes. As music for scenes in a film, it might just about be passable (despite this, the band performed this track live almost 50 times in their early concerts). The most interesting thing about 'Oberkorn (It's A Small Town)' is the story behind how the instrumental track was saddled with such a strange title – it was named for a tiny town in Luxembourg where they played a gig in March 1982.

'Excerpt From: My Secret Garden' 3:14
This B-side to the single release of 'Leave In Silence' is a reinterpretation of 'My Secret Garden' as a faster-paced instrumental with an even more melancholic overlay. As with many of Gore's instrumentals, it's a 'beefed up' electro-disco version of the original, out Kraftwerk-ing Kraftwerk, certainly in pace but also in musical virtuosity. It's a more dynamic take on the original, driving forward with insistent rhythms, but still retaining the lullaby-like core. Parts of it could easily have been used for the theme tune for a BBC early 1980s technology programme like *Tomorrow's World* or *The Computer Programme*.

Construction Time Again (1983)

Personnel:
Dave Gahan: lead vocals
Martin Gore: keyboards, backing vocals, additional vocals on 'Everything Counts'
and 'Shame', lead vocals on 'Pipeline'
Andy Fletcher: keyboards, backing vocals
Alan Wilder: keyboards, backing vocals
Recorded at The Garden, London, April–July 1983
Producer: Daniel Miller, Depeche Mode
All tracks written by Martin Gore, except 'Two Minute Warning', 'The Landscape
Is Changing' and 'Fools', written by Alan Wilder, and 'The Great Outdoors' and
'Work Hard' written by Gore and Wilder
Released: 22 August 1983. Label: Mute
Running time: 42:26
Highest chart placings: UK: 6; France: 16; Germany: 7; Holland: 32; New
Zealand: 44; Sweden: 12; Switzerland: 21.

Alan Wilder played the game Depeche Mode's way, providing live support
during the tour for *A Broken Frame*, but otherwise not contributing
creatively to the band's musical evolution. That was all to change with
1983's *Construction Time Again*. Wilder was a suitable replacement for the
departed Vince Clarke and was easily the most musically adept of the group
(Martin Gore was still developing, having tentatively stepped into Clarke's
shoes on *A Broken Frame*, and having recycled several older tracks for use
by Depeche Mode). Speaking to *Uncut* magazine, Wilder confessed: 'The
problem was that they had something to prove to themselves. The three of
them didn't want the press to say they'd just roped in a musician to make
things easier after Vince left.'

Playing the long game, touring with the band, as well as making
appearances in the last few music videos, marked Wilder out as a team player.
Those experiences on the road helped build up the relationship between the
original trio and the newcomer, so that they finally became an official quartet.
The Depeche Mode fan club newsletter broke the news in October 1982:
'Alan Wilder is now a permanent member of Depeche Mode... although he
didn't play on the last three hit singles or *A Broken Frame*, he will be joining
Dave, Martin and Andy in the studio from now on.'

The first recording that Wilder participated in was for the single 'Get The
Balance Right!', released six months before *Construction Time Again*. It was
Miller's idea to create a single to maintain the band's chart momentum, so
they gathered at Blackwing before Christmas 1982. With the new financial
success of Mute, Miller had invested £10,000 (about £25,000 in 2022) in a
Synclavier II digital synthesiser, famously used on Michael Jackson's best-
selling *Thriller* album. The attraction of this new piece of kit was its ability to
sample any real-world sound and manipulate it in a musical fashion. It was to

eventually impact dramatically on Depeche Mode's sound, but when they first encountered it, the band found it a very tricky piece of kit to get the hang of.

More international touring followed the one-off recording for 'Get The Balance Right!', and when the band returned to start work on their third album, it would be to an unfamiliar studio. John Foxx had quit Ultravox in 1979. Going solo, Foxx had produced a cutting-edge album of electronica, *Metamatic*, followed by 1981's *The Garden*. He invested in a newly built state-of-the-art recording studio in Shoreditch, also called The Garden. In early 1983, the band struck up an influential relationship with Foxx's engineer, Gareth Jones. Jones was reluctant to work with a 'pop group' as he preferred new wave and punk outfits. Jones was among the first to see the innovative musical potential in Depeche Mode that perhaps the band themselves were only beginning to recognise.

The recent tour had opened the band's eyes to obvious inequalities in the world, especially in places like Thailand, where they played two shows. Having been mobbed by fans in Hong Kong, they found their lifestyles to be quite a contrast to the poor of Asia. Returning home, Gore found he had a host of inspiration for new songs, revealing a previously unrealised political edge to Depeche Mode's lyrics. Wilder recalled the impact their trip to Asia had upon the band members as they returned to further inequality in Thatcher's Britain of the early 1980s. '[Martin] wrote pretty much all the next album in a couple of weeks straight after those trips,' said Wilder. 'It was obvious that all these bizarre places such as Bangkok had opened up a few eyes in the band.' The Mode men's new-found political outlook meshed with the musical ambitions of both Wilder and Gareth Jones as on *Construction Time Again* the band tentatively set out to explore their newly developing sound.

Working in a new studio environment with new equipment put the foursome on an equal footing. 'We all wanted to discover new sound worlds,' noted Jones, 'and give a sense of depth, scale and edge to the music.' 'Get The Balance Right!' pointed in the new direction that Depeche Mode were to head. Miller's Synclavier was installed in The Garden studio and its ability to handle 'found noises' was put to immediate use. In the early 1980s, Shoreditch was a run-down area of industrial landscapes, pocked with abandoned factories and unsupervised building sites. Inspired by Einstürzende Neubauten's use of industrial tools as musical instruments, Depeche Mode set out to fuse such 'metal bashing' sounds with their electronic pop. Armed with a Sony recorder, band members and Jones roamed through Shoreditch, seeking interesting sounds they could repurpose. 'We were going out, smashing pieces of metal with sledgehammers, raiding the kitchen drawer for utensils to make percussion sounds, anything we could get our hands on,' Martin Gore told the 2009 BBC documentary *Synth Britannia*.

In the studio, under the supervision of Miller and Jones, the quartet would meld these industrial 'found sounds' with Gore and Wilder's developing political lyrics to create a new sound that forever erased Depeche Mode's early 'plinky-plonk' synthesiser sound once and for all. The approach to *Construction Time Again* was to lay the groundwork for Depeche Mode's next two albums, *Some Great Reward* and *Black Celebration*, making them pioneers of a fresh, popular techno-industrial electronica the likes of which had never been heard before.

'Love In Itself' 4:29

A brave choice, both as an album opener and as a single, 'Love, In Itself' was released on 19 September 1983 (the month after *Construction Time Again*) and only reached number 21 in the UK Singles Chart, a major disappointment after hitting the Top 10 with 'Everything Counts'. It feels like Gore was consciously attempting to combine Vince Clarke's upbeat pop sensibilities with the 'break-up' songs from *A Broken Frame* and the new 'metal bashing' sound, with the result satisfying no one. Gahan faced an uphill task trying to realise the vocal, complaining that Gore's lyrics featured too many soft 'S' sounds. 'It had a very soft vocal, with a lot of S's,' noted Gahan in *No. 1* magazine in October 1985. 'It sounded awful. I was a bit disappointed with this – it could have been different.'

One guest critic enamoured of 'Love, In Itself' was comedian and actor Lenny Henry, who was reviewing for *Smash Hits* during the week of release. 'Nice tune,' said Henry. 'It's a very moody production and, hang on, did I hear someone playing guitar in there? And some (gasp) real piano?!' The *Top of the Pops* performance on 25 October 1983 did feature Gore on acoustic guitar and Wilder noodling around on a large, white Yamaha grand piano.

'More Than A Party' 4:45

Gore's new political outlook came to the fore on the album's second track, 'More Than A Party'. The start of Thatcher's second term in government and the fact that he'd had his eyes opened to widespread poverty first-hand during the Asian leg of a recent tour inspired Gore to write lyrics that switched from the personal (mainly doomed romance) to the political (mainly anti-capitalist). Life, according to Gore, is 'More than a party/It's a whole lot more'. There's much naivety in the lyrics, but the point comes across, even in lines like: 'Keep telling us we're to have fun/Then take all the ice cream so we've got none'. This is global politics couched in the terms of the playground, although it does suggest an awareness of the 'bread and circuses' aspect of British governance: keep the population amused or entertained (circuses) and provide them with enough food (bread), and they'll want for little else. In the 1980s, this consisted of television and video games, two of Depeche Mode's formative influences. It's the relentless beat that keeps 'More Than A Party' moving. Musically, it is more successful than the lyrics might suggest. Using elements from a children's party (blind man's buff, ice cream, a failed magician) to cast aspersions upon politics as practised at Westminster, the song is a slave to the insistent rhythm, clattering to a frenetic climax as

31

Gahan chants along. The endless scream of 'more, more, more' towards the end seemed to sum up the ruling Conservative Party's attitude: 'This isn't a party/It's a whole lot more'.

'Pipeline' 5:54
The train leaving the station sounds that closed out 'More Than A Party' bleed directly into the banging and chanting that opens 'Pipeline'. Slow and moody, this is Depeche Mode metal bashing at its finest. While dealing on the surface with concepts of industrial labour (the album title line 'construction time again' originates here), to quote 'More Than A Party', this is not just a song, it's a whole lot more. First, the metal bashing ... 'We went down Brick Lane and just hit everything and then recorded it and took it back to the studio and then put it into the keyboard,' Andy Fletcher told *Melody Maker* in 1984. 'That's how we made the track "Pipeline". We [were] smashing corrugated iron and old cars. The vocals were recorded in a railway arch in Shoreditch – you've got the train three-quarters of the way through and the aeroplane up above. It's really interesting doing that.' The previous year in *Sounds*, Gahan had claimed 'Pipeline' to be 'very experimental in that every sound on there has been made from us just out on the street hitting things.'

There is, however, a hidden subtext to Martin Gore's lyrics. The 'Pipeline' being sung about may not be just the bog standard oil or water pipeline, but a metaphorical one that's 'taking from the greedy and giving to the needy'. While 'trickle-down economics' have largely been discredited with the decline of neoliberalism in the 21st century, in the early to mid-1980s it was a theory that was all the rage in the Reagan and Thatcher governments. Indeed, 'Work's been sent our way/That could last a lifetime', in that it could take that or longer to rebalance between the rich and poor. Gore, even at this early stage, appears to have been unconvinced of 'trickle down' economics: 'From the heart of our land/To the mouth of the man/Must reach him sometime'.

It was a subject that Gore would return to directly with the track 'Poorman' on the 2017 *Spirit* album (which also saw Depeche Mode recapture their political edge after a long time). The lyrics 'Tell us how long it's going to take/For it to trickle down/When will it trickle down' are a direct call back to 'Pipeline', the construction of a pipeline that would syphon wealth from the rich and redistribute it to the poor. As 'Poorman' suggests, even 34 years later, people were still waiting.

'Everything Counts' 4:19
The first single released from *Construction Time Again*, 'Everything Counts' followed 'Get The Balance Right!' on 11 July 1983, peaking at number six in the UK Singles Chart, their first single since 'See You' (which also reached number six) in 1982 to breach the Top 10. More impactful than 'Get The Balance Right!', 'Everything Counts' pointed ahead to the direction Depeche Mode would be taking. Gore told *NME* that their recent experiences abroad

had directly influenced 'Everything Counts': 'You go over there and all the hotels are full of businessmen and they tend to treat people as though they're nothing. All they're interested in is their business; people just don't seem to matter. Just money.'

The song could also be a comment on the world of international pop that Depeche Mode now found themselves in. Ironically, their innovative deal with Mute and Daniel Miller had been sealed by a 'handshake' with no formal contract. It suggests what might have happened if the Mode men had been offered a huge advance from a bigger record company: a great holiday, followed by the come-down when they faced producing the work they'd already been paid for. Depeche Mode's deal had been 'the turning point of a career', but it had been much more equitable than the song suggests. There were no 'grabbing hands' at Mute or in the band 'grabbing all that they can'.

For the music video, the band re-enlisted Clive Richardson, who'd previously tackled 'Just Can't Get Enough' two years earlier. Featuring travelogue material shot in West Berlin intercut with shots of Gahan (with blond highlights) dancing and singing and the other three performing the chorus, it was a step up from some of their more questionable videos. The song rapidly became a live favourite, performed over 760 times right up to the early leg of the 2023 Memento Mori Tour. 'It's one of my favourite songs,' admitted Gahan of 'Everything Counts'. 'The lyrics are timeless. They talk of money, power and corruption.'

'Two Minute Warning' 4:13
In writing 'Two Minute Warning', Wilder showed he could be as youthfully naive as Gore if he really put his mind to it. 'It was about the nuclear arms race of the 1980s,' Wilder glibly said of the song in an online Q&A. Musically, it's actually interesting, even if the lyrics are a bit obvious being a combination of nuclear bomb anxiety and a Vince Clarke-style word salad. It was inevitable that the theme of nuclear destruction would be a topic for the newly politically awakened Depeche Mode, given the times they were living through. The first deployment of American cruise missiles in Europe happened in 1983, with the Campaign for Nuclear Disarmament (CND) stepping up their acts of civil disobedience in return. The Cold War was at the forefront of many people's minds, with the possibility of nuclear Armageddon a very real danger. In March, while the band were in the studio, US President Ronald Reagan had launched his Strategic Defense Initiative, a plan that involved satellites shooting down missiles in flight that inevitably became dubbed 'Star Wars'. Margaret Thatcher's Conservative government was re-elected in June 1983 with a landslide win, so nothing much was expected to change in terms of international relations.

On 1 September, just weeks after the release of *Construction Time Again*, Korean Air Lines Flight 007 was shot down by the Soviet Union, further increasing tensions which reached new heights with the 26 September 'false alarm' in which Soviet military officer Stanislav Petrov averted a possible nuclear strike on the US. In that context, however straightforward its lyrics might be, 'Two Minute Warning' was certainly topical. 'I really like the idea of people humming "Two Minute Warning" without realising what it's about,' said Wilder to *Sounds*. 'It's almost surreal, the possibility of a nuclear holocaust is so terrifying but to actually turn it round and make it beautiful – and the tune is very light and bouncy – is more of a challenge than making it doomy!'

'Shame' 3:51

This was another track inspired by the band's travels through Thailand. Gore translated his concerns directly into lyrics that held up the western powers' 'shame' about the state of the rest of the world; in the 1980s, it became evident that as the West prospered, the rest fell further behind. The 'businessmen' Gore and Gahan encountered are the ones who can't 'wash away your shame', the ones who can't 'improve your pain', and the ones whose 'good deeds' won't 'remove the stain'. 'Shame' contains one of Depeche Mode's simplest yet catchiest and most memorable refrains in the chorus: 'It all seems so stupid/It makes me want to give up/But why should I give up/When it all seems so stupid'. With *Construction Time Again*, Depeche Mode were rapidly becoming the masters of electro-pop protest songs, a kind of 1960s throwback, taking in 'More Than A Party', 'Pipeline' and 'Told You So'. Nonetheless, Gore makes a point of ending on a positive note, hoping 'That something can be done/to eradicate these problems/ And make the people one'. It's a nice thought, but we're still waiting over 40 years later ...

'The Landscape Is Changing' 4:49

Depeche Mode engaged with the issue of what's now called climate change early on with Wilder's song 'The Landscape Is Changing'. Back then, it was dubbed 'global warming', but the dangers of severe man-made environmental damage had been widely known about since the 1960s and had even been speculated about as far back as the 1930s at the height of the coal mining industry in Britain. There was a specific inspiration that caused Wilder to tackle this subject: 'I saw a TV documentary about acid rain which gave me the idea for "The Landscape...".' Rather than the metal bashing on other tracks, this one relies on 'parping' simulated wind instruments and a subtle series of backing rhythms. Indeed, 'Acid streams are flowing ill across the countryside', and Gahan's vocals urge listeners to 'take good care of the world'. In the studio recording of *Construction Time Again*, the musically and technically minded Wilder slipped easily into Vince Clarke's former role, working with studio engineer Gareth Jones to develop Depeche Mode's deeper and richer sound, certainly compared to some of the airiness of *Speak & Spell* and *A Broken Frame*, which can sound a little empty in contrast. However, he discovered that writing songs wasn't necessarily his forte:

> Songwriting didn't really come naturally to me, but I felt I should participate in the process. However, it became clear that my strengths were more to do with the placement of sounds and the structuring of the music, and I suppose my classical upbringing was a factor in this. What I really added was enthusiasm and a desire to experiment more. I was also desperate for us to be taken more seriously, which meant producing a darker, more weighty sound.

'Told You So' 4:26
For 'Told You So', Martin Gore reached back to his religious background for inspiration, presenting a pop version of William Blake's 'Jerusalem', a poem adopted as a hymn by the Church of England. Opening line 'And do those feet in modern times' clearly echoes Blake's opening line of 'And did those feet in ancient time'. Blake's religiosity is given an apocalyptic makeover suitable to the mid-1980s. On the surface, Gore may be suggesting that the message of Christ's redemption of mankind had not translated through to 'modern times' as 'Something went wrong along the way'. Suggestions of domination by the strong over the weak, and of violence as an enforcement tactic offer a lament for a fallen humanity that failed to comprehend the message of brotherly love due to 'Playing Chinese whispers'. It's a brave subject for an out-and-out pop group to tackle at that time, but it seems to sit comfortably amid the agitprop songs on the rest of the album.

'And Then...' 5:39
Thematically, this sounds like a throwback to *A Broken Frame*'s 'Shouldn't Have Done That', while musically, it looks forward to *Some Great Reward* and *Black Celebration*. It's a summation of the themes of *Construction Time Again*, highlighting that a process of change is needed to counter the greed and corruption highlighted in the other songs. Jokingly, Gore plays upon his own political naivety with the line: 'All that we need at the start's/ Universal revolution (that's all)'. Given that 'things couldn't turn out worse', Gore puts his faith in the next generation, 'All of the boys and the girls... To pull it all down and start again'. Remaking the world is Gore's ambition, the creation of a new world without borders or difference: 'Let's take a map of the world/Tear it into pieces'. Seemingly disconnected is the middle section about travelling by plane and car, but never really going far. Again, this could suggest that wherever one goes (in the title of a later Depeche Mode song) 'People Are People', but in a 21st-century context, looking back, it almost feels like a pre-echo of the arrival of the internet, the feeling of being permanently connected regardless of geographical distance or social difference. The very first day of 1983 – the year Depeche Mode conceived,

recorded and released *Construction Time Again* – saw the US Department
of Defense ARPANET complete its migration to the new TCP/IP protocol, the
foundation of remote computer networking. It's a technical achievement that
is now regarded as the true beginnings of the internet as we'd come to know
it. As ever, Depeche Mode were ahead of their time...

'Everything Counts (Reprise)' 1:00
A reminder, right at the end, that 'The grabbing hand grab all they can'.
Despite it all, greed always triumphs.

Related Tracks
'Get The Balance Right!' 3:12
'Get The Balance Right!' was produced as a stop-gap single between albums,
and as a result of the band's animosity towards the song – due to the difficult
and frustrating recording process – it was left off the album. Despite that, its
new sounds were to be a first harbinger of the direction that Depeche Mode
would move in now that Wilder was a full-time member. The lyrics show the
beginnings of Gore's political awakening. Lyrics like 'Concerned and caring/
Help the helpless/But always remain/Ultimately selfish' revealed the cynical
political outlook that would permeate the band's third album. The song
encompasses conformity and rebellion, the pressure to do what's socially right:
'Be responsible, respectable/Stable, but gullible'. It also anticipated the fact that
the band could not stay on the high of their recent success: 'When you reach
the top/Get ready to drop/Prepare yourself for the fall/You're going to fall'.
One of the most prolific Depeche Mode websites – Almost Predictable Almost –
took its name from the line: 'It's almost predictable/Almost'.

The track also reflected the band's own growth, as the former high
schoolers were now in their early twenties. The accompanying video
(directed by Kevin Hewitt, who would later work with New Order and, er...,
Donny Osmond) sees the Mode men don white coats as scientists studying
a young child in laboratory conditions before spiralling out to depict an
extended metaphor in which a funfair stands in for society at large. The
video concludes with the counting of large amounts of money (a theme
explored further in 'Everything Counts'). Hewitt has the band members lip-
synching to the song and he chose Wilder to front the track, believing him
to be the band's singer. Apparently, the rest of them were too embarrassed
to point out the error.

The group grew to dislike 'Get The Balance Right!' as they'd had such
trouble trying to work with the new Synclavier synthesiser that Daniel Miller
was keen to use. Gore had presented the song as the only one he had, and
the band always had reservations about it. Gore later identified it as 'our least
favourite single. It was hell to record. I hate it, and I wrote it!' Released on the
last day of January 1983, 'Get The Balance Right!' peaked at number 13 in the
UK Singles Chart on 5 March 1983. Although it didn't make the UK release of

Construction Time Again, the track did feature on the 1984 US compilation *People Are People*, released by Sire. The 12" Combination Mix version became an underground dance club hit in the US, paving the way for Depeche Mode's influence on Detroit's later hip-hop scene. Critic Kevin Saunderson dubbed 'Get The Balance Right!' to be 'the first House record'. According to *Smash Hits*, it was 'fascinating enough structurally to keep it around [the charts] longer than most', while *Sounds* labelled the single 'the sort of thing [Depeche Mode] do better than anyone else'. Not a live favourite, due to the band's antipathy, 'Get The Balance Right!' was performed 62 times, with the last performance in the summer of 1984.

'The Great Outdoors!' 5:04

The B-side to the single release of 'Get The Balance Right!', instrumental 'The Great Outdoors!' was the first work by Alan Wilder to be released by the band – he co-wrote the track with Martin Gore. On the *A Broken Frame* tour, 'The Great Outdoors!' replaced 'Oberkorn (It's A Small Town)' as the band's preferred intro music after an accident with their Revox tape machine obliterated the recording of the previous track. It's an odd track that recalls some of the early 1980s work by the BBC Radiophonic Workshop as showcased in episodes of *Doctor Who*. Written in the studio and 'all done very quickly', according to Wilder, 'The Great Outdoors!' reveals a couple of electronic musicians playing with their tools yet producing a track of little consequence.

'Work Hard' 4:24

Released as the B-side to the single 'Everything Counts', 'Work Hard' was co-written by Wilder and Gore. According to Gahan, 'Work Hard' 'mainly consisted of wood breaking. We ran around with a hammer and toolbox across the junkyards in East London and crashed everything we could find... we came back into the studio with loud, strange sounds, which we would put in a sampler or on an analogue tape, and cut up again and again until a good rhythm came out of it.' It's a prime example of Depeche Mode's 'metal bashing' period as the track opens with various clangs and bangs, as well as car horn sounds, before a programmed rhythm kicks in. The lyrics fit right in with the 'work' theme of *Construction Time Again*, extolling the need to 'work hard/If you want anything at all', which might be the opposite message from the single's A-side, 'Everything Counts'. Perhaps Wilder and Gore intended the song as a riposte to the flipside? As the track crashes to a conclusion, it's played out through more clanging metal and sounds like a typewriter or supermarket till.

'Fools' 4:17

The B-side to the single release of 'Love In Itself', this song was written by Alan Wilder. Recorded during the session for *Construction Time Again*, the track didn't make the cut for the album, although it would have fitted right in. From the bangs and clangs of the rhythmic opening, through the synthesised backbeat, to Gahan's vocals, it's an upbeat, fast-paced track of the kind that the album was perhaps missing. It's fully developed lyrically, a 'break-up' song (or at least about a domestic disagreement) in which 'fools don't run away', suggesting the need for persistence in relationships: 'So call me now and tell me that you're home'. It's enough to make you wonder what might have happened if this had been released as the single A-side rather than the morose 'Love In Itself'. It seems the band weren't yet ready to hand Wilder that kind of accolade...

Some Great Reward (1984)

Personnel:
Dave Gahan: lead vocals
Martin Gore: keyboards, backing vocals, additional vocals on 'Something To Do' and 'People Are People', lead vocals on 'It Doesn't Matter' and 'Somebody'
Andy Fletcher: keyboards, backing vocals
Alan Wilder: keyboards, backing vocals
Recorded at Music Works, London and Hansa Mischraum, Berlin, January–August 1984
Producer: Daniel Miller, Depeche Mode, Gareth Jones
All tracks written by Martin Gore, except 'If You Want', written by Alan Wilder
Released: 24 September 1984. Label: Mute
Running time: 40:18
Highest chart placings: UK: 5; US: 54; Canada: 34; France: 10; Germany: 3; Holland: 34; New Zealand: 44; Sweden: 7; Switzerland: 5.

In 1983, Depeche Mode discovered Berlin. *Construction Time Again* had been recorded at John Foxx's studio The Garden in London, but that studio could only offer 24-track facilities. Daniel Miller and Gareth Jones went looking for a higher spec facility where they could mix the album, finally settling upon Hansa in what was then West Berlin, where David Bowie had recorded his three late 1970s albums, *Low*, *Heroes* and *Lodger*. Located in the shadow of the Berlin Wall, Hansa boasted a 64-track mixing room, exactly what was needed to give *Construction Time Again* the 'sense of depth, scale and edge' that Jones was seeking.

While working at Hansa, the Mode men also discovered Berlin's nightlife. 'Everyone got the Berlin vibe,' noted Jones, 'and started wearing black leather.' Martin Gore, having split with his Christian girlfriend, found new life in Berlin, dating local woman Cristina Friedrich. 'I suddenly discovered all this freedom,' said Gore. 'It was a big turning point for me.' These new experiences matured Gore's songwriting, making the next album – *Some Great Reward* – their most ambitious.

The tour promoting *Construction Time Again* had bonded the band together, with Gore coming out of his shell, Gahan becoming a more confident frontman (his dancing had developed markedly), Fletcher securing his niche as the business manager and Wilder finally feeling fully accepted. The band's sense of performance also developed, with an integrated light show and an attempt to make the unimpressive spectacle of a trio of keyboard players look a bit more dynamic (they were placed upon tall podiums). As their popularity soared in Germany (where Gore was now living), the tour climaxed with three dates in Hamburg. The one market where Depeche Mode had singularly failed to make any significant inroads remained the US.

For their next recording, the rest of the band followed Gore to Berlin, setting up in Hansa. Engineer Gareth Jones joined them, with the first track recorded – as the Orwellian year of 1984 began – being the sonically adventurous but lyrically naive 'People Are People'. All but one of the songs would be written by Gore, with Wilder keeping his hand in with one track, 'If You Want'.

That same January, Gore attended a performance by Einstürzende Neubauten at London's Institute of the Contemporary Arts (ICA) where they performed a work entitled 'Concerto For Voices And Machinery'. The performance used various industrial 'instruments': acetylene torches, electric saws, a road drill, generators and even a concrete mixer. The collective 'metal banging' went off the rails, part of the stage was damaged, and the ICA called an early halt to proceedings.

That sound and drama were fresh in Gore's mind when Depeche Mode assembled at Hansa to begin work on their fourth album, *Some Great Reward* (the title a lyric in the song 'Lie To Me'). Of course, Depeche Mode were well down the road of 'metal bashing', having made huge strides on *Construction Time Again*. They'd take that further on *Some Great Reward*, especially on 'People Are People' and 'Master And Servant', two of the three singles from the album.

Wilder found himself heavily involved with Gareth Jones in building the band's sound in the studio. 'He was a total sound nut as well,' said Jones of discovering a sonic fellow traveller in Wilder. 'It was always me, Alan and Daniel [Miller, for Mute] for those three albums. We were always there from the beginning of the session to the end of the session.'

It was around this time that fans began to question Andy Fletcher's role. He didn't seem to play a hugely creative role in the studio, he didn't write music or lyrics, and his live performance skills seemed to lie in playing minimal keyboard parts in support of the others. That impression was – and continued to be – entirely erroneous. Although not seen as a key creative figure in Depeche Mode, much of the band's longevity in a business sense was no doubt down to Fletcher taking over Vince Clarke's former role of looking out for the band's business interests.

However, according to Jones, Fletcher did have a key role in the construction of the band's new sound during the mid-1980s. 'Martin (and Alan) wrote the songs, Dave sang most of them, and Martin sang some of them, and Martin and Alan sang backing vocals,' explained Jones. 'Everything was played by machines, so it was more about what atmosphere we teased out of the machines, and Andy was a really important part of that, a really important part of the group dynamic. He would put his foot down sometimes and say, "It's not weird enough; that sounds a bit too normal." Andy was very concerned that we should maximise the potential of Martin's songs. They were determined to do something that would earn them the respect of their peers.' *Some Great Reward* was the middle album of a trio of works, preceded by *Construction Time Again* and followed by *Black Celebration*, which achieved those ambitions.

'Something To Do' 3:45

It's a brave choice to open an album with a song that (at first hearing) appears to be about boredom, but turns into something very different. The refrain 'Is there something to do' that gives the track its title suggests as much, made explicit with 'I'm going crazy with boredom'. It's one of few tracks that recalls the original band members' teen years in Basildon: there can be little doubt about the lines 'Grey sky over a black town/I can feel depression all around'. The driving, industrial rhythm provide a scaffold for Gahan's vocals and Gore's backing. Everything stops at the 1:30 mark for a cacophony of noise, punctuating the song before the darker second half, which alludes to alcoholism and kinky sex. The 'leather boots' line recurs throughout but takes on a more sinister aspect as the song builds. The final verse is pure Gore circa 1984 when the (male) singer dons his girlfriend's clothes, with Gahan giving an especially breathy delivery to the climatic line 'I put your pretty dress on'. Gore's exploration of S&M was beginning to seep into Depeche Mode's lyrics and the band's visual style, both in Gore's dress and in the graphics accompanying their releases (which switched from the industrial look of *Construction Time Again* to chains and hooks, suggesting a more BDSM vibe). This was in tune with Gore's outlook, with him telling *No.1* magazine: 'Sexual barriers are silly. My girlfriend and I swap clothes, make-up, anything – so what?'

'Lie To Me' 5:04

There is a view that *Some Great Reward* was a collection of anti-love songs – taking in 'Lie To Me', 'It Doesn't Matter', 'Stories Of Old' and 'Somebody' – all of which put caveats on the process of falling in love. 'Lie To Me', in particular, was one of Gore's favourite songs and one that Gahan enjoyed performing live. It begins like a straightforward love song, but the addition of the lines concerning lies gives it an edge. Where it succeeds is moving from the personal ('Come on and lie to me/Tell me I'm the only one') to the social/industrial ('So lie to me/Like they do in the factory'), connecting romance with commerce. For Daniel Miller, 'Lie To Me' was 'one of the strongest songs that Martin had written up to that point. I thought it just had a great feeling to it.' According to Gore, the song wasn't so much an 'anti-love' song as concerned with paranoia, the fear that a partner is not being truthful. Looking back to 1984 from a 21st-century perspective, some of the words of the song take on an entirely new meaning in a time of 'fake news' and online disinformation: 'Truth is a word/That's lost its meaning/The truth has become/Merely half-truth'. As in so many other ways, in this Depeche Mode were ahead of their time.

'People Are People' 3:52

The next big step forward came on this track, the first recorded for *Some Great Reward* and the first single from the album (12 March 1984). It reached number four in the UK Singles Chart and – more importantly for the band's future – climbed to number 13 in the US *Billboard* Top 100, finally achieving the breakthrough that had eluded them so far. In Germany, 'People Are People' reached the top spot (it proved equally popular elsewhere in Europe, reaching number three in Belgium, number two in Ireland and number two in Poland).

The song had started life in a rehearsal room in Dollis Hill, London, where some of the preprogramming of the synth sounds was completed. They took their initial sampling experiments further than before, building a song almost entirely from 'found' sounds. 'There's very little playing in "People Are People",' admitted Wilder in *International Musician and Recording World*. 'Virtually everything was sampled into the Synclavier.' Gore saw this industrial sampling combining their pop sensibilities with the much more aggressive industrial sound of German bands like Einstürzende Neubauten. In 1986, he explained to *Electronics and Music* magazine: 'Usually we spend two or three days just sampling sounds. Then we sample as we go. If somebody has a good idea, we just stop recording and do some sampling. Sometimes we use old favourites – like one sample which we first used on "People Are People". It's a Hank Marvin-type guitar sound, an acoustic guitar plucked with a 50-pfennig piece. We've used that three or four times now.'

The track was built from various sounds: an acoustic bass drum at the beginning, a bit of metal bashing (what Gore called 'an anvil type sound'), and various vocal contributions from the band, as well as found sounds (Gore worked in, deep in the mix, part of an airline safety announcement he'd recorded). According to Wilder, once in the Synclavier the sounds could be altered:

> You sample in one note and then you can alter the length and dynamic of every note in the sequence for the guitar part so it will give expression, but it will still be completely in time. There's a Synclavier harp sound in the verses and an ARP sequencer playing very fast in the chorus. We got a lot of people singing the high, 'It's a lot,' and then a low, 'Like life'.

Where 'People Are People' falls down – entirely in retrospect, given how the band developed – is in the lyrics. Although it was their most catchy song since 'Just Can't Get Enough', and was basically 'pop' enough to get wide radio play, the lyrics display the naivety of youth. The core sentiment is admirable – 'People are people/So why should it be/That you and I should get along so awfully' – if a little laboured. It was what was needed at the time, but looking back, Gore came to recognise the lyrical simplicity and the band largely stopped performing the track live around 1988, just four years after it was released. Fletcher noted: 'We thought it was a good song. Now, we're not too keen on it. It's probably our biggest hit that we don't play.

Martin cannot stand this song now. He finds it not subtle enough.' Despite not being overly fond of 'People Are People' now, the band were smart enough to recognise the breakthrough the track was, both musically and in terms of their popularity. Dave Gahan said of 'People Are People':

It's not one of Martin's particular favourites, this one, and I don't think we've done it live since the mid-1980s. It's quite literal, very poppy, all major chords, something Martin doesn't like so much these days. [It] really propelled us into a new cosmos at that particular time, [and was a] hit in a lot of countries in Europe. It allowed us to then go off and create the music that we wanted to create.

Even Gore, despite his disdain for his simple sentiments, recognised the importance of the track to the band's overall progress. 'It was good that we recorded this, because it brought us to a newer, bigger level. It was our first big hit in America and also in Germany. Or our first number one, I think. I really don't appreciate the song any more nowadays, but without it, we might not have been around as a band right now.'

'It Doesn't Matter' 4:45
Only ever performed live a total of eight times (mainly during the 1987–88 Music For The Masses Tour), 'It Doesn't Matter' is a slight track that attempts to work in Gore's by-now trademark narrative twist where the song doesn't turn out to be about what it initially appeared to be. It first seems to be about lovers long parted, where one of the pair has moved on leaving the other behind with unrequited attraction. References to being far away, dreaming of someone else, friendship and jealousy all back up this idea of looking back at a lost love. Then, that's all undercut by the lines: 'But I'm praying/That we're staying/Together' that are repeated throughout and suggest a temporary separation while each considers their future. Whatever it means, it's a lovely, dreamy track that just washes over the listener, a sonic landscape perhaps at odds with the lyrics.

'Stories Of Old' 3:12
Another song from the lullaby school, after 'Shouldn't Have Done That' on *A Broken Frame* and 'And Then...' from *Construction Time Again*. This time 'Stories Of Old' plunders the fairy tale for its recounting of 'romantic' love between 'princes bold' and 'the girl of their dreams', typically undercut by the singer's statement that 'I couldn't sacrifice/Anything at all/To love'. It's a strangely constructed song (little wonder it has never been played live) that shows the growing maturity in Depeche Mode's sonic explorations. It's one of Gore's twist-in-the-tale narratives where the partners '[We] won't sacrifice/Anything at all/To love', yet simultaneously plan to '[Let's] surrender/To this love divine'. That's having your cake and eating it, right there!

'Somebody' 4:26

Infamously, 'Somebody' (also released as a double A-side single with 'Blasphemous Rumours') is the track that Martin Gore recorded naked. It's a straightforward, deceptively simple track, just a piano and ambient background sounds over which Gore delivers his vocals. The decision on who would take lead vocals on a track (given the long-standing tradition that Gore would sing one or two each album) came down to a gut feeling about which tracks were more suited to his higher register. Of the choice, Andy Fletcher said, 'It was really down to two things: If we thought it suited Martin's voice more, or if they were of a more personal nature, like "Somebody".' According to Wilder, 'Somebody' was 'probably the first of what you'd call an acoustic performed track on an album. In fact, Martin sang it naked. I turned the piano away as I was playing, but yeah, we recorded it live, just him and me, in the big [Hansa] Studio 2 hall, and he stripped off for that one.' In his recounting of the recording in *Melody Maker* in 1984, Gore managed to work in the words 'all together' and 'bare', as if he was trying to make a point: 'The song is... performed all together. It just needed three takes, mainly to get the sound okay, and really uses the bare essentials. In fact, I sang it completely naked in the cellar of the studio, which we use for ambience...'

It's a saccharine-sweet song about finding your soulmate, who'll nonetheless challenge your views while still being supportive. Surprisingly, Gore later turned against the song, even though it contains the kind of narrative twist in the closing lines he seems to think it doesn't feature: 'Though things like this/Make me sick/In a case like this/I think I'll get away with it'. Speaking to French magazine *Best* in 1989, Gore claimed: 'I don't like this song any more. Looking back on it, I think it's too soft and tender. Most of my songs are not as naive. I usually arrange songs in such a way that they take an unexpected turn at some point. I prefer it to contain doubt, when it doesn't rule out the possibility that a loving relationship may go wrong.'

'Master And Servant' 4:13

Building on the sound of 'People Are People', the second single from *Some Great Reward* (released on 14 August 1984) was the BDSM-themed 'Master And Servant', where Gore's lyrics were more complex and meaningful than those on the first single. It seemed that 1984 would be the year of sexually suggestive songs banned by Radio 1. Frankie Goes to Hollywood had hit the big time with 'Relax' (banned in January 1984, when Depeche Mode were in the studio recording for *Some Great Reward*), and Mode's 'Master And Servant' narrowly avoided a similar ban. Unlike the Frankie track, there was a deeper meaning hidden in Gore's song. 'I was going out to quite a few S&M clubs, and I just started seeing a correlation between what's happening there and life and politics...' The key line was 'Domination's the name of the game/ In bed or in life/They're both just the same' with the ribald kicker: 'Except in one you're fulfilled/At the end of the day'!

Dave Gahan saw Gore's embrace of a decadent lifestyle and manner of dress as a reaction against his strict religious upbringing (which was to inform so many of his songs). 'He missed out on his teens,' said Gahan, who'd spent quite a few of his teen years as a tearaway in trouble with the police. '[He] missed out on just going out, seeing different girls every night, getting drunk all the time. He's living that now. It's not a bad thing – everyone should go through that phase.'

If the lyrics had come together relatively easily for Gore, realising the sonic effects of 'Master And Servant' was an entirely more complicated matter. Daniel Miller called the track 'the monster of the album. There's always one monster in terms of getting it finished.' The band were wary of following the 'poppy' sound of 'People Are People' with another track that would enable easy radio play. Andy Fletcher was in large part driving the band to find a more provocative, experimental sound, while Gore was happy to emulate the industrial noise (albeit in a more mainstream vein) of Einstürzende Neubauten. 'We felt that the next single had to be a lot harder, kind of different again,' said Miller. By the end of a week-long mixing process, Miller, Jones and Wilder were so frazzled they discovered they'd managed to omit the track's snare drum sound. Rather than remix it all once more, they decided (in the words of Wilder) that 'nobody will notice'.

In a 1984 issue of *Star Hits* magazine, Gahan threw some light on the sounds that had been used: 'We've got a whip, an air compressor from a builder's nail gun, a water drop, a toy piano, and you can hear Andy being spanked by Martin...' That may have been a joke, as might Fletcher admitting (in a German magazine): 'I was once whipped. The result can be heard on "Master And Servant". That was really strange.' There is some debate as to whether the whip sounds on the track are genuine samples or synthesised sounds, with band members making conflicting claims. However, the track proved hugely popular. The single peaked at number nine in the UK but reached number two in Germany, with Top 10 placings in Belgium, Ireland, Poland, Sweden and Switzerland.

Sporadically banned from radio airplay in the US, 'Master And Servant' nonetheless broke the *Billboard* Top 100, reaching number 87 (although it only remained in the chart for three weeks). Speaking to French magazine *Best*, Dave Gahan noted: 'Ever since we recorded it, we have always played "Master And Servant" on stage. As soon as the first chords are heard, the audience recognises it. It is the hymn of Depeche Mode.'

'If You Want' 4:40
Alan Wilder's 'If You Want' would have been a better fit with *Construction Time Again*, rather than on *Some Great Reward*. The lyrical content, focusing on 'the working week', and containing the lines 'We could build a building site' seem more in tune with tracks like 'Pipeline' or 'Work Hard'. It's a musically upbeat track (with a hint of an Indian sound about it, more evident on Wilder's demo

than on the finished track) that is downbeat lyrically. It's a good match for Gore's tracks that also deal with teen life in Basildon: 'Something To Do' on boredom, 'People Are People' on racism and homophobia, and 'Blasphemous Rumours' on spiritual belief. Looked at through that lens, much of *Some Great Reward* could be seen as an adult looking back upon the experiences earlier in life that informed the man he has become. Wilder even manages to sneak in a Gore-like sexual edge with the 'If you want to be with me' line, and even works in a narrative reversal like on Gore's 'Somebody' with the kicker 'Even though you may still not want to.'

'Blasphemous Rumours' 6:21

The closing track on *Some Great Reward* was also the album's third and final single release. Weirdly, given the apparent lyrical subject matter of 'Master And Servant', it was 'Blasphemous Rumours' that attracted the greater controversy. Like 'Something To Do', this looks back to the experiences of the Basildon boys before Depeche Mode existed. Gore drew upon the period when as teens, he, Fletcher and original Mode member Vince Clarke were all keen churchgoers. For Gore, it was never a simple matter of belief or of a commitment to Christianity, as he told New York radio station WLIR: 'I just used to go along because they were my friends. I was never a practising Christian, although they were. When you're not involved in it, I think you really notice the hypocrisy...' It was that hypocrisy that captured Gore's attention, the questions that an unwavering belief in God can throw up. Every week there was a 'prayer list' for the unwell and dying. The deaths that followed, despite the prayers of the congregation, were then greeted as positive developments, as being God's will, where the dead individual has been 'relieved' of their suffering and taken to 'a better place'. It got Gore thinking, and the result was 'Blasphemous Rumours' that plays upon the seeming arbitrariness of life and the supposed role of 'God' in events.

For his part, Fletcher took against the song upon first hearing: 'The song "Blasphemous Rumours" stems from our experiences... When Martin first played me "Blasphemous Rumours", I was quite offended. I can see why people would dislike it. It certainly verges on the offensive.' It's a narrative song that tells a story, contrasting the fates of two individuals – one a teenager who tries to commit suicide, but lives, and another God-fearing girl who is killed in a car crash (or perhaps it tells the tale of just one girl who undergoes a transformation in outlook). The controversy came from the lyrics that formed the chorus: 'I don't want to start/Any blasphemous rumours/But I think that God's/Got a sick sense of humour/And when I die/I expect to find him laughing'.

Reviewing for *Smash Hits*, then assistant editor Neil Tennant (later of the Pet Shop Boys) dubbed 'Blasphemous Rumours': 'a routine slab of gloom in which God is given a severe ticking off'. Fearing the single was an attack on the deity, many radio stations refused to play it on the basis of the title alone, so limiting its chart potential to Top 20 only (hitting a high of number 16); it largely failed to build upon the success of the previous two singles across Europe. Depeche Mode's dedicated song plugger Neil Ferris felt the track was 'a very, very difficult record, and there were a lot of people who felt that that song, lyrically, and just the title of it, shouldn't be on the radio.'

While Gahan recognised that the track got a lot of underground play in the US (paving the way for 'Personal Jesus'), Gore felt in 1989 that 'Of all of our songs, this is one that gets the most response. When it was released, I received a lot of letters from people who were shocked by the lyrics. They wanted to have "Blasphemous Rumours" banned on the radio.' There was a last-minute compromise that saw 'Blasphemous Rumours' released as a double A-side single with 'Somebody', but it was widely recognised which track was the 'real' single. In 1985, Gahan (in Steve Malins' *Depeche Mode: The Biography*) was relatively upbeat about the controversy. 'I think the problem arose because it had the word "Blasphemous" in the title, so the record itself must be, whereas it's just the thoughts of one man looking for some kind of reason in the goings-on in the world. We did get response from Christian associations saying that they understood what we were trying to say.'

Related Tracks
'In Your Memory' 4:06
Alan Wilder's second songwriting contribution to *Some Great Reward*, 'In Your Memory' was relegated to B-side status on the single 'People Are People', ironically giving it a brilliant showcase for one of Depeche Mode's lesser-known tracks. Wilder outlined his writing process to *Electronic Soundmaker & Computer Music* magazine in 1984: 'Where this writing differs from perhaps more conventional writing is that chord changes are far less important: the use of sound changes takes their place to produce atmosphere, and the attention is on lyrics, melody and sound.' As well as the Drumulator, the Roland MC-4 and the Synclavier, Wilder sampled a metal pipe being struck mixed with the natural decay of an acoustic bass drum. Musically, the track fits with 'People Are People' and 'Master And Servant', so it is surprising it wasn't included on the album. Gahan's vocal performance is strong, and the insistent rhythms drive the track onwards to its conclusion.

Never played live, 'In Your Memory' was first announced in the pages of the Depeche Mode Information Service in March 1983 under the title 'Place It In Your Memory'. Like 'Fools' on *Construction Time Again*, 'In Your Memory' is a low-key, atmosphere-driven track with lyrics very different to those normally composed by Gore. The 12" release of 'People Are People' also featured a reworking of 'In Your Memory' on the B-side that incorporated some melancholic piano in the middle, dubbed the 'Slick Mix' (running time 8:15), supposedly after the band's nickname for Wilder due to the increasing size of his slicked back hair (seen to great effect in the video for 'Master And Servant') – a nickname he professed to disliking.

'(Set Me Free) Remotivate Me' 4:18

Released as the B-side to the single 'Master And Servant', '(Set Me Free) Remotivate Me' continued the lyrical themes of the A-side. Driven by the chants of 'Set me free', the track opens with a light melody that is transformed as it goes along into something weightier. Gore's S&M tendencies come through in the lyric 'My body is yearning/For a new lease on life/Add a little spice', but beyond that, the song could be interpreted in line with the boredom explored in 'Something To Do'. 'Give me something/To get excited about' and 'It could be my imagination/But wasn't there more than this numb sensation' speak to the same lyrical concerns as *Some Great Reward*'s opening track, even if it is very different musically.

Black Celebration (1986)

Personnel:

Dave Gahan: lead vocals

Martin Gore: keyboards, backing vocals, additional vocals on 'Here Is The House', 'Dressed In Black' and 'Shake The Disease', lead vocals on 'A Question Of Lust', 'Sometimes', 'It Doesn't Matter Two', 'World Full Of Nothing' and 'Black Day'

Andy Fletcher: keyboards, backing vocals

Alan Wilder: keyboards, backing vocals

Recorded at Westside/Genetic, London and Hansa Mischraum, Berlin, November 1985 to January 1986

Producer: Depeche Mode, Gareth Jones, Daniel Miller

All tracks written by Martin Gore, except 'Black Day', written by Martin Gore, Alan Wilder and Daniel Miller, and 'Christmas Island', written by Martin Gore and Alan Wilder

Released: 17 March 1986. Label: Mute

Running time: 41:01

Highest chart placings: UK: 4; US: 90; Austria: 26; Canada: 47; France: 11; Germany: 2; New Zealand: 34; Sweden: 5; Switzerland: 1.

By the mid-1980s, Depeche Mode had evolved. No longer were they the 'plinky-plonky' teen exponents of synth-pop from Basildon, Daniel Miller's Silicon Teens made flesh. The original band members had matured together, having stepped up their game following the departure of Vince Clarke. Martin Gore's songwriting had also matured, with him beginning to explore darker themes over the past two albums, while Dave Gahan had developed a strong stage presence for the band's ever-changing live performances. Andy Fletcher was also doing his organiser thing as they began to finally make serious inroads into the American market.

With the belated success of 'People Are People' in the US, the band decided to strike while the iron was hot and release a follow-up single to bolster their upcoming tour of the States, set to begin in March 1985. Ticket sales had been encouraging, so it finally looked like America was waiting to be cracked. Having conquered Germany and in the process of becoming increasingly popular across Europe (if still regarded with some suspicion in Britain), Depeche Mode were ready for a new adventure. Playing to sold-out crowds in sports stadiums and vast halls, like the San Diego Sports Arena and the Oakland Civic Auditorium, was a sign of things to come.

Miller proposed a singles compilation for the UK and the American market just discovering Depeche Mode. *The Singles 81>85* was released in October 1985, while America got *Catching Up With Depeche Mode* the following month. Where *The Singles 81>85* was a collection of the band's 7" releases (with two new singles, 'Shake The Disease' and 'It's Called A Heart'), the American release had to be different as there'd already been the *People*

Are People compilation from July 1984 that featured several of the singles alongside selected album tracks (like 'Pipeline' and 'Told You So') and B-sides (like 'Now This Is Fun' and 'Work Hard'). *Catching Up...* featured those singles not on the previous compilation, with the addition of two other B-sides, 'Flexible' and 'Fly On The Windscreen', as well as the two new singles. While *Catching Up...* reached number 113 on the US *Billboard* Top 200 Chart, *The Singles 81>85* hit number six on the main UK Album Chart but topped the UK Independent Albums Chart. It hit the Top 40 across Europe (notably number nine in Germany).

Work on the band's fifth album, *Black Celebration* – a pivotal work – began in November 1985 at two London studios, Westside and Genetic, and continued at Hansa. The band worked on the project for three months, right through to the end of January 1986, but Gore and Wilder, in particular, had been laying the groundwork for the songs and the sounds that appeared on the record. It was a fraught time in the studio as their future direction seemed unclear and Gahan was concerned with Gore's control over the musical direction of Depeche Mode. The non-stop four-month working period didn't help, while Miller became concerned that Gore's demos were not producing obvious single-worthy tracks.

Cabin fever and claustrophobia set in at Hansa, compounded by the bleak nature of many of Gore's songs that concerned themselves with the darker side of sex and death.

The resulting *Black Celebration* – unlike the preceding albums – played through like a unified whole, with many of the short tracks cross-fading one into another. The theme is consistent throughout, with most dealing with love and sex, often the dark side. *Black Celebration* resembled an electronic prog rock album (albeit with shorter tracks). The music flowed, sometimes feeding back upon itself, with the same lyrical concerns reoccurring. The sound was a consolidation of the last two albums – as they were all recorded or mixed at Hansa, they essentially formed Depeche Mode's own Berlin trilogy. A period that had begun with the jaunty sounding 'Shake The Disease' and 'It's Called A Heart' ended with the deeper, darker sounds of 'Stripped' and 'Fly On The Windscreen'. It was the last album to be produced by Miller and Jones, drawing a line under the first era of Depeche Mode.

'Black Celebration' 4:55

The opening title track of *Black Celebration* was a declaration of intent. Their sound was evolving, taking the metal bashing in a more controlled direction, but with Martin Gore honing his songwriting with a strong focus on the topics of sex and death. The sound was, according to Gore, 'a lot heavier, harder and darker', and this was reflected in the lyrics. The songs on *Black Celebration* often adopted unconventional structures (made possible by the use of electronic instruments and sampling), and that begins here.

This use of samples and unconventional sounds and structures made 'Black Celebration' in particular, a difficult track to perform live. The increasing complexity of the band's sound meant they'd moved far beyond backing tracks and a trio of synth keyboards. Keeping the backing vocals – mainly by Gore and Wilder – in tune with the complex build that makes up the track proved difficult in a live context. In a commentary for the concert DVD *101*, Gore noted: 'The [backing vocals] just seemed to be so removed from the music. Everything always just sounds in a totally different key to me. I like the song; it's just that actually trying to perform it [was difficult]. Putting all the computer stuff together took quite a while as well. Well, Alan used to do most of that... Unfortunately, it is not really a "dance song" and it did not fit with the rest of the [live] show.'

'Fly On The Windscreen (Final)' 5:18
First released as a B-side to non-album single 'Shake The Disease', this is a slightly extended 'final' version, but it's not all that different to the B-side (discussed in detail under Related Tracks). The lyrical concerns darken and deepen from those featured on the preceding track.

'A Question Of Lust' 4:20
Second single released from *Black Celebration*, on 14 April 1986, 'A Question Of Lust' was only the second time that Gore performed lead vocals on a single (the first was 'Somebody'; his third and final – to date – single release on lead vocals would be June 1997's 'Home'). Given that Gore sings lead vocals on four tracks on *Black Celebration* (the most to that point), and provides co-lead vocals on two others ('Here Is The House' and 'Dressed In Black'), it's no surprise that he'd end up fronting a single.

It's a very big 1960s Phil Spector 'wall of sound' approach, albeit through electronic pop, with Gore comparing the track to something The Beatles might have done in their heyday. In the Mode fanzine *Bong #37* in 1998, Gore looked back at 'A Question Of Lust': 'This track has always been almost like an old 1950s or 1960s classic pop song. It's a really good song to do live and it's got a great melody.' The video was shot by Clive Richardson (who'd previously helmed 'Just Can't Get Enough' and 'Everything Counts'). Mixing concert footage with specially shot material (in which Gahan is relegated to waving a tambourine) and an opening sequence of a near-naked Gore messing about in the studio, it's a pretty basic affair, although it is notable as the final Mode video prior to the arrival of Anton Corbijn who would have a dramatic effect on the band's image.

Smash Hits made reference to the track's 'black electro clanks' that open this 'floating, melancholic tune', although from the suggestive title, critic Tom Hibbert was disappointed not to get something 'pervy' from it. *No. 1* magazine dubbed it Depeche Mode's 'first fully-fledged ballad', while describing it as a 'haunting track, mournful without being depressing'. It didn't fare too well on the UK Singles Chart, whether due to its slowness or the fact that Gahan was missing in action is unclear. 'A Question Of Lust' peaked at number 28, the band's worst single performance since their debut release 'Dreaming Of Me' five years earlier.

'Sometimes' 1:53

The only track on *Black Celebration* never played live, 'Sometimes' is another Gore ballad. Opening with the title sung gospel style, this anticipates the full-on gospel grunge of 'Condemnation' from 1993's *Songs Of Faith And Devotion*. At just 1:53, 'Sometimes' is the shortest non-instrumental Mode album track. Once described by Gore as a 'funny song', it's a piano ballad sung by Gore about questioning 'everything' with one of his narrative twists where the listener is branded as being 'as embarrassing as me'. The pseudonymous 'Betty Page' (actually Beverley Glick) in *Record Mirror* dubbed it 'one of the rather too many sweet little ballads [on *Black Celebration*]. Although the melodies are gorgeous, Martin seems preoccupied with sounding like the gawky school choirboy. Mr. Gore is again lyrically concerned with tenderness, sweetness, closeness with another, and putting his heart on his sleeve. That's fine, balanced against Depeche Mode's more exciting, sinister side.'

'It Doesn't Matter Two' 2:50

A 'sequel' song, following 'It Doesn't Matter' from *Some Great Reward*, 'It Doesn't Matter Two' is another shorter track that contributes to the overall tapestry. There's something of the 1980s vogue for 'systems music' – the kind of thing produced by Steve Reich, Philip Glass and Michael Nyman. The chant-sound rhythms (which echo some elements of the original 'It Doesn't Matter') that underlie the melody drive the morbid lyrics forward (Gore called the song 'very desperate, very, very morbid'). Chronicling early sexual experience as if it were a momentous event, though such intense feelings must fade: 'It might last for an hour'. The systems music feel was reinforced by the slow unwinding of the song as it collapses in on itself towards the end. This was a trick of technology, with the Friend Chip SMPTE controller allowing the track to be slowed in production without affecting the pitch. Gore admitted: 'Probably we were remotely inspired by [Philip] Glass, though I hardly ever listen to that kind of music. It wasn't a piss-take or something. It was serious.'

'A Question Of Time' 4:10

The third single from the album, 'A Question Of Time', is notable in being the first Mode music video to be directed by Anton Corbijn. Taking a totally fresh approach, Corbijn produced short films rather than the very literal video clips the band had previously been lumbered with. Shot in black and white, it sees a rider on a motorcycle and sidecar crossing rural America on a mercy mission to rescue an abandoned baby, which he then delivers to a waiting

Alan Wilder. This is intercut with concert performance footage featuring the rest, who all appear at the end. It doesn't make much sense or relate to the song, but it is far better than many of the videos the band had previously had to suffer through.

The lyrics of 'A Question Of Time' are, in retrospect, a bit dodgy as a twenty-something (and now married) Gahan sings about stalking a 15-year-old, presumably for sexual purposes (the same accusation can be made against 'Little 15' on *Music For The Masses*). It's redeemed by the final lyric: 'And then I condemn them/I know my kind/ What goes on in our minds'. Mixed into the chorus was a subtle sample from what Gore called 'an old doo-wop disc', 'She Wants To Mambo' by The Chanters released in 1954. 'At the end of each verse, the woman sort of moans,' said Gore to *Electronics and Music* in 1986. 'We sampled this moan and played it up a few notes, which made it sound like a girl. We used it on the chorus section of "A Question Of Time".'

'Stripped' 4:17

The first single to come from the album – following the two non-album single releases – was 'Stripped', a song that illustrated the changes the band were going through in 1986. According to Andy Fletcher: 'The idea of "Stripped" is to get away from technology and civilisation for a day and get back to basics in the country. It's about two people stripping down to their bare emotions.' The opening sounds were the ignition of Gahan's new Porsche. There were further engine sounds in the rhythms of 'Stripped', according to Gore. Buried in the mix was 'the sound of an idling motorbike played half an octave down from its original pitch'. The contrast of this vehicular noise and the lyrical appeal to the countryside is compelling. The filmic lyric 'Metropolis/Has nothing on this/You're breathing in fumes/I taste when we kiss' combines the themes of environmental degradation and eventual planetary death with sex once more (as on 'Fly On The Windscreen'). There's a call back to 'Lie To Me' on *Some Great Reward* in the lines 'Let me hear you/Make decisions/Without your televisions' that like much of that earlier song, has as strong a resonance in the 21st century as it did in the 1980s.

Released as a single on 10 February 1986, 'Stripped' was the band's sixth consecutive single to hit the UK Top 20, peaking at number 15 (slightly higher than the previous two singles; it also reached the Top 10 in Finland, Sweden and Switzerland, and reached number four in Germany). It was supported by the final video directed by Peter Care (who'd done 'Shake The Disease' and the bizarre cornfield video for 'It's Called A Heart'), filmed just outside Berlin's Hansa studio. Flowers and fumes imagery is matched to the band members demolishing a car with sledgehammers and melting a television. Care had managed to move the quality of Depeche Mode's videos up a gear, a process that would be completed only with the arrival of Anton Corbijn as their visual director.

'Here Is The House' 4:15

With the exceptions of this and 'New Dress', the vast majority of *Black Celebration* deals with lust and sex. Many of those tracks take a darker view of the topics than 'Here Is The House', which manages a more positive spin on adolescent sex. It serves as a 'come down' track after the raucous 'Stripped', although the sudden start might come as something of a jolt. There's a sense of togetherness lacking from most of the other relationships suggested on the other tracks, many of which deal with alienation and shame. Musically and lyrically, 'Here Is The House' is a throwback to Depeche Mode's earlier poppy output, and while not entirely out of place, it certainly stands out thanks to its positivity. The ticking clock that concludes the song, however, hints that the idyll described here might be running out of time.

'World Full Of Nothing' 2:50

After the respite of 'Here Is The House', Gore returns to the pointlessness of life and love in 'World Full Of Nothing', charting the first experience of adolescent love and concluding that in a cynical world where trust is lacking, whatever experience is available will just have to do: 'In a world full of nothing/Although it's not love/It means something'. From the bleakness of the title through the sentiment of the chorus, 'World Full Of Nothing' suggests that 'Here Is The House' was a moment of positive madness on behalf of Gore, who also provides the vocals here. *NME*'s Sean O'Hagan dubbed this track an 'evocative exploration of loneliness'.

'Dressed In Black' 2:32

The kink is strong on 'Dressed In Black', the second of two subsequent tracks that run under three minutes. Encompassing voyeurism and S&M, Gore is just putting it all out there. It describes one partner's total subjugation to the whims of another, simply because she's 'dressed in black again'. A pre-release version was included on a free 7" EP issued by *Record Mirror* magazine, with this rougher around the edges and less smoothly produced version being the first many heard of it.

'New Dress' 3:42

A throbbing attack on the popular media (specifically, in a 1986 context, popular tabloids) and their tendency to distract from 'real' news, 'New Dress' is a somewhat dated but nonetheless effective political statement. It powers along, with the admittedly juvenile lyrics given some punch by Gahan's chanting delivery. Although the royal of the time is the focus ('Princess Di is wearing a new dress'), the sentiment is easily transferable to current tabloid obsessions with her sons and their respective spouses. Again, like 'Lie To Me' (on *Some Great Reward*) and some of the lyrics of 'Stripped', there's an anticipation of the impact of 'fake news' and disinformation in the chorus line

'But you can change the facts/And when you change the facts/You change points of view/And if you change points of view/You may change a vote'. The tabloid media obsession with celebrity, particularly of the royal variety, has never left us, and 'New Dress' nailed that in 1986. It stands out on *Black Celebration* as being forthrightly political and real-world engaged, in contrast to the bulk of the songs that deal with the personal politics of relationships and sex. It brings the album to a strong close, and in many respects, points the way forward to *Music For The Masses* and *Violator*.

Related Tracks
'Shake The Disease' 4:49
Recorded at Hansa in March 1985 while the band were mid-tour, 'Shake The Disease' was one of two tracks issued to promote the compilation albums *The Singles 81>85* (UK) and *Catching Up With Depeche Mode* (US). Recorded under the title 'Understand Me' (a backing line from the chorus), Daniel Miller insisted another line would make a better title: 'Shake The Disease'. Released at the height of the AIDS/HIV epidemic that had kicked off in 1981, just as Depeche Mode were finding their fame as pop stars, many assumed the title was a reference to AIDS. Instead, 'Shake The Disease' was a simple love song, using the metaphor of infection for the state of being in love. It was a track the band were never entirely happy with. In *No.1* magazine, Gahan noted: 'I think it's a great song where we didn't really give it enough [attention] in the studio.'

For Gore (in the Dutch magazine *Hitkrant*, August 1985), the subject matter was simple: '[It's] the story of a one-sided relationship between a girl and a boy. They realise that it is as good as over for them, so it's a poignant song.' According to Gahan (on ITV show *No. 73*): 'It's basically a love song, and it's really about the problems of trying to get across what you really mean in love, when you're actually trying to talk to someone [when] it's very difficult.' Fletcher (in July 1985's *Popcorn* magazine) saw it as a tribute to the band members' girlfriends who 'have not always had it easy with us. [It's about] how difficult it is to keep a relationship.' Gore even included a call back to 'Stories Of Old' from *Some Great Reward* with the lines 'Now I've got things to do/And I've said before/That I know you have too'. Gore said: 'I really like references to other songs.'

The single reached number 18 in the UK Singles Chart (hitting the top spot in the UK Independent Singles Chart) and was Top 10 across Europe (number four in Germany and number two in the Netherlands). The music video – which received widespread airplay, especially on MTV – featured the band members apparently tumbling through the air (along with the required leather jackets and metal bashing) and was directed by Peter Care. 'Shake The Disease', despite the band's ambivalent feelings towards it, proved to be a popular live track that continued to be played right through to two outings during the 2017–18 Global Spirit Tour.

'Flexible' 3:14

The B-side to the single 'Shake The Disease', 'Flexible' was recorded at Hansa during the same sessions. Chanting over driving rhythms, 'Flexible' is Depeche Mode displaying a relaxed 'let's all have fun' attitude. On the surface, it deals with the result of the kind of fame that the band (Gore in particular) had experienced. As the lyrics note: fame, money, drink and girls 'can have strange effects'. The chorus and title, however, raise another possibility, one enhanced by the track featuring on the flip side of 'Shake The Disease'. The song asks: 'I ask myself/Is it a sin/to be flexible'. In the light of Gore's newfound interest in S&M and his explorations of the Berlin nightlife, is it a stretch to suggest such 'flexibility' might also encompass sexuality? Coming into adulthood on the cusp of the 1980s, the individual members of Depeche Mode cannot fail to have encountered (or experienced) homosexuality, especially in the club culture in which Gahan, in particular, was extremely active.

'It's Called A Heart' 3:48

Musically and sonically, Depeche Mode's 14th single – 'It's Called A Heart' – is something of a greatest hits package in just over three minutes. All the usual expected rhythms and 'found sounds' are present, while the lyrics hark back to the band's more 'poppy' past. The second fresh track included on the 1985 compilations, 'It's Called A Heart' was released on 16 September 1985.

Like the preceding single 'Shake The Disease', it was a track that the band would ultimately fall out of love with (somewhat ironic, given the song's subject matter). As a result, it was only ever played live during the 1986 Black Celebration Tour. According to Gore (in *Popcorn*), it dealt with 'the dangers within a romantic relationship... it's about feelings in general, how to deal with them.'

There was a fierce debate among the band and their advisers as to whether 'It's Called A Heart' or the far darker 'Fly On The Windscreen' would be the A-side. Wilder argued passionately for 'Fly', while others (including plugger Neil Ferris) expressed concern about a track where the opening lines featured 'death' as a repeated motif. 'I was vehemently against it,' Wilder said. '[Gore] had other songs that were much better, like "Fly On The Windscreen", that was the B-side. It was a stronger song, and I tried to argue to get it flipped to become the A-side.' The other band members, Daniel Miller and Ferris argued in favour of 'It's Called A Heart', so 'Fly' was relegated to B-side status. The single charted in the UK at number 18 (number one on the Independent Chart), and was Top 10 in many European countries (Ireland, Sweden, Switzerland and Germany). The choice didn't stand the test of time, with Gore noting it was 'probably my least favourite track we've ever released!'

'Fly On The Windscreen' 5:07

This became the B-side to the single 'Shake The Disease' after a furious row over the two songs' respective merits between Wilder and the rest of the band. Opening, according to Gore, with the sounds of 'a Black & Decker drill' and 'Daniel Miller breath sample noises', it's a dark track that suits the rest of *Black Celebration*, and so was revised and included as 'Fly On The Windscreen (Final)' (vindicating Wilder's faith). Of all the many Mode tracks that used sampling, 'Fly On The Windscreen' is one of the most 'built'. Gareth Jones (at website Almost Predictable Almost) recalled: 'Depeche [Mode] had an interesting philosophy and working practice. Because they were an electronic group, the work on the tracks was collaborative. It didn't matter who made or found a noise as it was just an element of the piece. It didn't matter who did what or who made what noise as we were all sculpting the same sonic world.'

Unusually for a B-side, 'Fly On The Windscreen' was widely played live, particularly as part of the Black Celebration Tour, but also during tours in 1993 and 2009. First released as a B-side, 'Fly On The Windscreen' was the darkest Depeche Mode song released to that point, totally unlike the poppy and upbeat 'It's Called A Heart'. The song deals directly with mortality and death. It mixes sex and death in a way that would later become second nature, opening with the bold declaration 'Death is everywhere' (no wonder Ferris didn't see it as single material). For all the 'flies on the windscreen' and 'lambs to the slaughter', the song concludes by highlighting sex (or perhaps love) as the antidote to inevitable death: the end is coming, but let's have a good time before we get there.

'But Not Tonight' 4:19
This track was the B-side for the single 'Stripped' and was included as a 12th track on the US release of *Black Celebration*. Used in promotion for the 1986 film *Modern Girls* starring Virginia Madsen and Daphne Zuniga, it was released as a 'promo single' in the US, accompanied by a music video directed by Tamra Davis (who shot promos for Hüsker Dü, N.W.A. and Sonic Youth).

It wasn't the first time a Mode track had featured in a movie. That honour belonged to 'Just Can't Get Enough', heard on the soundtrack of 1982's *Summer Lovers*. That same year the darkly romantic 'Photographic' had featured in *The Last Horror Film*. In 1986 – the same year as *Modern Girls* – both 'Stripped' and 'A Question Of Lust' had featured in the high school vigilante movie *Dangerously Close*. Television would quickly latch on to the Mode sound too, with multiple tracks featuring in a pair of *Miami Vice* episodes in 1986 and 1987. This was only the beginning, as Depeche Mode became the go-to band for movies and television episodes that wanted an aura of edgy cool.

'But Not Tonight' was never part of the band's live set (the single having failed to make a mark in the US) until it was reinvented as an acoustic piano piece for the 2013–14 Delta Machine Tour. Gore explained to *Rolling Stone*: 'We played a small show at the Troubadour in LA and we did "But Not Tonight" for the first time ever. We did [it] acoustic and it was surprising how much people loved it. America is really the only place where the fans love that song. It was a single in America, but not in the rest of the world. It's like a forgotten gem.' It was last performed live in October 2017 at the Hollywood Bowl in Los Angeles, California, as part of the Global Spirit Tour.

'Breathing In Fumes' 6:08

A dramatic remix of the elements that made up 'Stripped', 'Breathing In Fumes' was one of three B-side tracks featured on the 7" UK release (the others were 'But Not Tonight' and 'Black Day'). Samples and other sonic elements (distorted and reordered lyrics) from 'Stripped' were remixed at Hansa by Thomas Stiehler and the band during the production of *Black Celebration*. This was just one of several extended mixes or experimental remixes of elements of 'Stripped' and other *Black Celebration* tracks that played into the pollution and environmental themes.

'Black Day' 2:39

A third B-side featured on the UK 7" single release of 'Stripped', 'Black Day' is the only co-writing song credit from the *Black Celebration* sessions for Wilder, and the only Depeche Mode co-writing song credit for Daniel Miller. Both worked on developing the track with Gore, who also sings. It's a deconstruction of some of the lyrics from the album's title track, reworked against an electronic harmonica rhythm.

'Christmas Island' 4:52

Since the likes of 'Big Muff' on *Speak & Spell* and 'Nothing To Fear' on *A Broken Frame*, instrumentals had been relegated to B-sides, 12" releases and other curiosities. Co-written by Gore and Wilder, 'Christmas Island' was the B-side to the single 'A Question Of Lust', and unlike many B-sides and instrumentals, it featured multiple times throughout the 1986 Black Celebration Tour as an introductory theme. Continuing the naming of tracks after places (as in 'Oberkorn (It's A Small Town)'), it's named after the nuclear test site of Christmas Island. Web blog Almost Predictable Almost described 'Christmas Island' as a 'doom-laden, nuclear-themed instrumental... a quite marvellous booming instrumental full of the sort of satisfying noises that Depeche Mode specialised in around that time. [It's] a cracking track.' Long after it was recorded, 'Christmas Island' featured over the end credits of the second episode of the Disney+ Marvel superhero show *Hawkeye* (2021), whose first season was set during Christmas.

Music For The Masses (1987)

Personnel:
Dave Gahan: lead vocals
Martin Gore: keyboards, backing vocals, lead vocals on 'The Things You Said'
and 'I Want You Now', additional vocals on 'Behind The Wheel'
Andy Fletcher: keyboards, backing vocals
Alan Wilder: keyboards, backing vocals
Recorded at Guillaume Tell (Paris), Konk (London), Puk (Denmark), February–
July 1987
Producer: Depeche Mode, Dave Bascombe, Daniel Miller
All tracks written by Martin Gore
Released: 28 September 1987. Label: Mute
Running time: 44:04
Highest chart placings: UK: 10; US: 35; Australia: 60; Austria: 16; Canada: 26;
France: 7; Germany: 2; Italy: 7; Spain: 26; Sweden: 4; Switzerland: 4.

With their Berlin period (*Construction Time Again*, *Some Great Reward* and
Black Celebration) over, Depeche Mode next delivered an album that was
transitional, moving on from the dark and murky sounds of those Berlin
albums to the cleaner, brighter sounds of *Violator*, their first work of the
1990s. *Music For The Masses* was a culmination of all that had come before,
a consolidation of their work throughout the 1980s, emphasised by the
celebratory concert film and documentary that made up the *101* package. It
was the end of an era and a fresh start.

Unlike many of the British synth-pop bands and performers of the early
1980s, Depeche Mode had developed into a strong live outfit. The band
toured almost constantly, stopping only to produce a new album or singles
to keep their presence in the charts across Europe alive. From 1980's initial
tour – largely playing small local venues in Essex and London – Depeche
Mode had developed into a formidable live act. Every year, up through 1988's
Music For The Masses Tour, the band had played extensive live dates, honing
their performance skills, converting their synth-heavy sound to a subtle live
performance, and benefiting from Dave Gahan's growing showmanship.

Alan Wilder was now an important contributor to the band's sound,
working sometimes in tension with Martin Gore, to craft songs that both
impressed on vinyl (and, increasingly, CD) yet could also be played live to
an arena full of thousands of fans. Few in 1980 could ever imagine Depeche
Mode filling the Pasadena Rose Bowl in the US to capacity, yet that gig on
18 June 1988 was the climax of the Music For The Masses Tour, the 101st
performance. That gig was filmed for the *101* project (Wilder devised the
title), which consisted of the live gig, a documentary film following fans
across the US, and the band's first official live album release (also titled *101*).
Acclaimed American documentary film-maker D. A. Pennebaker (*Primary*,
1960; *Don't Look Back*, 1967; *Ziggy Stardust And The Spiders From Mars*,

1979) helmed both the concert film (an incomplete record of the entire performance) and the documentary, which were released in 1989.

The ironic title chosen for Depeche Mode's sixth studio album, *Music For The Masses* – which was released on 28 September 1987 – came true with *101*. Andy Fletcher told Depeche Mode biographer Jonathan Miller that the title was 'a bit tongue in cheek, really. Everyone is telling us we should make more commercial music, so that was the reason we chose the title.' With new producer Dave Bascombe, Depeche Mode began to move away from Miller and Jones' focus on sampling and metal bashing, paving the way for the cleaner sounds of *Violator*.

In previous years the Mode brand had been a haphazard affair, relying on Brian Griffin's abstract photography (a swan, a peasant in a field, a worker up a mountain), but the process had proven fraught on *Black Celebration*, resulting in an album sleeve no one was entirely happy with. Designer Martyn Atkins had been working on single sleeves for the band as far back as 'Get The Balance Right!' and he directed the music video for 'Little 15' from *Music For The Masses*. Atkins' work was seen in 1983's 'Everything Counts' sleeve and 1984's 'People Are People', among others. *Black Celebration*'s unsatisfactory cover saw Atkins' graphic designs clash with Griffin's photographic work (it would be Griffin's final contribution). For *Music For The Masses*, Atkins built upon the logos he'd introduced on *Black Celebration*, designing a unique graphic element for each track. His Bong megaphone concept carried across the album, singles and even the music videos.

Another major creative contributor to *Music For The Masses* was pop photographer Anton Corbijn. Dutch-born Corbijn began contributing photographic work to the *NME* in the 1970s, photographing David Bowie, Siouxsie Sioux, Bob Dylan, Kate Bush and, notably, Joy Division. He'd photographed Depeche Mode's first-ever magazine cover for the 22 August 1981 edition of *NME*, which was notorious for featuring Dave Gahan out of focus. Beginning with the video for the 1986 single 'A Question Of Time', Corbijn became a major force in Depeche Mode's graphic and filmic look, as well as their concert performances. Corbijn would ultimately direct 21 videos for the band (up to 2023's 'Ghosts Again'), design album covers and single sleeves from 1990's *Violator* onwards, and design the band's live sets.

While *Music For The Masses* was important (it reached number 35 on the US *Billboard* Top 200 Chart, securing their hold on the American market), it was the *101* project that served as the end of the first phase of Depeche Mode's musical evolution. The performance in front of over 60,000 paying fans at the Rose Bowl saw the band reach an apotheosis, something that was clear to frontman Dave Gahan: 'I had a strange feeling at that concert. I remember at the end of it, I really felt like it was all over, there was nowhere to go now with this caravan that we had been dragging around for the last ten years. What were we gonna do now? It was almost like we'd reached our destination.'

'Never Let Me Down Again' 4:47

A strong opener, and the second single release (on 24 August 1987, reaching number 22 in the UK and number two in Germany, and a Top 10 hit across Europe), 'Never Let Me Down Again' is a text book example of the dangers in attempting to interpret Martin Gore's lyrics. Speaking to *Rolling Stone*, Gore recalled: 'Two separate people came up to me after a show one night and said, "I really like that song." One of them thought it was a gay anthem and the other one thought it was a drug anthem.' The 'gay' reading is obvious: 'I'm taking a ride/With my best friend/I hope he never lets me down again'. A male singer referring to his 'best friend' as 'he' makes that reading inevitable. That's reinforced by one of Gore's more notorious attempts at rhyming: 'Promises me I'm safe as houses/As long as I remember who's wearing the trousers'. The drug angle is suggested by the chorus: 'Never want to come down/Never want to put my feet back down/On the ground'.

An obvious single, 'Never Let Me Down Again' quickly became a live favourite. Gahan recalled this as one of the highlights as the band played to larger audiences in stadium gigs: 'For me, this is one of the most intense moments during the concert, firstly because this track has a very strong emotional charge, and every time I play it the [hand] waving goes well with the crowd.' The song was part of the band's standard live line-up right through to the 2023 Memento Mori Tour.

The song's opening guitar riff was one of the first times they foregrounded 'traditional' rock 'n' roll instruments, although the sound was (inevitably) sampled and manipulated. Real orchestral sounds, such as strings and horns, began to make themselves feel part of the Depeche Mode sonic repertoire. Said Wilder (at his website): 'It stood out as an obvious single and suggested a "Stripped"-like feel. It has a very definite anthemic quality, which is especially demonstrated when the song is performed live and the whole audience wave their hands in unison at the end – a Depeche high-point I think.' The video was another black-and-white Anton Corbijn special, picking up with the fade-out orange Bong megaphone from the end of the 'Strangelove' video. It's a strange video, shot in the Danish countryside, featuring Gahan driving around in a tiny bubble car and the other band members seemingly larking around in some fields. It's clear, however, that the Bong megaphone was to be the unifying image of *Music For The Masses*, appearing in the videos, with three of them on the album sleeve, and showing up on some of the single packaging too.

'The Things You Said' 4:02

Martin Gore (who sings this) suggested it was 'the opposite' to 'Somebody', being about 'treason, about a man who is disappointed by someone he loved, but luckily he has real friends by his side', as he told French magazine *Best* (April 1989). It would become one of those Mode tracks featured in Gore's acoustic solo slots, performed throughout the Music For The Masses Tour (on 94 of the 101 dates) and then revived for the 2017–18 Global Spirit Tour for 12 dates. 'This is one of the songs I have performed right at the front of the stage,' said Gore. 'I like having a slot of one or two tracks, but I could not go on for any longer, it's way too stressful...' Also from *Music For The Masses*, 'I Want You Now' was another song frequently featured in Gore's solo acoustic set.

'Strangelove' 4:56

The first single released from *Music For The Masses* – on 13 April 1987 – signalled Depeche Mode's latest musical evolution. Although lyrically Gore continued to push the envelope, following the S&M theme of 'Master And Servant', with the sexual masochism suggested by 'Strangelove' ('Pain, will you return it'), in terms of their sound, this was a much more straightforward, even 'poppy' track that wrapped the lyrics in accessible sounds.

The single stalled at number 16 on the UK Singles Chart (while reaching number two in the ever-reliable German market, and Top 10 across much of the rest of Europe). 'Strangelove' made the Single of the Fortnight in *Smash Hits* and was reviewed by synth-pop pioneer Gary Numan: 'This is very much their style, isn't it... Quite metallic, quite a hard sound. I do like this, actually.' For Gore (in *Bong* #37, 1998), 'Strangelove' was on the edge of what he felt the band could get away with: 'Occasionally we've stepped on the wrong side of commerciality, not very often, and "Strangelove" is just on the right side. It's like "Enjoy The Silence", it's just on the right side of commerciality.'

As was so often the case for Depeche Mode, 'Strangelove' was constructed from complex sounds. Daniel Miller supervised the final mix, according to Wilder (on his website): 'The single was released before the final mixing of *Music For The Masses* and it was during this late stage that Daniel [Miller] visited the studio to assist with it – an act that demonstrated the still close production relationship he had with the band. He contributed a 12" version (Blind Mix) and by the time the band was ready to mix "Strangelove" for the LP, it was decided that the album version should incorporate elements of this. The result was an amalgamation of the original and Dan's remix.'

Anton Corbijn returned to shoot the black-and-white video for 'Strangelove', filmed in Paris. Amid the tourist attractions (the Eiffel Tower), the band are seen peering from balconies and pursuing a variety of leather- and rubber-clad models. The 'Bong 13' megaphone – an icon of the *Music For The Masses* period – pops up throughout (and bursts into full colour – red/orange – for the finale). As the Almost Predictable Almost fan site noted: 'This is the exact point Depeche Mode began to look incredible.' In the *NME*, Jane Solanas asked: 'What I want to know is, are Depeche Mode pervs? Their minds are veritable sewers. Leastways, Martin Gore's is and the rest of the Modes appear to encourage him, happily singing and playing his bizarre songs.'

'Sacred' 4:47

Love as a religion is the subject of 'Sacred', an underrated track. Effectively a bridge between *Black Celebration* and *Violator*, it draws upon the best of the past to point towards the future. Gore draws upon the churchgoing past he shared with Fletcher and Clarke, giving a song about sex and/or love (deleted as applicable) a veneer of religiosity. It contains references to 'duty', 'confession' and being a 'believer' and 'one of the devout', all connected with religion. There's reference to being a 'missionary', spreading the Gospel, but also a sex reference (no doubt). The 'devout' line was hijacked by Mode fans to refer to themselves as 'the devout'. As a live track, 'Sacred' didn't survive beyond the Music For The Masses Tour, being played on every date. During the Rose Bowl performance – recorded for the *101* film – the line '...then came the rain...' from 'Blasphemous Rumours' saw a short-lived burst of rainfall, only for the following song, 'Sacred', to apparently cause the rain to stop. Wilder quipped: 'We had a word with 'im upstairs!'

'Little 15' 4:18

The fourth and final single from *Music For The Masses* was the dubious 'Little 15', in which married mid-twenties Dave Gahan appears to be lusting after a 15-year-old (again). Gahan claimed (to KROQ Radio in 1987) the song was one of innocence about a young boy and his mother. '"Little 15" is actually about a boy. See, a lot of people have taken that song in the wrong way, they think it's about a small girl, but it's not. His mother is talking to him. She's saying, "Look, you're gonna grow up, and this is what it's gonna be like. It's not a bed of roses, and you're gonna be going out into the big, bad world soon." It's actually one of my favourite songs – but when he [Gore] brought it to me, I thought immediately it was about a little girl, one of his, you know, "things"... But we won't talk about those!' Despite Gahan's protestations, Gore did come clean that there was a little 'kink' on 'Little 15'. In Swedish magazine *Slitz* in 1987, he said: 'To me, it's about a bored, middle-aged housewife trying to find a new lease on life through a young boy. It doesn't have to be sexual. Although this particular song is about one of our classmates who did have an affair with a middle-aged woman when he was 15!'

The song was not intended as a single and barely made the final cut of the album. It was recorded towards the end of the sessions, and Wilder claimed inspiration from Michael Nyman's music for the 1985 Peter Greenaway film *A Zed & Two Noughts*. Wilder said: '"Little 15" was never intended as a single – in fact, from the outset, it was touch and go as to whether [it] would even be recorded. However, encouraged by Dan Miller, an experimental approach in the studio gave rise to a simple ballad based around a Nymanesque opening string arrangement.'

It was Mode's French record company that championed this and wanted it put out as a stand-alone single. Ironically, the single (released only in France, although it charted in Austria and Switzerland and reached number 16 in Germany) didn't chart there, but it did reach the UK Singles Chart at number 60 through import sales (it even reached number four in the

UK Indie Chart). The video was shot by Depeche Mode's then-design guru Martyn Atkins and was filmed in London's notorious Trellick Tower.

'Behind The Wheel' 5:18

The third single (released after the album on 28 December 1987), 'Behind The Wheel' was a return to the themes of domination and submission that had run through *Black Celebration*. In *Smash Hits* Sue Doyle deconstructed what she believed to be the 'found sounds' mixed into the track:

> Not unnaturally, since this is, after all, Depeche Mode, several odd noises immediately come into play here, not least the sound of a car hub cap falling off to begin proceedings. A door opens and closes and then – zwoom! – we're off at fairly moderate speed, Dave Gahan in the passenger seat and some weird girlie (not only weird but no doubt a bit of a perv on the quiet since Martin Gore wrote the thing) driving.

The 'hub cap' sound was actually a spinning saucepan lid, while the track also featured a hand striking the end of a Hoover tube, a guitar pick and sampled pan pipes (all according to Wilder). The Corbijn video continued his serialised adventures of Depeche Mode, as Gahan abandons the bubble car he'd been driving in 'Never Let Me Down Again' before embarking on new escapades in Italy with model Ippolita Santarelli on a shared Vespa SS180. Arriving in a small village, where the other band members are waiting, Gahan (complete with Midge Ure-style moustache) and Santarelli proceed to dance the night away. The single version was a lighter remix, while the album version plays out the song in its full dark majesty. A live favourite, 'Behind The Wheel' has been played at concerts almost 600 times, right up to the Delta Machine Tour of 2013–14.

'I Want You Now' 3:44

Another song about sexual desire and lust, 'I Want You Now' kicks off with distinctive sounds of breathy moaning before Gore's vocals. According to Dave Bascombe, the breathing sounds were originally sampled from a porn film before being replaced instead by sounds generated by a couple of French models summoned to the studio during Fashion Week in Paris. Proving that Gore has failed to 'Shake The Disease', he sings lines like 'My heart is aching/ My body is burning/My hands are shaking/My head is turning' as if suffering from a major malady. The end mixes more industrial 'breathing' ('It was actually an accordion just with no keys held down. There's a button you press on the accordion which lets all the air out. It does sound really disgusting.' – Dave Bascombe) with the sound of Russian spoken on a radio channel (which leads right into 'To Have And To Hold'). In 1988, 'I Want You Now' was released as a single in Japan, a double A-side with 'Behind The Wheel' that fades out before the Russian language sample kicks in.

Above: Depeche Mode's leather phase - including Martin Gore's dodgy S&M fashion choices!

Below: The older Mode men rediscovering their Spirit in the 21st century.

Left: The enigmatic cover for Depeche Mode's 1981 debut album *Speak & Spell*, photographed by Brian Griffin. (*Mute*)

Right: Brian Griffin's cover for 1982's *A Broken Frame* - a widely-acclaimed image that made the cover of *Life* magazine in 1990. (*Mute*)

Right: The cover for 1983's *Construction Time Again* combined with *A Broken Frame* suggested a political agenda matched by the songs. (*Mute*)

Left: The romance of industry inspired Brian Griffin for 1984's *Some Great Reward* album cover. (*Mute*)

Left: A young and innocent looking Dave Gahan dressed to the nines for a 1981 appearance on *Top Of The Pops*. (*BBC*)

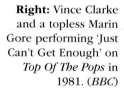

Right: Vince Clarke and a topless Marin Gore performing 'Just Can't Get Enough' on *Top Of The Pops* in 1981. (*BBC*)

Left: Andrew Fletcher, Alan Wilder, and Martin Gore in the music video for 'Everything Counts'. (*Mute*)

Right: Fletch blows the shawm while Wilder strikes the marimba in Clive Richardson's 'Everything Counts' video. (*Mute*)

Left: The band relishing their 'pop star' status, performing 'Everything Counts' on a 1983 edition of *Top Of The Pops*. (*BBC*)

Right: Andrew Fletcher, Depeche Mode's 'man of mystery', on *Top Of The Pops* in 1983. (*BBC*)

Left: Brian Griffin's final album cover photography - for 1986's *Black Celebration* - proved disappointing to the band. (*Mute*)

Right: Iconic artwork for 1987's *Music For The Masses* from Martyn Atkins. The ironic album title proved to be rather prophetic. (*Mute*)

MUSIC FOR THE MASSES
DEPECHE MODE

Left: Cover image for the CD releases of *Strangelove*, labelled Bong 13 in Mute's Depeche Mode numbering system. (*Mute*)

Right: Music for a new decade: Anton Corbijn's evocative design for 1990's *Violator*, which pushed the band to greater musical heights. (*Mute*)

Left: First *Violator* single, 'Personal Jesus' set the stage for the 1990s and gave Depeche Mode a hold on the US. (*Mute*)

Right: In 1993, *Songs Of Faith And Devotion* brought a harder rock edge to Depeche Mode's evolving sound. (*Mute*)

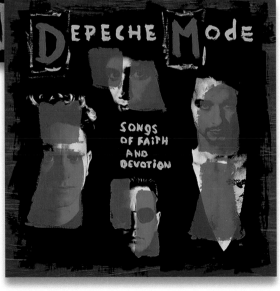

Left: The *101* documentary film captured the final date on Depeche Mode's *Music For The Masses* Tour at Pasadena's Rose Bowl. (*Mute*)

Right: Depeche Mode's stage presence had evolved dramatically by the time of *101*. (*Mute*)

Left: Martin Gore and Andrew Fletcher 'Shake The Disease' during the *101* concert film and documentary. (*Mute*)

Right: 'King' Dave Gahan in Anton Corbijn's video for 'Enjoy The Silence', shot in Scotland, Portugal, and the Swiss Alps. (*Mute*)

Left: Mean and moody: the Mode men 'Enjoy The Silence' while posing in studio. (*Mute*)

Right: 'Enjoy The Silence' won Best British Single at the 1991 Brit Awards; the band gave the ceremony a miss. (*Mute*)

Left: The album many thought could never exist: *Ultra*, Depeche Mode's 1997 album following the departure of Alan Wilder. (*Mute*)

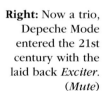

Right: Now a trio, Depeche Mode entered the 21st century with the laid back *Exciter*. (*Mute*)

Right: *Playing The Angel* saw Depeche Mode recapture their experimental edge in 2005. (*Mute*)

Left: Heavily electronic, 2009's *Sounds Of The Universe* met a mixed reception from fans and the music press. (*Mute*)

Left: In 2013, *Delta Machine* was regarded as one of the band's strongest albums this century. (*Mute*)

Right: A dramatically simplified sound and a return to political engagement were central to 2017's *Spirit*. (*Mute*)

Left: 'Where's The Revolution' was the first Depeche Mode single not to chart on the UK Singles Chart. (*Mute*)

Right: Dave Gahan - no longer the shy teen who first fronted Depeche Mode gigs - in Berlin on the *Delta Machine Tour.* (*Mute*)

Left: The band perform 'Should Be Higher' on stage in Berlin on the *Delta Machine Tour.* (*Mute*)

Right: 'Reach out and touch Dave' - fans greet Gahan during the *Delta Machine Tour* in Berlin. (*Mute*)

Left: *Memento Mori*, the first Depeche Mode album following the death of band member Andrew Fletcher. (*Mute*)

Right: Now a duo, Dave Gahan and Martin Gore playing chess on a New York rooftop in the 'Ghosts Again' video. (*Mute*)

Left: Thing take a grave turn in Anton Corbijn's 'Ghosts Again' music video. (*Mute*)

Right: Dave Gahan fronts the performance with the BBC Concert Orchestra for Radio 2's *Piano Room.* (*BBC*)

Left: Depeche Mode take to the BBC's Maida Vale studios with the BBC Concert Orchestra. (*BBC*)

Right: The band performed 'Ghosts Again' and 'Walking In My Shoes' for Radio 2's *Piano Room.* (*BBC*)

Facing mortality: Martin Gore and Dave Gahan promote *Memento Mori*. (*Mute*)

'To Have And To Hold' 2:51

The radio Russian that cross-fades from 'I Want You Now' translates as: 'The evolution of nuclear arsenals and socially psychological aspects of the arms race was considered in these reports.' Although the band claimed not to know the source at the time (or exactly what the words meant), the sample came from a Cold War-era news report featuring the voice of well-known Soviet news anchor Igor Kirillov. This track has been the source of some disagreement among the band, with two versions released. The original recording was the album track, which Wilder called 'possibly one of DM's darkest tracks'. The alternative version, a rerecording of Gore's original demo, was released as the B-side to 'Never Let Me Down Again' as the 'Spanish Taster' version. 'The Spanish Taster is basically Martin's demo which he insisted on recording as well,' said Wilder on his website. 'I don't think there is a more perfect example of the musical differences between myself and Martin. His original [take] was too lightweight for my tastes, and – I felt – for the mood of the album. I pushed it in a darker, more atmospheric direction.'

Never played live (perhaps due to these musical differences), the lyrics of 'To Have And To Hold' are certainly darker than most Mode songs at this point, and the sonic approach taken by Wilder points towards the future work on *Violator* and *Songs Of Faith And Devotion*. Concerns with 'damage', 'disease', 'sin', 'dirt' and 'decay' are balanced by the need to be 'cleansed' amid calls for 'amends' and 'forgiveness'. The 'Spanish Taster' is sonically significantly lighter and seems at odds with the lyrical content (with Gahan's vocal so buried in the mix as to be near inaudible), an odd misstep for Gore, whose music and words are usually much more in alignment. As it is, at under three minutes, either version of 'To Have And To Hold' is simply an often overlooked sketch that points strongly to the future direction the band would take.

'Nothing' 4:18

Nihilism writ large is the message of 'Nothing'. Previously, Depeche Mode declared there was 'Nothing To Fear' (*A Broken Frame*) or that they lived in a 'World Full Of Nothing' (*Black Celebration*). By the time they reached *Music For The Masses*, this outlook had been reduced to a succinct, simple 'Nothing'! The suggestion is that there's nothing to be expected from life (certainly not satisfaction – 'Life... advertises nothing'), that nothing is promised to you ('Learn to expect/Nothing'), and nothing is likely to be delivered ('Anticipating/Nothing')! As ever, Gore falls back upon religion for the final kicker: 'God is saying/Nothing', as even the deity has checked out. These are among the bleakest lyrics Gore had written, delivered – rather incongruously – by a rather upbeat-sounding Gahan. To put a positive spin on 'Nothing', perhaps the intention is to suggest that it's best simply to 'go with the flow' and not expect any particular outcome. That's rather undercut by the dark, muscular sound, leavened by a slightly brighter melody.

'Pimpf'/'Interlude#1 – Mission Impossible' 5:00

This instrumental, originally recorded and released as the B-side to 'Strangelove', was liked by the band so much that it was included as the final track on *Music For The Masses*. While the band were off with Anton Corbijn filming the video for 'Strangelove', back at Puk Studios in Denmark producer Dave Bascombe remixed the 'Pimpf' B-side. The strength of 'Pimpf' saw it used as their opening music for the Music For The Masses Tour. Wilder noted (in *Best*, April 1989): 'All our concerts on the tour started with "Pimpf", so now whenever I hear this melody, it evokes a very precise memory: it was a signal that we were about to enter the stage, a moment when I started to have cold sweats. "Pimpf" – I think that's what the young members of the Hitler Youth were called. This music reflects the political climate... at the time of the rise of Nazism. It's because of its orchestral, quite distressing aspect...' (*Der Pimpf* was actually the title of the magazine of the Hitler Youth.)

Unusually, for an instrumental, there was a Corbijn-directed video for 'Pimpf' that saw Gahan, Wilder and Fletcher launch an attack on a wooden shack labelled 'Museo Depeche Mode', within which Gore is seen playing the piano. 'Pimpf' was also used on the soundtrack of the 1994 Indian-made 'Bollywood' knock-off of Wes Craven's *A Nightmare on Elm Street* called *Mahakaal* (aka *Demon*), directed by the prolific Ramsay brothers, Shyam and Tulsi. It also turned up in an episode of the apocalyptic animated series *Broken Saints* (2001–03) and on the 2006 DVD documentary *Doctor Who: Origins*.

On the album, 'Pimpf' is followed by the hidden track 'Interlude #1 – Mission Impossible', which consists of ambient studio noise, a dissonant woodwind sound and a sitar-style instrument playing the chorus riff from 'Strangelove'. Wilder admitted to an influence from minimalist composers on 'Pimpf' that spread across the whole of *Music For The Masses*:

> Quite a lot of the tracks on there do go in that way, where they keep going on a theme and build and build... 'Pimpf', for example, is very much like that. You end up with the kitchen sink, starting from one little riff that turns around on itself. I'd been listening to a lot of Philip Glass at the time, and the minimalists, so you've got this one theme and we just kept adding and adding to it.

Related Tracks
'Agent Orange' 5:05

This instrumental was the second B-side to 'Strangelove', alongside 'Pimpf', and was named after the notorious herbicide mixture used by the US in Vietnam – the poisonous dioxin continues to have an impact many decades after the conclusion of hostilities. It's a slower, quieter track than many recorded during the *Music For The Masses* sessions, coming across like the soundtrack to an imaginary film (making it all the odder that it has never been taken up by film or TV producers when so many other Depeche Mode tracks have been, even 'Pimpf'). It's a piece of mood music, haunting in a way some of the more bombastic Depeche Mode tracks simply aren't allowed to be.

'Fpmip' 5:24
An additional track on the 'Strangelove' 12" release, 'Fpmip' is an impish reworking of 'Pimpf'.

'Pleasure Little Treasure' 2:53
A rather unsung little B-side (to the 'Never Let Me Down Again' single) that has been played live a surprising number of times (a total of 95 performances on the Music For The Masses Tour), 'Pleasure, Little Treasure' was 'a good old rock 'n' roll [song that's] fun to play on stage,' according to Andy Fletcher (in *Best*, April 1987).

'Route 66' 4:11
The B-side to the 'Behind The Wheel' single, 'Route 66' continued the vehicle theme being (that rare thing) a Depeche Mode cover version, the Bobby Troup song '(Get Your Kicks On) Route 66' from 1946. The track draws its title and lyrics from US Route 66 (US66) that crosses the western two-thirds of the US, from Chicago to Los Angeles. Recorded by Nat King Cole and released as a single in 1946, 'Route 66' reached number three on the US *Billboard* Top 100 Chart. It's been covered countless times, including by Bing Crosby, the Rolling Stones (in 1964) and Manhattan Transfer (in 1982). Billy Bragg adapted the song in 1985 using UK landmarks and cities under the title 'A13 (Trunk Road to the Sea)'.

The Depeche Mode interpretation includes an entire middle section that draws musically from 'Behind The Wheel' (as does parts of 'Pleasure, Little Treasure'). It was Gore's idea to make the B-side of 'Behind The Wheel' a complementary driving song, with the Depeche Mode take being mixed by The Beatmasters (who also worked with the Pet Shop Boys, David Bowie and, er, Girls Aloud). According to Fletcher, songwriter Bobby Troup called Gore to declare the Mode take to be among his favourites. '"Route 66" was complete DIY,' declared Gore in *Best* in 1990. 'We did this song in less than a day in the studio and it was mixed immediately the next day. For us, there was nothing very serious about it, it was just a good B-side for "Behind The Wheel", a song for the road. Everyone was crazy about it and we used it a lot for the movie *101*. The Americans even wanted to put it on the A-side.' 'Route 66' turned up in the film *Earth Girls Are Easy* (1988) and was featured in the car racing video game *Burnout Paradise Remastered* in 2018.

'Stjarna' 4:25
The French 'Little 15' single release featured two B-sides: 'Stjarna' (Swedish for 'star') on the 7" and Beethoven's 'Moonlight Sonata #14' on the 12". Both tracks were solo instrumental piano performances by Alan Wilder, played for

pleasure during production on *Music For The Masses*, but recorded by Martin Gore (who'd written 'Stjarna', misspelt on the record label as 'St. Jarna').

'Sonata No.14 in C#m (Moonlight Sonata)' 5:36
See 'Stjarna'

Violator (1990)

Personnel:

Dave Gahan: lead vocals (except 'Sweetest Perfection' and 'Blue Dress'), backing vocals on 'Sweetest Perfection', Guitar on 'Interlude #2 – From Crucified'

Martin Gore: keyboards, guitar, backing vocals, lead vocals on 'Sweetest Perfection' and 'Blue Dress', additional vocals on 'Waiting For The Night'

Andy Fletcher: keyboards, backing vocals, distorted vocals on 'Interlude #2 – From Crucified'

Alan Wilder: keyboards, programming, drums on 'Clean', drum machine, electro-drums on 'Personal Jesus', backing vocals

Recorded at Logic (Milan), Puk (Denmark), The Church (London), Master Rock (London), Axis (New York), May 1989 to January 1990

Producer: Depeche Mode, Flood (Mark Ellis)

All tracks written by Martin Gore

Released: 19 March 1990. Label: Mute

Running time: 47:02

Highest chart placings: UK: 2; US: 7; Australia: 42; Austria: 4; Belgium: 1; Canada: 5; Finland: 7; France: 1; Germany: 2; Greece: 1; Italy: 6; Japan: 46; Spain: 1; Sweden: 6; Switzerland: 2.

Depeche Mode were different after playing the Rose Bowl in Pasadena. It dramatically changed the perception of the band in the UK and across the world, and gave the critics pause. How had the real-life Silicon Teens turned into a stadium-conquering behemoth set to dominate the 1990s? Over 60,000 people welcomed the foursome to Pasadena, cementing their growing popularity. As an album title, *Music For The Masses* had turned out not to be such a joke, after all.

Martin Gore had given up on Germany and his German girlfriend and returned to London. Dave Gahan had married his teen sweetheart Jo Fox and their first child was born along with *Music For The Masses*. Alan Wilder had built a home studio and was recording personal electronica under the name Recoil, an outlet for his musical experimentation. Andy Fletcher remained the most grounded, becoming involved in the business side while maintaining a presence in the studio and on stage: his was the tie-breaker when it came to disputes between the band's biggest egos, Gore and Gahan.

On the road, playing the 101 dates of the Music For The Masses Tour, Gore and Gahan finally adopted the part of the rock stars they had belatedly become, with Gahan perfecting his combination Mick Jagger and Iggy Pop dance moves. Gore was single and threw himself into partying, while the previously strait-laced, if not entirely abstemious Gahan deliberately pursued sex, drugs and rock 'n' roll (despite being married). Cocaine and dope joined the previously most abused Depeche drug, alcohol, with Gahan setting down a path that would see him come to the edge of death.

Indicative of the band's booming success in the US was the event to promote the release of *Violator* known as 'The Wherehouse record store incident' or more simply 'the riot'. A signing on the evening of 20 March 1990 at Los Angeles record store The Wherehouse on La Cienega Boulevard was expected to draw a few thousand fans (there was an in-store capacity for 150), but actually saw in excess of 20,000 turn up, filling up the streets around the store for six blocks. Never a riot, the sheer weight of numbers caused some minor injuries. For their own safety, the members of Depeche Mode where whisked away from the signing. The *Los Angeles Times* reported that 100 LAPD officers attended in riot gear, some on horseback, to disperse the frustrated crowds while police helicopters circled shining spotlights on the scenes below. In the end, there were very few actual arrests. Covering the event in *Melody Maker* (18 August 1990), Ted Mico wrote:

Nothing like this had happened in LA for years – even when U2 shot their video for 'Where the Streets Have No Name' on a Downtown roof. Depeche Mode bigger than Jesus? Not quite, but they'd give Bono a run for his money and are taken as seriously and followed as fanatically here as The Cure or New Order are in Britain.

The album that kicked off this chaos was *Violator*, the product of a new approach to recording provoked by Wilder. Rather than devote pre-production time to programming synthesisers, Wilder felt a less restricted approach might prove productive. Gore told Stuart Maconie in *NME* (17 February 1990): 'Over the last five years, we'd perfected a formula; my demos, [then] a month in a programming studio. We decided that our first record of the 1990s ought to be different.'

New producer Flood (Mark Ellis) worked closely with Wilder advancing the Depeche Mode signature, developing a cleaner electronic sound. The band's roles in recording had developed over many years, but now they knew enough to allow each to contribute from their individual strengths. Gore wrote the songs and provided an initial take in his home-produced demos. Wilder and Flood would take those and develop them further, layering sampled and created sounds throughout. Gahan's vocals would be the final layer that brought the songs to life. Early work in Milan produced 'Personal Jesus', setting the tone for *Violator* and securing the appeal of the band, particularly in America.

The bulk of the recording took place in Puk Studios in Denmark, but largely without Fletcher. Focusing on administrative management (an important background role that goes largely unsung), Fletcher could sometimes find himself at a loose end in the studio, beyond passing judgement on the sounds the others were producing. Fletcher, citing depression caused by delayed grieving for his sister, Karen, who'd died of cancer several years before, was persuaded to return to the UK where he signed into The Priory. Recording *Violator* would be completed without Fletch, although he later played the role of band spokesman following The Wherehouse record store incident, dealing with the media response. He was the one who, in *Q* magazine in May 2001, noted Depeche Mode's new level of success: 'Before this, we'd been going along quite nicely... Then when it came to *Violator* we inexplicably went huge. It was just incredible, and in many ways, we never really recovered from that.' The scene was being set for the carnage that would ensue during the 1993 Devotional Tour promoting their next (and best) album, *Songs Of Faith And Devotion*.

'World In My Eyes' 4:26

The fourth and final single from *Violator*, released on 17 September 1990, 'World In My Eyes' was selected as the album's opening track. It's an effective scene-setter, grabbing the attention from the opening bars and with a distinctive, cleaner electronica sound. It was one of the earliest tracks developed and one of the most reworked during the first recording sessions in Milan. Talking to Depeche Mode fanzine *Bong* #37 (1998), Martin Gore recalled:

> The original demo [was] slightly faster and slightly more obvious. While we were recording it in Milan, Dave was away for a couple of days, so we worked on it and turned it into this really moody piece. Dave arrived back in the studio, slightly jet-lagged and totally shocked, thinking we'd ruined the song, but half a day later he said, 'That's really good, the way it's turned out.' It always takes a while to get used to things.

The 'electro' sound of 'World In My Eyes' was no accident – it was a deliberate approach, making the opening track familiar to Mode fans, while laying the groundwork for what was to follow. On his website, Wilder noted 'with its "drop" third verse and use of vocal double-tracking to fill out and build the later choruses, ["World In My Eyes"] was probably the most "electro" sounding track on the LP – something of a homage to Kraftwerk, in a rhythmical sense at least.'

Critic Stuart Maconie (in *NME*, 17 February 1990) suggested to Gore the song was 'saying "Just for this moment, pleasure and gratification are all that matters". It's almost like (deep breath) existentialism.' In response, Gore declared 'World In My Eyes' to be 'a very positive song. It's saying that love and sex and pleasure are positive things'. Despite that positivity, 'World In My Eyes' only peaked at number 17 in the UK Singles Chart (although it reached number two in both Denmark and Spain). In *Q* magazine (May 2001), Fletcher flew the flag for the track: 'Whenever I'm asked which of our tracks is my favourite, I always say "World In My Eyes".'

'Sweetest Perfection' 4:43

Martin Gore provides the vocals for 'Sweetest Perfection', an epic track that any other band might have considered positioning as the album closer.

Instead, it's the bridge between two iconic songs. Built from all sorts of swirling noises and orchestral sounds, it's a truly epic construction, one that was difficult for studio engineer Kevin Paul to effectively recreate when remastering the album in 2006. He told *Sound on Sound* magazine in November 2007 that the track was 'completely crazy. It had lots of tape loops, lots of phasing, all sorts of sounds going on.' Gore gives his all to the vocal, spinning an obsessive love song into a towering sonic structure that threatens to collapse come the conclusion. Wilder (on his website) wrote that the finale of the track was perhaps the trickiest element: 'The weird stuff at the end came together during the mixing stage. It's the kind of thing you resort to when you haven't got an ending.' The dead-stop, hard out that wraps up 'Sweetest Perfection' was absolutely necessary in order to clear the decks for what was coming next...

'Personal Jesus' 4:56

Released seven months before *Violator*, 'Personal Jesus' was the first single (out on 28 August 1989, their final release of the 1980s) from that album and continued the evolution of their signature sound. The first recording sessions for *Violator* took place in Milan under new producer Flood (Mark Ellis). The immediate sonic difference from the former Mode sound is the foregrounding of the guitar riff. It wasn't the first time the band used guitars: they featured on 'Behind The Wheel' and were integral to their cover of 'Route 66', but guitars had been used subtly as far back as 'Love In Itself' and 'And Then...' from *Construction Time Again* and in acoustic form on *Black Celebration*'s 'Here Is The House'. For a band that had long eschewed 'traditional' rock instruments like guitar and live drums in favour of 'modern' synths and manipulated samples, the prominence of a blues-inspired guitar riff with a strong rhythm was a departure.

There was some internal debate about the song's commercial prospects as a lead single. As reported in Depeche Mode fanzine *Bong* #37, Gore recalled:

> We were really happy with the song and we realised it was a potential single, but we didn't have any idea of the mass appeal. We thought it was the sort of thing we liked but the radio programmers would hate, and we'd be lucky if it reached 25. We were especially worried about America, because the moment you mention the word Jesus in the title, you're asking for trouble...

As Gore knew from experience, his lyrics could stir up controversy in the US ('Blasphemous Rumours') or meet with resistance even within the Mode in-house promotional machine ('Fly On The Windscreen'), so his concerns over 'Personal Jesus' were understandable.

Although the track appears to feature what sounds like a live drum sound, that was yet another real-world manipulated sound sample that had been produced in their trademark idiosyncratic way. On his website, Wilder explained:

> The track was a significant move forward but still retained elements of [Depeche Mode's] former experimental self. The main 'stomp' was a recording of two or three people jumping up and down on flight cases alongside Martin's John Lee Hooker guitar riff and the Kraftwerk-style synth parts.

Gore found inspiration for what Johnny Cash – who did an acclaimed cover version in 2002 – described as 'a very fine evangelical gospel song' in Priscilla Presley's 1985 book about her husband, Elvis Presley. 'It's a song about being a Jesus [-figure] for somebody else, to give you hope and care. It's about how Elvis was her man and her mentor and how often that happens in love; how everybody's heart is like a god in some way.'

It had been over a year since Depeche Mode's previous single 'Little 15' (in May 1988) and almost two years since the release of *Music For The Masses*, their previous studio album (excluding the live *101* project). Therefore, 'Personal Jesus' was a 'comeback' requiring special promotion. The unique promotional strategy involved placing small ads across the UK's newspapers (in a pre-social media world) and on the London Underground with white text on a black background inviting those seeking 'Your own personal Jesus' to call a phone line where you could hear a rather tinny rendition of the new Depeche Mode track.

The resulting boost saw the track hit a high of number 13 in the UK Singles Chart (as usual, it fared better across Europe, reaching number five in Germany, three in Italy and three in Spain). 'Personal Jesus' was the first Mode song since 'People Are People' to hit the *Billboard* Top 40, reaching a high point of number 28 (though it hit number three on the *Billboard* Alternative Chart).

The distinctive promotional video directed by Anton Corbijn was shot on standing movie sets in the Tabernas Desert in Almeria, where various 1960s 'spaghetti westerns' had been filmed, including Sergio Leone's *A Fistful of Dollars* (1964). In keeping with the western theme, the four Mode members were depicted wearing cowboy hats and shades.

There were a plethora of remixes and extended versions (the track was Warner Bros. biggest selling US 12" release to that point), and it was covered by many artists, including Johnny Cash, Marilyn Manson, Def Leppard and others. The track was widely heard in film and TV productions, including *Mystery Science Theatre 3000* (1994), *Law of the Lawless* (2002), *Saved!* (2004), *Almost Human* (2013), *Fear the Walking Dead* (2019), *The Last Days of American Crime* (2020), *Lucifer* (2020), *Russian Doll* (2022, accompanying a drug trip), and on the soundtrack of the video game *Grand Theft Auto: San Andreas* (2004), to name just a few. This anthemic track not only proved popular with the media, it was a much-favoured banger played live almost 900 times.

'Halo' 4:30

The flip side of 'World In My Eyes', Gore explores the downsides of helpless indulgence in 'Halo'. Gore told *NME* (17 February 1990): 'On "Halo"... I'm saying "Let's give in to this", but there's also a real feeling of wrongfulness. I suppose my songs do seem to advocate immorality, but if you listen, there's always a sense of guilt.'

The percussion was a second-hand sample from Led Zeppelin's 'When The Levee Breaks' via an unnamed rap record, combined with string samples that Wilder remembered were lifted from classical composer Edward Elgar. He admitted (in the *Electricity Club*, 2011): 'One of my techniques is to find classical strings and transpose [or] stretch these, then add my own samples, to formulate new and unusual arrangements.' For a while, 'Halo' was on the shortlist of potential singles from *Violator*, but – according to Wilder – it was 'never really a major contender'. Despite that, a video was produced by Anton Corbijn for 'Halo' released as part of the *Strange Too* VHS compilation (a tale of love among circus folk, with Gore as a juggling clown, Gahan as a strongman, Wilder and Fletcher as undertakers and Corbijn as a donkey minder!).

'Waiting For The Night' 6:07

A near duet between Gahan and Gore, 'Waiting For The Night' falls at the mid-point of *Violator*. The slow-moving, expansive track was inspired by 1970s prog rock electronic pioneers Tangerine Dream, then a favourite of Wilder and producer Flood. The vocals floated over what Wilder described as 'the bubbling bass part'. Both Wilder and Flood came to rely upon the imperfections of the ARP2600 synth sequencer, which meant that 'slight tuning and timing variations' led to what Wilder described to the *Electricity Club* (2011) as 'happy accidents and almost random events... we arrived at that particularly hypnotic end result'. It's another much-covered track, performed live a surprising 227 times, running through to the 2023 Memento Mori Tour. The video backing played out during early live performances featured Gore done up as some kind of bondage angel.

'Enjoy The Silence' 6:12 (including 'Interlude #2 – From Crucified', 1:52)

The second single from *Violator* was 'Enjoy The Silence', released in advance of the album on 5 February 1990. While still foregrounding the guitar sounds core to 'Personal Jesus', this was a very different, cleaner sound. Originating as a ballad written by Gore, 'Enjoy The Silence' was heavily revamped by Wilder, who thought the original sounded like a Pet Shop Boys song, to become a more up-tempo, smoother, synth-driven take. Gore told *Mojo* magazine (September 2012):

The original demo was very slow and minimal, just me and a harmonium, and Alan had this idea of putting a beat to it. We added the choir chords and [producer] Flood and Alan said, 'Why don't you play some guitar over the top?' That's when I came up with the riff. I think that's the only time when we all looked at each other and said, 'I think this might be a hit.'

Unusually for Depeche Mode, 'Enjoy The Silence' was a positive song lacking the darkness (either lyrical or sonic) that pervaded many previous Mode releases. On MTV's *120 Minutes*, Gore explained: 'It's just about a feeling of not wanting anything else, feeling totally satisfied, even words seem an intrusion.' That was why Gore was originally resistant to Wilder's revisions. 'Alan had this idea to speed it up and make it a bit more disco, which I was really averse to at first, because I thought "it's supposed to be about serenity, and serenity doesn't go with the disco beat".'

Not only was it a hit (reaching number six in the UK and number eight in the US, the band's highest position), but 'Enjoy The Silence' also won the Brit Award as Single of the Year for 1990. Perhaps in reaction to the way the UK music industry had long shunned them, the band didn't attend the ceremony.

'Enjoy The Silence' came with another memorable music video, again directed by Anton Corbijn. Heavily featuring Gahan (and in some long shots, a double – actually video producer Richard Bell) dressed as a king, complete with crown and ermine cloak, it was filmed in the snow-covered landscapes of the Swiss Alps, in Alvor, Portugal and in Scotland. Throughout, he is seen lugging a seaside deckchair everywhere as if seeking the perfect location to enjoy the silence. Corbijn, in liner notes for the 2005 documentary *Anton Corbijn – The Work*, recalled he had 'one idea for the video, which was the image of a king walking around the world looking for peace, in silence, and bringing his deckchair with him. It took a lot of persuasion to get a go-ahead...'

Critically, 'Enjoy The Silence' was very well received, marking something of a change in the UK media's attitude to the band that *NME* dubbed 'teen corruptors'. It was the *NME*'s selection as Single of the Week ('[a] brooding, tender piece'), while *Melody Maker*'s Simon Reynolds declared the track '[a] glum, earnest vibrato... new romanticism infected with miserabilism'. For *Music Week*, 'Enjoy The Silence' was simply 'the best Depeche Mode single in years'. Like 'Personal Jesus' before it, 'Enjoy The Silence' was phenomenally popular with other artists who covered it, including Tori Amos (in 2001), Lacuna Coil (2006), Keane (2007) and Carla Bruni (2017). It was also often used in film and TV, including documentary short *NotNa* (2005), *Tell Me You Love Me* (2007), *Coach Trip* (2011), *Laurence Anyways* (2012), *My Mad Fat Diary* (2014) and *Narcos: Mexico* (2021). As a live track, it was almost as popular as 'Personal Jesus', with 885 performances, sealing its position as one of Depeche Mode's best live tracks.

'Policy Of Truth' 4:55

Released as the third single from *Violator* on 7 May 1990 (two months after the album), 'Policy Of Truth' is an often overlooked yet significant Mode track. Martin Gore (in *Bong* #37) certainly saw it as one of his best works:

> It has been one of my all-time favourite songs that we've ever recorded. I really like the words to it and the whole concept of having to lie to keep up appearances, maybe it's better to do that ... I think a lot of the time, [some] songs are overlooked, disregarded or not taken seriously...

Gore put that lack of attention down to the electronic instrumentation that Depeche Mode usually favoured over traditional guitar-and-drum rock sounds. As is clear with *Violator*, the band were now incorporating such 'traditional' instrumentation more than ever before, but using it in a signature Mode way. The introductory melody that opens 'Policy Of Truth' was a single note sampled from a guitar, but looped and played from a synth keyboard. According to Wilder, 'The loop is what gives it the vibrato effect.' This incorporation of guitars, filtered through the imaginative pioneering approach of Depeche Mode, served to give them such a distinctive sound.

'Policy Of Truth' was first developed and recorded during the sessions in Danish studio Puk. The band's approach to the track changed dramatically, and it was still in a state of flux when they reconvened in The Church studio in London's Crouch End. Wilder wrote that these revisions 'would signify problems with a song, although in this case, we knew it was a strong track, not least a potential single. The main riff proved such a problem to get a sound for, we must have tried 100 different variations before settling on what had become the sound of the album: slide guitar.'

The critical reception for 'Policy Of Truth' was rather bizarre, as if the collective pop music rags had decided they'd given the band they loved to hate too easy a run recently with 'Personal Jesus' and 'Enjoy The Silence'. *Melody Maker* first referred to 'Enjoy The Silence' as having been 'cute' before damning 'Policy Of Truth' as 'ineffectual' and 'the runt of the litter' from *Violator*. *NME* described it as 'f***ing boring' (the censorious stars are theirs). It was left to *Smash Hits* to recognise that 'Policy Of Truth' would be an overlooked classic: 'this is a thumpingly-good dance floor stomper.' In the US, the *Boston Globe* praised the song's 'alluring synth line tipped by a sliding bass note, a tiny infectious hook courtesy of Gore's treated guitar'.

Whatever the critics said, the track was a Top 20 hit on both sides of the Atlantic, reaching number 16 in the UK but going one higher on the *Billboard* Hot 100 by hitting number 15 (the only single to do so, but the usual story of Top 10 status across Europe applied: number seven in Germany and Spain, and number five in Finland and Italy). Corbijn's mostly black-and-white video was shot around the shadow of the Manhattan Bridge as the various

Mode members find themselves unlucky in love, presumably after confessing some dark truth – it's an unusually literal interpretation by the often abstract Corbijn.

'Blue Dress' 5:41 (includes 'Interlude #3', 1:23)

The second Gore-fronted vocal on *Violator*, 'Blue Dress' was the album's 'pervy song' – according to Gore in the *NME* (17 February 1990). The song was built around 'the idea of watching a girl dress, and then realising that "this is what makes the world turn".' Wilder (online) recalled the track being built from 'washy sounds' and 'drone guitars' in the style of Suicide to provide a 'deliberately wet sound to give it some atmosphere'. For Wilder, 'Blue Dress' was relegated to the penultimate spot on *Violator* as essentially a 'filler' track. 'It's not really one of my favourites,' he deadpanned. Rarely performed live, 'Blue Dress' nonetheless became one of Gore's occasional live acoustic tracks, including on his solo tours apart from Depeche Mode.

'Clean' 5:32

Album closer 'Clean' is rather ironically titled given what was to come next in the Depeche Mode story (especially concerning Dave Gahan). Gore got to combine his two favourite topics – 'a lot of Holy imagery that intertwines with the sex theme' (*Select*, December 1990) – with sounds that echo Pink Floyd (in particular 'One Of These Days' from *Meddle*, 1971). Wilder recognised the comparison, but denied that song had been sampled, even if the opening sounds like a slowed-down take on that Floyd track. It was the second track – after 'Halo' – to have an accompanying video (although it was not a single release) put out on the *Strange Too* VHS video compilation.

Related Tracks
'Dangerous' 4:22

The B-side to 'Personal Jesus', 'Dangerous' was a throwback, lyrically and musically, but also in having a completely new song as a B-side, rather than a 'throwaway' remix or instrumental. It's clearly a track that doesn't fit with the rest of *Violator*, so was rejected for being a bit too *Black Celebration* or *Music For The Masses* in tone. The track is given a different, freer musical interpretation on the longer 'Sensual Mix' (by Flood) that featured on the 12" release of 'Personal Jesus'. Daniel Miller also offered his take on the track with the 'Hazchemix' version that limits the vocals, but unleashes an electro storm verging on acid house for over five and a half minutes.

'Memphisto' 4:03

Released as the B-side to 'Enjoy The Silence', 'Memphisto' was intended as an 'atmosphere' piece accompanying an imaginary movie. In *Bong* #18 in April 1993, Gore confirmed 'Memphisto' 'was the name of a make-believe film about Elvis as the Devil...' The title was a corruption of the name

Mephisto, a shortening of Mephistopheles, the name of a major demon in German folklore often thought of as synonymic with Satan. It was used as the title of movies in 1930 and 1981, and was a Marvel Comics character and a Swedish black metal band (Mefisto). The alteration of the title to 'Memphisto' combines Memphis, Tennessee, closely associated with Elvis, and the name of the Devil, Mefisto (or Mephisto).

'Memphisto' is a rather sedate, laid-back piano-led outing that builds from a simple repeating melody to something altogether darker, with electronic hums, drones and background vocal harmonies, with increasingly dissonant percussion over the top. In 1990, *Poster Seductores* quoted an unnamed Mode member commenting: 'We like cinema and we like to create special [atmospheres]. In a way, "Memphisto" is our homage to esoteric cinema.'

'Sibeling' 3:18
Also released as a B-side to 'Enjoy The Silence', 'Sibeling' has some similarities to 'Memphisto' in that it is a piano-led instrumental but with a more 'spacey' and spooky sci-fi feel than the horror overtones of Gore's 'Elvis as the Devil' inspired tune. There is something of the nursery rhyme ballad buried deep within the track's approach.

'Kaleid' 4:18
The B-side to 'Policy Of Truth', 'Kaleid' (apparently pronounced close to 'collide' as in 'kaleidoscope') forgoes the simplicity of 'Memphisto' and 'Sibeling' for something more acid house. Mixed with a version of 'Interlude Crucified', 'Kaleid' was used as intro music for the World Violation Tour of 1990. It's an instrumental driven by its percussion, with throbbing beats and chunky sounds making for a powerful track. None of the band, however, have ever commented on the fact that the title is an anagram of 'I Dalek'...

'Happiest Girl (Jack Mix)' 4:58
Originally intended as an album track for *Violator*, 'Happiest Girl' was relegated to B-side status on the fourth single, 'World In Your Eyes'. The 'Jack Mix' featured on the B-side is the original version, which according to Wilder, was simply not 'strong enough' for the album. It's a middling track, a bit of a throwback to earlier Mode sounds mixing elements of *Black Celebration* and *Music For The Masses*. Gore delves into his love and pain themes, asking if happiness can be real and if it can survive deliberately induced pain, either in a physical BDSM context or as a form of emotional violence. Expressing the desire to 'see the pain she'd feel' and almost wanting to steal her happiness in a vampiric way ('Wanted to feel her joy/ Penetrate my skin'), 'Happiest Girl' is a throwback. It was later remixed by The Orb (a band that owed a huge debt to Depeche Mode) as 'Happiest Girl (The Pulsating Orbital Vocal Mix)' in 2004.

'Sea Of Sin (Tonal Mix)' 4:46

This B-side to 'World In My Eyes' was classed by Almost Predictable Almost as 'a real lost gem in the Depeche catalogue'. As with 'Happiest Girl (Jack Mix)' the 'Tonal Mix' is the original, first-released version of 'Sea Of Sin', later reworked in various 12" formats. An example of the moody electronica that Mode were past masters of, 'Sea Of Sin' was given an even heavier electronica remix in the 'Sensoria' version that plays down the evident darkness of the original B-side. Although produced during the 1990 recording sessions for *Violator* there is no suggestion that this – unlike 'Happiest Girl' – was intended for the album. As a B-side, it's quintessential Mode music, but another song that might have disrupted the flow of the album. While the song is a basic deep dive into instant sex, Gore can't resist including references to 'God' and 'lies', as was his wont.

Songs Of Faith And Devotion (1993)

Personnel:
Dave Gahan: lead vocals (except 'Judas' and 'One Caress'), sampler
Martin Gore: keyboards, guitar, backing vocals, lead vocals on 'Judas' and 'One Caress', sampler
Andy Fletcher: keyboards, sampler
Alan Wilder: keyboards, programming, bass guitar, drums on 'I Feel You', 'In Your Room' and 'Rush', drum machine, sampler
Recorded at Madrid, Spain; Chateau du Pape, Hamburg, Germany; February 1992 to January 1993
Producer: Depeche Mode, Flood (Mark Ellis)
All tracks written by Martin Gore
Released: 22 March 1993. Label: Mute
Running time: 47:26
Highest chart placings: UK: 1; US: 1; Australia: 14; Austria: 1; Belgium: 1; Canada: 5; Finland: 1; France: 1; Germany: 1; Greece: 1; Italy: 6; Japan: 31; Spain: 2; Sweden: 2; Switzerland: 1.

'There's been a big change in each individual member of the group, which I couldn't sum up in a few sentences, but particularly over the last few years,' is how band member Alan Wilder perceived the state of Depeche Mode a few years into the 1990s. The follow-up album to the world-beating *Violator* was *Songs Of Faith And Devotion*, a controversial Mode release that also proved to be Wilder's last involvement with the band. Following the excesses of the Devotional Tour, promoting that album, and the following extended Exotic Tour, Wilder quit the band in 1995. The fallout from the tours and the departure of Wilder was the biggest crisis in Depeche Mode history since the departure of founding member Vince Clarke over a decade earlier.

After the World Violation Tour in support of *Violator*, the members of Depeche Mode scattered to the four winds to recover. Their lives had changed dramatically since the early 1980s, when they were young lads on the make, playing at being pop stars. During the *Violator* period both Andy Fletcher and Martin Gore had become fathers (Fletcher with his long-term partner Gráinne Mullan and Gore with his American girlfriend Suzanne Boisvert, whom he'd met in Paris two years earlier; they would marry in 1994). Dave Gahan was married and had a son, but he'd split from Jo Fox as a result of his adoption of a full-on rock 'n' roll lifestyle in the wake of the *Music For The Masses* album, including taking full advantage (in all senses) of the groupies that Depeche Mode attracted. Gahan was now based in Los Angeles, living with American girlfriend Teresa Conroy, who'd worked as a US publicist for Depeche Mode.

'Since we've got to our thirties,' noted Wilder of the changes in the circumstances of the band's four members, 'certain aspects of our lives have become much more important to us. We've had a significant break away from each other before we started making this record [*Songs Of Faith And Devotion*], and when we came back together, you could really see the changes in us.' As with the other three, Wilder had also got married, to his girlfriend Jeri Young, and had continued to stretch himself musically and creatively by producing a new Recoil album.

According to a 'Mode camp insider' in *NME* in 1993, each member – beyond Dave Gahan being singer and frontman – had a clearly defined role to play in Depeche Mode: 'If it wasn't for Martin, there'd be no songs. If it wasn't for Alan, the records wouldn't sound the way they do. If it wasn't for Fletch, there probably wouldn't be any money.'

These changes weren't only in their personal lives. By the end of 1991, Martin Gore had completed demos of a couple of tracks that would be central to the new album, 'I Feel You' and 'Condemnation'. Gahan had been out of contact with the rest of the band for over a year and the others were unaware of the changes that had taken place in his lifestyle. Isolated with Conroy in an LA mansion, Gahan had taken on the full 1990s rock star junkie persona: long, shoulder-length hair, additional tattoos (a Celtic dagger, a Hindu symbol, among others), and a well-entrenched heroin addiction. The band agreed to reconvene in Madrid, Spain, in January 1992 to begin work on a new Depeche Mode album, but the other three were in for a shock when they saw Gahan.

'I had changed,' Gahan told *Q* magazine in 1997, 'but I didn't really understand it until I came face to face with Al [Wilder] and Mart [Gore] and Fletch [Andy Fletcher]. The looks on their faces... it battered me.' Gahan's musical tastes had also changed considerably, and along with Conroy, he was much more into the early 1990s American 'grunge' scene populated by the likes of Nirvana, Jane's Addiction, Pearl Jam, Alice in Chains and Rage Against the Machine. Such was his dedication, Gahan was no longer sure he wanted to continue with the 'dance electronica' of Depeche Mode. The more blues-oriented and rockier-sounding demos Gore had come up with were a huge relief to Gahan: 'I was so glad Martin was moving away from the dance music formula. When he started sending me demos for the new record, I thought, "Great!"'

The last time the band had reconvened to produce an album under some pressure and amid changing lifestyles, the result was *Black Celebration* – it was a fine record, but the process of making it took its toll. The same was about to happen all over again on *Songs Of Faith And Devotion*, but in an even more disruptive way. The pressure this time was to produce something worthy as a follow-up to *Violator*, the album that had at last launched Depeche Mode to international – but especially American – super-stardom. What could they possibly do as an encore?

Producer Flood was fresh from working with U2 on *Achtung Baby* (1991), and he chose to recreate the all-in, 24-hours-a-day creation process that had resulted in that album. A villa was rented in a palatial estate some 30 miles

81

from Madrid and converted into a recording studio where the band would also live. The plan was for two six-week working periods to be separated with a month off, but it quickly became clear that the 'communal living' approach was not working. Mute's Daniel Miller visited early on to see how things were progressing, only to immediately become aware that all was not well in Mode-land:

> They'd spent time apart, they'd all gone through quite big changes in their lives, some of them had kids, [and] there wasn't that natural coming together any more... It was the worst vibe. Everyone seemed to be in their own little space and nobody was relating to each other at all... You'd expect a bustle of activity, but it felt like they had burned out before they'd even started.

Gahan wanted a harder rock sound, Gore was feeling the pressure of following *Violator*, and Fletcher was struggling with his own mental health issues, while Wilder was beginning to feel creatively unfulfilled, fearing his strong musical contributions were being taken for granted. When they regrouped in Hamburg for the rescheduled second session, things began to progress (Fletch sat out this part). The rough studio jam sessions of the first tracks were reworked effectively by Flood with input from Wilder to sound like a rockier take on the signature Depeche Mode sound. The album was wrapped up in London at Olympic Studios, where a gospel choir was recruited to add the finishing touch to 'Get Right With Me'. By the end, Flood had also decided to call it quits with Depeche Mode, calling *Songs Of Faith And Devotion* the 'hardest album he'd ever made'. There would be worse to come, as the Devotional Tour almost tore the band apart. After almost 15 years, the end appeared nigh for Depeche Mode just as they'd reached a new creative high.

'I Feel You' 4:35

The difference in the 'new' Depeche Mode is obvious right away from the shock of noise (a synthesised and manipulated tyre screech) that opens 'I Feel You', the first single from *Songs Of Faith And Devotion* (released on 15 February 1993, in advance of the album). It's a million miles away from 'Enjoy The Silence' and it's hard to believe this is from the same band who just a decade before were producing such 'bubblegum' electro-pop as 'Everything Counts'. The disorienting opening would be repeated with variations on several future albums (such as 'Barrel Of A Gun' on *Ultra*, 'A Pain That I'm Used To' on *Playing The Angel*, and 'In Chains' on *Sounds Of The Universe*).

The blues guitar (played by Gore) and much more rock-sounding 'live' performance feel is upfront and in your face (or ears). According to Martin Gore, this was a deliberate and very different way for Depeche Mode to work in studio:

The whole *Songs Of Faith And Devotion* project started off with the basic principle that we wanted to become more live, spontaneous and have a lot more performances involved. So that whole album turned out to be the rockiest that we've ever achieved. 'I Feel You' is probably the pinnacle of that and it's about the closest we're going to come to sounding like a real authentic rock band.

There are two immediate differences that repeat across the album: Dave Gahan's voice is pushed in new directions and Alan Wilder's live drums give a totally different feel than the preprogrammed sounds previously used. Even so, Depeche Mode remained fundamentally themselves: Wilder may have played 'live' drums, but they were sampled and sequenced into loops that made them more consistent. The feel is still 'live' (more than on anything the band had previously produced in studio), but the traditional Mode control is present.

Another black-and-white music video by Anton Corbijn featured British actress Lysette Anthony. Just as the track recalls the bluesy guitar riff of 'Personal Jesus', so the music video shares some iconography, shot in Red Rock Canyon, Nevada. Wearing shades, gloves and a pinstripe suit, a very different-looking Gahan features: long-haired, additional tattoos and bearded. It's all a long way from Basildon. Also wearing shades are Wilder on drums and Fletch on keyboards, while the only one not sporting eyewear is Gore on guitar. The live version of the track rapidly became a firm favourite from the Devotional Tour onwards, racking up over 715 performances.

Strangely, this disruptive track was first played on Simon Mayo's Radio 1 *Breakfast Show* in late January 1993 – not exactly music to enjoy your cornflakes to. The promotion must've worked (combined with an audience waiting to see what might follow *Violator*) as 'I Feel You' crashed into the UK Singles Chart, peaking at number eight (the band's highest placing since 'Enjoy The Silence' reached number six; the previous highest position was 'People Are People' at number four). Across Europe the song hit the Top 10 (number seven in Austria; two in Denmark; five in France; four in Germany; and one in Finland, Greece and Spain). In the US, the song proved that Depeche Mode were bigger than ever, reaching number 37 on the *Billboard* Hot 100, number three on the Dance Chart, and number one on the Alternative Chart). 'I Feel You' was used in a variety of television series episodes, including instalments of *Skins* (2008), *Misfits* (2012), *Absentia* (2017), *Sense8* (2018), and on a trailer for *Thirteen Reasons Why* (2018), and the films *Bullfighter* (2000), *Head-On* (2004), *The Collector* (2009) and *Floating Skyscrapers* (2013).

'Walking In My Shoes' 5:35
The live performance aspect continued through the second track (and second single, released on 26 April 1993). Said Wilder (online): '[This] was constructed using an unusual method for us, [by] jamming together. Martin

played guitar, I played bass and we ran a rhythm machine – just to get the basic feel – and after much trial and error, the chorus bass line and guitar pattern fell into place.' That was followed by Wilder working with Flood to develop the drum loops, the strings and the main riff on piano and harpsichord (altered by being processed through a distorted guitar amp).

Lyrically, the song is the first on this album to put the singer on trial. Questions of 'absolution' and 'forgiveness' abound, but it may be Gore's take on Gahan's excesses during the World Violation Tour: 'The countless feasts laid at my feet/Forbidden fruits for me to eat' suggests the world of tour groupies and drugs. Gahan refers to 'my judge and jurors', while the following track 'Condemnation' includes reference to being 'tried', 'the book in my hand' and 'my sentence'. Gore rarely reveals exactly what his songs are about, but it is clear he was presenting Gahan with lyrics that encompassed their recent experiences. 'Walking In My Shoes' also seemed to be a particularly meaningful and successful track for Gore (*Bong* #37, 1998):

> If I really had to stick my neck out and choose my all-time favourite song, it would probably be 'Walking In My Shoes'. I think it has a great melody – the words and the subject matter really complement each other perfectly. The instrumentation is also interesting.

Reviewers seemed mixed on the new rockier Depeche Mode, although *NME* dubbed this 'eerie and powerful' while doubting it was strong enough to be a single. U2's Bono picked 'Walking In My Shoes' as one of his favourites, calling it 'deeply moving and profound... a uniquely European fusion between blues and gospel... a blunt and beautiful declaration of a need for healing.'

For the video, Corbijn finally abandoned his long-term devotion to black and white (mostly), instead opting for a bonkers full-colour evocation of madness as bird-headed beasts and purple-clad priests cavort at the base of the mountain of the demon king (or something). The single was the only one of the four from *Songs Of Faith And Devotion* not to reach the UK Top 10, hitting a high of number 14 (despite arguably being the best single). Across Europe, it was better appreciated reaching the top 5 in Denmark (five) and Portugal (three). In the US, 'Walking In My Shoes' reached number 69 on the *Billboard* Top 100, number 15 on the Dance Chart and number one on the Modern Rock Chart. A favourite of Wilder (alongside 'In Your Room'), it was used in a second-season episode of the television show *Mr. Robot* (2016).

'Condemnation' 3:20

For the third single from *Songs Of Faith And Devotion*, released on 13 September 1993, Depeche Mode went full gospel. It was a sound they'd been flirting with, notably on 'Personal Jesus', a touch on 'Sacred', and even in the opening of 'Sometimes'. The machine sounds of the past were gone, as were the synths and sampling that Depeche Mode had so long relied on.

Instead, this is a fairly straightforward gospel grunge take on an excellent Gore song. In the May 1993 edition of *Keyboard* magazine, Wilder described how the baseline piano that forms the solid foundation to 'Condemnation' was put through 'some kind of wobbly pitch-shifter' with the aim of enhancing the gospel feel while steering clear of any parody or pastiche. The other important element was the band's sonic representation of the song having been performed in a large, empty space, without relying on echo or reverb. Each member performed their parts in the same recording space, the garage of the house that had been converted into a recording studio in Madrid. Said Wilder:

Fletcher was bashing a flight case with a pole, Flood and Dave were clapping, I was playing a drum, and Martin was playing an organ. We listened back to it. It was embryonic, but it gave us an idea for a direction.

Canadian magazine *Exclaim!* interviewed Gahan in 2021, with the vocalist looking back at the moment his grungy, gospel-sounding, larynx-punishing vocal was captured:

[It] wasn't necessarily completely accurate to the way Martin wrote the melody line or the phrasing or the timing. I just sang it, and [after] I sang it, the tape stopped rolling and it went quiet. I've got my headphones on and I hear Flood's voice go, 'Yeah, I mean, you could do another one, but I think we got it.'

Ever the perfectionist, Gore was never entirely happy with the outcome on any of his songs. The addition of gospel backing singers to the single version helped, and this would be replicated to a spine-tingling effect on the gruelling Devotional Tour. The single was a Top 10 UK hit, peaking at number nine on its first week, Depeche Mode's highest chart entry point. The *NME* dubbed the song 'perv-gospel', while *Music Week* labelled it 'subtle and stylish'. Despite that, Gore lamented: 'I am still not sure that's the optimum we could have got,' while Gahan was more satisfied: 'It's got everything in there: soulfulness, redemption, longing to belong. I feel that in all these songs.'

'Mercy In You' 4:17
Opening with a much more traditional, if heavier, Mode sound, 'Mercy In You' is the closest *Songs Of Faith And Devotion* has to offer to a throwback. However, the heaviness of the rockier sound makes it the ideal bridge between the gospel of 'Condemnation' and 'Judas'. There's a lot of reversed vocals built into the track, backwards trickery that adds to the uncanny middle eight and extended fade-out. Reports of the recording process suggest that Gahan actually learned the vocals backwards phonetically so he could perform them live, singing over a 'mirror image' of the melody. The tape was

then reversed, giving the vocal performance a 'ghostly' effect. It certainly adds some sneaky sonic trickery to an otherwise straight-up rock track, all about transgression and forgiveness, doing wrong full in the knowledge that the 'mercy' that follows will be so much the sweeter.

'Judas' 5:14

Opening with sampled Celtic uilleann pipes mixed with what Wilder called 'backwards reverb', 'Judas' is the first of two tracks featuring vocals from Gore (the other is 'One Caress'). It's a slow burner, springing into life after a minute when the drums hit. Featuring the religious and darkly romantic lyrics that Gore was famous for, the song is (according to Gore) about 'wanting one hundred per cent of someone in a relationship, [it's] the ultimate arrogance'. At a time when AIDS was still big, the line 'Risk your health for me' struck a particularly uneasy chord, motivating Gore to tell Australian newspaper *In Press*: '[It's] an arrogant love song, [but] we are not condoning unsafe sex!' The song concludes with an atmospheric Wilder-constructed 'come down' instrumental following Gore's vocal climax. The track moved in and out of the Depeche Mode concert tour set-lists, being performed just short of 100 times up to 2017–18's Global Spirit Tour.

'In Your Room' 6:26

Fourth and final single from *Songs Of Faith And Devotion*, 'In Your Room' was released on 10 January 1994 and went one better than 'Condemnation' hitting a UK chart Top 10 high spot at number eight (the third of the four singles to crack the Top 10, making this the band's highest ever singles per album success rate; it also reached number two in Denmark, Finland and Sweden). It had proven to be one of the more difficult songs for the band to get to grips with, and it originally existed in three distinct early forms: an austere ballad, a more soulful version, and – finally – a rock anthem. The final version was a Frankenstein monster-style mix of all three, building upon the best aspects of each. The lyrics and structure had been straightforward, it was just the specifics of the sound that had proven to be so elusive. Driven by a thundering, grinding drum backing that kicks in at two minutes, the song is an epic exploration of the darkness that surrounded Gahan during the Devotional Tour, making it one of his favourites to perform live. The result was a longer epic that was strong enough to be a hit but too ungainly to become a single that would win much radio play. Gore told *Rolling Stone* in December 1993:

> I think 'In Your Room' could be potentially bigger [as a hit single than 'I Feel You'], but it's six and a half minutes. It could be edited, but I think part of its beauty is its length.

The resulting single was dubbed the 'Zephyr Mix', a radical reworking by Butch Vig that ran for a somewhat trimmer 4:52. Gahan brought in Vig, who'd produced Nirvana's *Nevermind* and Smashing Pumpkins' *Siamese Dream*. Initially, the rest weren't sold on Vig's revamp, but slowly they came around to Gahan's point of view. 'It's an interesting mix, completely different to what we would have done, though we prefer our own original mix,' Fletcher told *Drum Media* in February 1994. 'We still like to consider ourselves European and away from that American grunge sound, we're not jumping on that bandwagon.' Wilder was a champion for the album version but found himself outvoted when even Gore gave up on his reservations to the grunge-infected take. According to Wilder (online), the single version of 'In Your Room' 'lost much of its Depeche Mode character, falling short of its intended sensuality and intensity'. These kinds of developing musical differences would play on Wilder's mind, contributing to him coming to a monumental decision. 'In Your Room' would be Depeche Mode's last single as a four-piece.

'Get Right With Me' 2:55 (and 'Interlude #4 My Kingdom Comes', 0:57)
A return to the gospel-inflected approach exemplified by 'Condemnation', 'Get Right With Me' saw Gore resist the further addition of backing vocalists. Talking to Swedish magazine *POP* in 1993, Gore said:

> We had already done the vocal tracks on all the songs, but Flood had this idea about a gospel choir. I was very suspicious, I thought we would lose what we'd already achieved. Which was actually quite good! But as soon as they came into the studio and started singing, the song was given a whole new dimension.

The gospel singers were Hildia Campbell and Samantha Smith, who joined the Devotional Tour, providing lively backing vocals on this, 'Condemnation', 'Death's Door', 'I Feel You' and several others. Originally, Gore intended to sing 'Get Right With Me', but Gahan found himself challenged by the track and insisted he take over. Despite Gahan's enthusiasm, and seemingly becoming more discontented with the musical direction Mode were going in, Wilder dubbed this track 'filler', comparing it with 'Blue Dress' on *Violator*. Despite that, it has a solid, crunchy sound, with hints of 1990s hip-hop infiltrating the rock gospel. The accompanying 'Interlude #4' is an airy instrumental featuring elements of the Swamp Mix of 'I Feel You', a buffer between tracks.

'Rush' 4:37
Driving drums open 'Rush', a track whose pace lives up to the song's title with a 109BPM tempo. It slows and changes tone dramatically about two minutes in. In the May 1993 edition of *Keyboard* magazine, Wilder noted:

> There's a part in the middle of 'Rush', the sort of progressive rock track near the end of the album, where the voice has lots of backwards reverb;

that really sets the vocal part off. The nice thing about backwards reverb is that it adds space to a sound without making it washy. I'm against using a lot of reverb, because I can't stand the distancing effect. I do often want to hear sounds in a space, or the clarity of a sound. Backwards reverb can do exactly that.

'One Caress' 3:32

The recording sessions for *Songs Of Faith And Devotion* did not produce much in the way of rejected, discarded or additional material. As a result, 'One Caress' was first released as the B-side to the initial single, 'I Feel You'. In the US, the track – featuring Gore on vocals, only his second (the other being 'Judas') – was released as a promo single. A hugely interesting musical departure, 'One Caress' features a string quartet (who also performed on the track on selected 1993 tour dates). Talking to the Swedish *POP* magazine in 1993, Gore explained how the sound came about:

> The best thing about it was that it was so spontaneous. [The string quartet] came in and played and I sang with them live. We recorded the song in three hours, usually every song takes about a month... there's something special with musicians, real string players. They've studied many years to play their instruments... my music was suddenly taken more seriously... suddenly hearing 'real' musicians performing your song makes it, in a way, come off as more serious.

It's a powerful, hugely emotional vocal from Gore, singing meaningful lyrics that provide a dash of light (despite all those references to 'darkness'). The 28-piece string quartet performed the score, arranged by Will Malone (Massive Attack's 'Unfinished Symphony'), and recorded at Olympic Studios in London. The three-hour start-to-finish process put 'One Caress' on a par with 'Somebody' for the song completed in the shortest time. Originally intended as a mere B-side (according to Fletcher), it was added to the album as it turned out so well. The US promo single was accompanied with a rare album-track music video (directed by Kevin Kerslake), featuring imagery of snakes and insects with a sense of rural folk horror as the band are taken away by the Ferryman!

'Higher Love' 5:56

The climax of *Songs Of Faith And Devotion* comes with 'Higher Love', a track the band were considering as a potential single. After a slow, measured start, it proves to be an energising and dramatic finale that is the perfect capper for one of the band's finest albums. A complex mix of many of the elements that had played throughout the preceding tracks, there's a dash of gospel, a pinch of hip-hop, a host of electronica, all wrapped up in Gahan's vocal rock swagger. Fan site Almost Predictable Almost dubbed 'Higher Love' as 'a lost Depeche classic'. Overlooked, it was performed 127 times live, and effectively wrapped up Wilder's time as a member of Depeche Mode in some style. The rigours of the Devotional Tour, Gahan's out-of-control addiction and near death, Fletcher's depression-driven breakdown and increasing musical differences accumulated to push Wilder into a major decision that would significantly affect the future direction of Depeche Mode.

Related Tracks
'My Joy' 3:57
Released as the B-side to the single of 'Walking In My Shoes', 'My Joy' was considered for the album. It has the same heavy, insistent rhythms of many of the other tracks, but with more obvious electronica. The distorted Gahan vocals make it a different beast, however, a lighter overall sound that bends towards the upbeat, happy and optimistic – not *Songs Of Faith And Devotion* material! Lyrically, it's a bit thin, a paean to God, devotion (whether religious or more earthly), and pleasure, but remains something of a 'lost' track, adrift in the world of B-sides and other ephemera.

'Death's Door' 6:38 ('Jazz Mix'), 3:54 (Soundtrack Mix)
Recorded as a contribution to the soundtrack of the epic Wim Wenders 1991 film *Until the End of the World* (the soundtrack album version was released on 10 December 1991, so the track didn't represent the forthcoming rockier, bluesier Depeche Mode to be), 'Death's Door' turned up as a B-side on both single releases of 'Condemnation' (as a 'Jazz Mix' by Depeche Mode and Steve Lyon) and 'In Your Room' (on the 12" vinyl; by this point 7" single releases were falling out of favour, replaced by CDs). According to engineer Steve Lyon, the track was completed quickly, using 'real' instruments (apparently to fit with the overall sound of the wider soundtrack), over a period of 'two to three days'. Only Gore and Wilder were involved, with Gore providing the vocal, as well as lifting musical elements from 'Clean' (steel guitar) and 'Blue Dress' (Gore's own guitar licks). Other artists represented on the movie soundtrack were Talking Heads, Julee Cruise, Neneh Cherry, Nick Cave & the Bad Seeds, Lou Reed, U2, R.E.M. and Elvis Costello – fine company for the Mode. Surprisingly, for a song made explicitly to support a movie, 'Death's Door' was performed around 60 times during 1993's Devotional Tour.

Ultra (1997)

Personnel:
Dave Gahan: lead vocals (except on 'Home' and 'The Bottom Line')
Martin Gore: keyboards, guitar, backing vocals, lead vocals on 'Home' and 'The Bottom Line'
Andy Fletcher: keyboards, backing vocals on 'Barrel Of A Gun'
Recorded at Abbey Road, Eastcote, Westside, Strongroom, RAK, London; Electric Lady, New York City; Larrabee West, Los Angeles, January 1996 to February 1997
Producer: Tim Simenon
All tracks written by Martin Gore
Released: 14 April 1997. Label: Mute
Running time: 60:04
Highest chart placings: UK: 1; US: 1; Australia: 7; Austria: 5; Belgium: 1; Canada: 2; Finland: 3; France: 2; Germany: 1; Greece: 1; Italy: 2; Japan: 39; Spain: 1; Sweden: 1; Switzerland: 4.

The Devotional Tour, in support of *Songs Of Faith And Devotion*, almost destroyed Depeche Mode. After a string of European dates in the spring and summer of 1993 and a 50-date North American tour in the autumn, the band went straight into a run of pre-Christmas dates in the UK in Dublin, Birmingham, Manchester, Sheffield and London. It featured the biggest stage set designed by Anton Corbijn, who also put together the film projections that accompanied the songs. Raised at the back, Gore, Fletcher and Wilder managed their keyboards while Gahan strutted his stuff in the large space at the front of the stage, occasionally joined (or replaced) by Gore on vocals.

The band were not in good shape before they began the tour: Fletcher (newly married that January) was suffering from depression, Gore's alcohol addiction was having an effect, while Gahan's drug habit escalated and the married Wilder grew 'close' to support act Miranda Sex Garden's Hepzibah Sessa. The tour included among the entourage a $4,000-a-week psychiatrist in an attempt to keep the show on the road. 'We weren't confident he [Gahan] was going to make it to the end of the tour,' confessed Wilder, who also took on an expanded role behind the drum kit. The 97 dates would see Depeche Mode performing a gruelling live set for a full seven months (13 months, including the Exotic Tour). Britain's *Q* rock music magazine later dubbed it 'the most debauched tour ever'!

As he had during the recording of *Songs Of Faith And Devotion*, Gahan separated himself from the rest during the tour. He would regularly retreat to his dark dressing room, indulging his drug habit, a sight described in detail in *NME*: '[It was] a darkened cavern. Candles burn on table tops... jasmine incense sticks are burned... there's a red carpet hung against a wall... a full rock 'n' roll Parnassian set-up... [Gahan is] playing the role of a Rock God!'. The band members would often arrive at venues separately (Gore and Fletcher tended to stick together). Wilder was giving serious thought to his future, but he – like the others – had to get through the tour first (in a break between live dates, Wilder mixed the live *Songs Of Faith And Devotion*, so he was still committed). Despite all the backstage strife and collapse of inter-personal relationships, the Devotional Tour was a huge success, with massive venues worldwide selling out. Crowds chanted back the chorus of 'Personal Jesus' as 'Reach out and touch Dave', such was his growing cult of personality.

During the late 1993 North American dates, Gahan spun further out of control. He and co-tour manager Daryl Bamonte were arrested in Canada after Gahan assaulted a security guard. Coming off stage following a performance on 8 October in New Orleans, Gahan collapsed, leaving the rest to play the encore (which ironically included 'Death's Door'). Gahan suffered a drug-induced heart attack and was warned off further touring. The following day's show was cancelled, but after that, Gahan returned to deliver his full performance after just one day off. Six weeks later, in Los Angeles, Gore suffered a drink-and-drug withdrawal seizure.

Due to the cost of the elaborate tour stage set and assorted costs (drink, drugs and psychiatrists), the Devotional Tour wasn't making much in the way of profit. Despite all the foreboding, the band decided to extend their live gigs (Miller and Fletcher were against the plan) into 1994's Exotic Tour, taking in more US dates, as well as Mexico, South America, South Africa, Singapore and Australia. Wilder was hospitalised for two days in South Africa, suffering from alcohol-induced kidney stones. Fletcher participated in just 21 of the additional 60 dates before dropping out altogether in April 1994. Gore summed up events in the *NME* in January 1997:

We lost the plot. We overplayed it. It's really difficult at our level to just do a few key dates around the world. The minimum we'd have to tour is nine months. Maybe we should have stuck to that, [like] *Violator,* which was 90 concerts. [Even that] is too much, heavy and gruelling. We decided to do a 14-month tour – those extra 30 to 40 gigs were the straw that broke the camel's back.

Gahan finished the final date of the 156-night double tour by jumping into the crowd, but misjudged and crashed shoulder-first into the seats and concrete floor, cracking two ribs. He was taken to hospital. 'I was so drunk, it took me 24 hours to feel anything,' the singer admitted. With that, the Devotional/Exotic Tour strife came to an end.

The other three members took the opportunity of the post-tour downtime to recover. Fletcher left the Priory a new man and welcomed a second child, while Gore married Suzanne Boisvert in August and moderated his drinking. Wilder left his wife for Hepzibah Sessa, surviving a near-death experience with her when an RAF Tornado crashed in front of their open-top car in Perthshire. Gahan, on the other hand, brazenly accepted his death spiral, continuing to party hard before retreating with his now-wife Teresa Conroy into an empty mansion in Los Angeles, where they continued their dark 'junkie' lifestyle. Paranoid and addicted to heroin, Gahan was barely functioning in the autumn of 1994. He overdosed more than once, but survived, and tried rehab (at the urging of his family) in Arizona over Christmas 1994, which carried on intermittently throughout the first half of 1995. His relationship with his wife collapsed, and further overdoses followed.

At that point, Wilder quit Depeche Mode. Feeling taken for granted and frustrated over the uneven sharing of the creative workload, Wilder reluctantly decided he had to leave. In particular, he objected to being paid the same as the largely non-musical Fletcher, despite spending many hours in the studio honing the Mode sound. Wilder informed Gore and Fletcher of his decision in a meeting in London, but Gahan proved uncontactable. On his 36th birthday, 1 June 1995, Wilder issued a press statement confirming his departure and outlining his reasons, criticising the 'internal relations and working practices of the group'.

Speaking to *The Quietus* in 1997, Wilder elaborated on the circumstances of his departure. There was 'a lack of vision' in the band, he said. 'I always felt everything was too safe – we could have gone so much further, but lethargy was a big enemy. Perversely, we did create some of our very best work under the tensest of circumstances, but it just wasn't much fun – like pulling teeth trying to get anything agreed upon with any enthusiasm.' Alan Wilder had been a member of Depeche Mode for 13 years. Just weeks after he announced he was quitting, on 17 August, Gahan attempted suicide by slitting his wrists. The question of Depeche Mode's future had never been in greater doubt ...

'Barrel Of A Gun' 5:35
The first single from *Ultra* – out on 3 February 1997 – emerged from the second set of sessions with Gahan and Gore at Eastcote Studio in London (the first sessions produced 'Sister Of Night' and two other tracks). Many of the songs on *Ultra* reflected the turmoil the band underwent in the wake of the Devotional/Exotic Tour excess, from Fletcher's breakdown to Wilder quitting, from Gahan's near-death experience (see 'Sister Of Night') to Gore's alcoholism. With Gahan largely absent when Gore was writing, Gore and producer Tim Simenon developed the sound of *Ultra*. Gahan finally joined the others – following his recovery – at Abbey Road Studios in London to lay down the vocals. Gahan felt the song and video (by Anton Corbijn, shot in Morocco and featuring a fidgety Gahan) closely reflected his experiences: '[It was] quite autobiographical... I wanted it to be like you're constantly running away from your life, avoiding life, avoiding your feelings... it's [about] being a junkie, basically.'

From the opening extended disruptive sound (as pioneered on 'I Feel You') through the trip-hop-inspired approach mixed with techno synths, metallic guitars, industrial sounds and Gahan's rough, distorted vocals vying for attention, 'Barrel Of A Gun' sounds like nothing less than an off-cut from the darker *Songs Of Faith And Devotion*. The song deals with the compulsion of addiction (with Gahan making the line 'mark of Cain' sound uncannily like 'my cocaine') and the ultimate acceptance of responsibility. Gahan sings of how 'A vicious appetite/Visits me each night/And won't be satisfied/Won't be denied', later telling *Entertainment Weekly* in 2017: 'I think Martin was also playing with this imagery... sort of pointing the finger at me. When I perform that song now, it really describes the way I felt at that time: This creature that was barely existing but somehow still thought he had it going on [laughs]. Martin was spot-on with his lyrics.'

According to Gore (in *NME* in 1997), 'Barrel Of A Gun' is 'about understanding what you're about and realising that you don't necessarily fit into somebody else's scheme of things. You can have slight diversions from your path, but I think there is something written for us, that is meant to be.' Gore believes to an extent in destiny: 'I'm not being totally fatalistic, I think we do have a say in things, but I don't think that say is very strong...' In *Uncut* magazine in 2001, Daniel Miller described Ultra as 'the sound of a band picking up the pieces, trying to figure out where it's going'.

Faced with making a comeback, having been absent from the scene for four years and following the departure of Wilder, Gore (in Mode fanzine *Bong* #37) selected 'Barrel Of A Gun' as Depeche Mode's first single from *Ultra* because '[it] wasn't necessarily so Depeche Mode-like. We felt that "Barrel Of A Gun" was probably about the furthest from what we've done in the past.' To his surprise, Fletcher, Gahan and Simenon concurred, so first-choice single 'It's No Good' was relegated to the second release. It proved the right choice, reaching number four on the UK Singles Chart (equalling 'People Are People' from 1984), number five in the US *Billboard* Dance Singles Chart, and Top 10 positions across Europe (reaching number one in the Czech Republic, Hungary, Spain, Sweden and Italy, as well as on the UK Indie Chart). A review in *Music Week* commented: 'After four years away, this atmospheric epic hints at an even darker approach. As the first taster of their new album, this is a certain smash.'

'The Love Thieves' 6:34

A complete change of pace and sound, 'The Love Thieves' introduced a mellower Mode, certainly in comparison to 'Barrel Of A Gun' and much of *Songs Of Faith And Devotion*. The aim with *Ultra* was to get the band established again, following their various troubles and the departure of Wilder. It was a pivotal time, as recognised by Fletcher, talking to *Dot Music* in May 2001: 'I think there was a feeling of us having to prove ourselves, a bit like after Vince [Clarke] left. It gave us a new challenge and in some ways, it's spurred us on to do better things.' This track revealed a mellow Mode sound, as also heard on the single version of 'Home' (the next track on the album). It was a laid-back approach to the serious subject of obsession, something Gore repeatedly returned to.

'Home' 5:42

The third single from *Ultra* was yet another change of pace. Issued on 16 June 1997, 'Home' featured vocals by Gore, singing with great emotional resonance. It was recorded at the Westside Studio in early June 1996, where much of *Black Celebration* had taken place. The strings last heard on 'Walking In My Shoes' and 'One Caress' make a welcome return, but the elegiac, almost melancholic lyrics came from a period of despair in Gore's life. 'That song was written at a pretty dark period when I was recognising the amount that I was depending on alcohol to fill my daily existence,' Gore told *Bong #37*. 'I saw that my whole lifestyle was affected by that and I think the song was a way of recording my "resignation" at the situation.' Playing up the strings and dominating synth riffs, 'Home' made a swing for the cinematic.

The video by Steve Green was relatively low-key, focusing on Gore with Gahan and Fletcher lurking in the background. A bald-headed, black-clad figure (a lookalike for erstwhile member Vince Clarke) representing Death stalks various dramatic scenarios that play out in the 'Pink Motel', before shooting off to space as a twinkle (so maybe he was an alien, experiencing human emotions?). It was an odd choice (perhaps confirmed by its poor UK chart performance, reaching a high point of number 23, although it was number two on the UK Indie Chart and it made number one in Italy) that failed to build on the amazing 'comeback' success of the previous singles (although *Billboard* hailed 'Home' as 'the act's best mainstream single in a good long time'). Despite that, 'Home' became a firm fan favourite when played live as part of later tours, featured in Gore's lone acoustic set, being played over 500 times in various forms from piano ballad to full-string support.

'It's No Good' 5:58

Bumped back to become the second single (released on 31 March 1997), 'It's No Good' is a stark contrast to 'Barrel Of A Gun'. A more traditional Mode sound, it might not have made such a splash as a debut single (although it rode the returned Mode momentum to number five in the UK Singles Chart). Lowering the temperature, 'It's No Good' was a return to ambient electronica, a song *Billboard* magazine dubbed 'the single die-hard Depeche Mode disciples have been starved for... the music cruises at a funky, electro-pop pace with minimal sound effect clutter'. It was certainly instantly recognisable as a Mode track, quite unlike 'Barrel Of A Gun', and it pointed to the sonic diversity of *Ultra*. Other reviewers called this cleaner Mode sound 'minimal', 'spartan', 'smooth', and 'retro'. For the promo video, Gahan, the band and director Anton Corbijn take the mickey out of the whole pop star business, featuring Gahan as a no-hope lounge singer playing unlikely New York venues (including the foyer of the Hotel Ultra), where spontaneous bar brawls break out and there's a simple (and unresolved) narrative about stolen money. The live television performances of this track during 1997 – particularly those on British show *TFI Friday* and *The Tonight Show* with Jay Leno in the US – show an increasingly confident Gahan slowly rediscovering his mojo. The critic-baiting title proved to be, in fact, very good indeed, hitting the Top 10 all across Europe.

'Uselink' 2:21
The first of two curious interstitial instrumentals on *Ultra*, 'Uselink' features Mute's Daniel Miller playing around on his classic System 100 modular synth and feels like a throwback to a different Mode era. Tim Simenon, in *Classic Pop* in August 2019, remembered:

'Uselink' and 'Jazz Thieves' were... links between tracks to give the album more atmosphere. I spent an afternoon at Daniel [Miller]'s house with his amazing collection of synths, processing a bunch of stuff. We built up loops which we ended up using on the album.

'Useless' 5:12
Released as the fourth and final single from *Ultra* (on 20 October 1997, and placing at a poor number 28 on the UK Singles Chart), 'Useless' was one of the first songs that Gore created as a demo, laid down in November 1995. Speaking in Mode fanzine *Bong* #37, Gore said of 'Useless':

It's one of the rockiest pieces that we've ever done and it's probably up there with 'I Feel You'. I think we're on that right side of another line when it comes to rock, but I don't think we'll ever be a rock band or a heavy metal band. We might branch out and do things like pop or we might do some rock, but we'll still retain some [Depeche Mode] identity.

The single remix by Alan Moulder altered the album version intro and presented a faster and louder version of the track with additional synth work in the chorus and scruffier vocals. It was released in the US as a double A-side with 'Home'. Anton Corbijn returned to direct the video, which saw the band performing in a quarry (in Aberystwyth in Wales). Fletcher, playing enigmatic, is easily the coolest (excluding the donkey, the leafleteer and the plane flying past promoting *Ultra*!). It was to be Corbijn's last video for eight years, until 'Suffer Well' in 2006, though he continued to contribute to the visuals for albums and singles. The compelling bass line that provides a driving rhythm was provided by Doug Wimbish (session musician and member of Living Colour). Drummer Gota Yashiki (of Soul II Soul and Simply Red) also contributed. In one of the more unusual Mode tie-ins, a Kruder & Dorfmeister instrumental remix of 'Useless' was used by Victoria's Secret for a US bra advertising campaign!

'Sister Of Night' 6:04
One of the first tracks developed during the exploratory six-month recording sessions without Gahan at London's Eastcote Studios (the others

being 'Useless' and 'Insight'), 'Sister Of Night' was properly recorded with Gahan's vocals during the third recording period for *Ultra* in New York. The vocals were pieced together by Simenon and Gore from multiple partial takes as Gahan was incapable of providing the complete vocal in a single sitting. Ironically, it turned out to be one of his favourites (talking to *MSN Music Central*): '"Sister Of Night" is actually my favourite, in terms of the vocal. I sometimes find it really hard to listen to myself, but on that particular song, that's really "me". It's a really honest vocal. I particularly got into the song quite a bit.'

A break in efforts to put together the new album was agreed following this recording, with Gahan instructed to return to Los Angeles and kick his habit if the band were to proceed further. Gahan agreed to spend time with singing coach Evelyn Halus in an attempt to get his voice in shape. In between, Gahan hooked up with actress Jennifer Sklias, whom he'd met in rehab in Arizona (the pair would marry on Valentine's Day in 1999 and were still together by 2023). Shortly thereafter, on 28 May 1996, Dave Gahan died – for at least three minutes. Gahan overdosed once more with a cocaine-heroin speedball and his heart stopped. He was revived in an ambulance on the way to Cedars-Sinai hospital by paramedics who already thought they'd lost him. Gahan's ongoing drug addiction became much more public when he gave a statement to the press outside the hospital:

I'm a heroin addict. I've been fighting to get off heroin for a year. I've been in rehab twice and I don't want to be like people like Kurt [Cobain, who died an addict in 1992, aged 27]. I want to be a survivor. I died last night... [being an addict] has taken everything away from me. I'm going to rebuild my life.

Recovering addict Sklias helped Gahan overcome his addiction, while Mode management staged an 'intervention' forcing him back into a hard-line rehab regime at a facility in Marina del Rey. Comprehending he had a choice, to die or live on, Gahan finally chose life.

All this resulted in a necessary break in the production process on *Ultra*. 'Sister Of Night' clearly captures that period of Gahan's life, combining a grungy opening with cathedral-like bells, that quickly settle down to a more mellow sound, with Gahan's yearning vocal smothered over the top, finishing up with more rock-oriented drums. Gahan told *Q* magazine (in March 1997) that the track was a reminder of a dark time: 'I can hear how scared I was. I'm glad it's there to remind me. I could see the pain I was causing everybody.'

'Jazz Thieves' 2:54
The second of two curious interstitial instrumentals on *Ultra*, 'Jazz Thieves' is a moody dollop of synth noodling that doesn't really go anywhere except to link to the next track...

'Freestate' 6:44

'Freestate' suffered from being reworked one time too many. It went through multiple iterations before the version on the album was arrived at. Tim Simenon recalled the collective frustration with 'Freestate' in *Classic Pop* (August 2019):

> There must have been seven or eight versions of "Freestate". We were throwing so many ideas at it.

There's the country music twangy guitar of 'Personal Jesus' in 'Freestate', but the song lacks that previous effort's rock 'n' roll majesty. No doubt another attempt at a mellow Mode track, like 'Jazz Thieves', the song only springs into life after about two minutes with the 'Step out of your cage' chorus.

'The Bottom Line' 4:26

Gore was once more on vocals for 'The Bottom Line', delivering a blistering performance of one of Depeche Mode's best songs. Like 'Freestate', it aspires to be a riff on country music. Obsessional love is the subject, backed by haunting musical tricks, from whelps and hums to plucked guitar and soft percussion. Whispered echoes back Gore's vocal, a ghost playing alongside the central track as the music swirls around. The poor deluded subject of the song's narrative is compared to a rain-bedraggled cat, a sacrificial pawn and a moth compelled by a flame, all in pursuit of the often unattainable. It builds to a lovely, spangly finish that continues after Gore's vocal ends, wrapping up in a very Mode-like drone. An underrated gem buried in the middle of an album, 'The Bottom Line' surely deserves to be wider known.

'Insight' 6:26

One of the earliest tracks developed for *Ultra*, 'Insight' has become one of Gore's occasional vocal performances during tours with a piano solo from Peter Gordeno. It's well placed as the final track on the album (with a Gahan vocal), as it builds to such an upbeat crescendo that it provides the perfect wrap-up for *Ultra*. The repeated backing mantra of 'You've got to give love' offers a clue to Gore's worldview. Yes, there's obsession and desire and kink, but none of it means anything unless you offer up the same depth of love that you hope to receive. 'The fire still burns' can be suggestive of either a long-running romance or a long unfulfilled desire. Either proves the meaning of love...

'Junior Painkiller' 2:11

A short extract from 'Painkiller', originally presented as a 'hidden' track attached to 'Insight'. Tim Simenon, in *Classic Pop* in August 2019, said: "'Junior Painkiller" was Martin['s idea]. He liked the idea of a surprise, having the album creep back in when you didn't expect [it].'

Related Tracks
'Painkiller' 7:29
Released as a B-side to the US 7" single of 'Barrel Of A Gun', the instrumental 'Painkiller' was used as intro music on *The Singles 86>89* Tour, and also released in a remix as the B-side on some editions of 'Only When I Lose Myself'. Its dark, guitar-and-drums atmosphere matches quite well with 'Barrel Of A Gun', with grungy synth sounds crashing into assorted bleeps and bloops. Running for almost seven and a half minutes, it's a robust instrumental, the kind of thing many thought Depeche Mode had left in the past.

'Slowblow' 5:25
Released as a B-side to the 'It's No Good' US 7" single, 'Slowblow' sounds like the title suggests, a slow-moving instrumental that atmospherically plods along for five minutes or so...

'Only When I Lose Myself' 4:34
The next single released after 'Useless' was 'Only When I Lose Myself', created as a promo for the compilation album *The Singles 86>98*, a follow-up to the earlier *The Singles 81>85* (which was also reissued at the end of September 1998). The single preceded the album by a few weeks, hitting stores on 7 September 1998. It was the band's 35th single and one of the few not to feature on an album of new music (the others being 'Dreaming Of Me', 'Shake The Disease' and 'It's Called A Heart', up to that point). *Melody Maker* called the track 'a low voltage charmer', while *NME* noted its 'lovely harmonies'.

Gore (talking to the Associated Press) described it as 'slow' and almost a 'ballad, but a rockin' ballad. It's about relationships – one of my favourite topics! I've always found love quite obsessional. People talk about co-dependency, [and] to me, I've always found there's something co-dependent about being in love.' The song is perhaps more about it being necessary for someone to 'lose' themselves, their sense of their own separate identity, in order to be truly in love with another. In losing yourself in another person, you ultimately find your real self, your real reason for being. For Gahan, this song was part of his work to rehabilitate his voice. Speaking in the electronic press kit that promoted *The Singles 86>98*, Gahan said:

> I've become a lot more confident about my singing. I felt like I was doing something not for everybody else. I challenge myself, I wanna get better. I wanna feel myself improving, and for a long time now, I felt like I wasn't improving. I lost my way a little bit there, and fortunately, I am very grateful for the opportunity to make *Ultra*. I had the chance, musically, to feel like I'm actually producing something that really adds to it, [and] is really part of the sound of Depeche Mode.

Gahan described the track as 'very soulful', telling the *Baltimore Sun*: 'It's got an intense feel about it. There's something about the song that I think makes you want to drive harder. It pumps along quite well. We had the time to actually relax with this one, and it went in quite a few different directions'. It was the first sign of a new direction the band would explore further in *Exciter*.

'Surrender' 6:19

Released as an additional track (the term 'B-side' doesn't really apply with CD releases) to the single 'Only When I Lose Myself', 'Surrender' was the first exclusive vocal 'B-side' track since 'My Joy'. Recorded under the working title 'Tempt', it's another that falls between *Ultra* and *Exciter* that exhibits sonic aspects of both and shows a band once more in musical transition. Gahan's vocal is more confident and solid. It's a song that, rather than finishing as expected turns into something else altogether near the end when the 'We're living in a world of illusion' section kicks in. The 'Rapture rushing through my veins' is another sign of Gore working Gahan's tribulations into the lyrics he's giving him to sing. Gore felt 'Surrender' was a 'lost' Mode track, overlooked by fans and critics. He told *AllStar* in 1998: '"Surrender" is quite slow. It's very melodic. It's good to sing. It's about surrendering to your desires – maybe you don't really have a choice. It is an extension of *Ultra*.'

'Headstar' 4:23

An alternative B-side to some single versions of 'Only When I Lose Myself', 'Headstar' is a rather groovy if largely ignored Depeche Mode instrumental.

Exciter (2001)

Personnel:

Dave Gahan: lead vocals, except on 'Comatose' and 'Breathe'

Martin Gore: keyboards, guitar, acoustic guitar on 'Dream On', backing vocals, lead vocals on 'Comatose' and 'Breathe'

Andy Fletcher: keyboards

Recorded at RAK Studios, Sarm West Studios, London; Sound Design, Santa Barbara; Electric Lady Studios, Sony Music Studios, New York City, June 2000 to February 2001

Producer: Mark Bell

All tracks written by Martin Gore

Released: 14 May 2001. Label: Mute

Running time: 56:40

Highest chart placings: UK: 9; US: 8; Australia: 20; Austria: 2; Belgium: 5; Canada: 3; Finland: 2; France: 1; Germany: 1; Greece: 1; Italy: 2; Japan: 79; Spain: 2; Sweden: 1; Switzerland: 2.

Depeche Mode entered their 20th year one man down and very much in recovery mode. Reaching their tenth studio album across those two decades meant the band had released a new album once every two years on average (annually early on, but with ever-growing gaps later). That was quite a track record for a group often written off by the pop press in the early 1980s. They changed and evolved through those two decades, with incredible highs and despairing lows (collectively and individually). Could they once more move forward creatively as a trio?

Lead singer Dave Gahan was now clean, a recovered heroin addict, following a punishing and wasted five years. 'Dave came good in the end,' said Andy Fletcher, who was in recovery from his own mental health issues. 'He gave up drugs and drink.' Working on *Ultra* and engaging with a vocal coach had allowed him to rediscover his voice, and the few live television appearances the band had made promoting the album had seen his confidence in front of audiences increase. Needless to say, after the damaging hedonism of the Devotional Tour, there was no full tour to promote *Ultra*.

Martin Gore, himself recovering from his alcoholic excesses, said frankly: 'We don't feel we can survive another tour!' Instead, through 1997 the band had played what were termed *Ultra* Parties, mini television performances that were strictly controlled and featured just six dates: two in London, one in Paris, Sweden and Germany, finishing up in Los Angeles' Shrine Exposition Hall featuring a six-track setlist. It was the first tour to feature Christian Eigner on drums (replacing the departed Alan Wilder), who – along with Peter Gordeno – would become central to Depeche Mode as a live band into the future.

By 1998, the band were recovered enough to embark upon a full international tour of 66 dates to promote *The Singles 86>98*, featuring a full setlist of 20 or so songs. Two dates were played at London's Wembley Arena.

Playing in a sober state for the first time in a long time came as a revelation to both Gahan and Gore, who found new joy in celebrating their music alongside hugely appreciative audiences who were happy the band members had survived their recent troubles.

Towards the end of 1999, Gore turned his attention to developing new songs for another Depeche Mode album, the band's tenth, only to come up against something he'd never really experienced before: writer's block! He started several potential songs, only to abandon them unfinished, feeling dissatisfied. He recruited some trusted help to aid him in developing a new sound for Depeche Mode: Gareth Jones, their former engineer and producer on *Construction Time Again*, *Some Great Reward* and *Black Celebration*, and who'd most recently worked on *Ultra* mixing and engineering tracks, and programmer Paul Freegard, who co-produced Gore's solo work *Counterfeit²*.

By the time the band began looking for a producer to supervise the studio recording sessions, Gore and company had produced demos of five tracks for what later became *Exciter* (it began life under the more explicit title *Lover*). Gore had been listening to late 1990s experimental electronica, and he wanted to bring those vibes to the new Mode sound. Gore had Mute's Daniel Miller approach Mark Bell, one of electronic trio LFO (Low Frequency Oscillation) with DJ Martin Williams and Gerrard 'Gez' Varley. Bell had been working with Björk, and as a fan of Depeche Mode from his teen days, found it hard to say no. Gahan was living in New York, Fletcher in London, and Gore had relocated to Santa Barbara with his family. It was on Gore's new home turf that the first work on *Exciter* would take place.

The new album benefited from the new relaxed vibe of the band – all seemed to be in better places in their lives as the new millennium kicked off, and they wanted to express this new optimism in their music (in stark contrast to the darker *Songs Of Faith And Devotion* and *Ultra*). Gahan described the recording of the album, in London and New York as well as the west coast of the US, as 'pretty laid back' and 'a very positive experience'. The resulting album may have been regarded by some diehard fans as notably unexciting (contrary to its title), but it suited the band to adopt a back-to-basics approach, stripping back the layers and noise that had increasingly come to swamp their sound, opting for cleaner atmospheric electronica.

Despite some disappointment, *Exciter* provoked largely positive notices in the music press. *NME* were onside, declaring: 'Not many long-running groups could make an album this fresh and confident in their 20th year, never mind one which bridges timeless soul-man crooning and underground techno...' *Rolling Stone* detected Kraftwerk vibes in Bell's production, while *Q* took a harsher tack: '*Exciter* is superficially attractive; an exercise in good taste that mixes contemporary droning with shuffling drums and guitar. It's pleasant enough wrapping that slips easily around Gahan's recharged vocals. This time it's Gore who's out of puff. No amount of fashionable tweaking can hide the flimsiness of his offerings.'

Q may have been on to something. While even the weakest Depeche Mode albums have something to offer, after a run of record-breaking highs, the band had to stumble sometime. Many expected *Ultra* to be the album that would prove surplus to requirements, given what it was following. Instead, it renewed interest in Depeche Mode. Given all they'd been through, if the band wanted to kick back a little on *Exciter*, who could begrudge them that?

'Dream On' 4:19

The first fans heard of the new, more relaxed Mode sound came with the release of the first single on 23 April 2001, a few weeks ahead of the album. It was the first new music from the band in three years. The breathy vocal delivery of 'Can you feel a little love' from Gahan continued the tradition of each opening track having an unusual initial sound. Gore's acoustic guitar, with some latent country twangs, kicks in before Bell's electronic overlays and Gahan's vocals take over. Overall, it's a rather subdued track compared to some, but it set the tone, putting expectations into a more realistic vein. Gahan noted (in *Entertainment Weekly* in 2017) that his vocals benefited from Bell's guidance, bringing some of the techniques Bell had used with Björk to Depeche Mode:

> I learned how to [whispering] sing very quietly and very close to the microphone, to use all the noises in my voice... 'Dream On' was one of those songs lyrically, where it was a character that I was becoming, that I could be without all the misery. I could step into it, and step out...

Speaking on the electronic press kit (EPK) for *Exciter*, Fletcher revealed that 'Dream On' was one of the first tracks Gore completed, and one of the first recordings the band tackled: 'It's the real defining track of the album: the mixture of electronic beats with acoustic blues guitar and some really good lyrics and a great catchy chorus. So it was great that we recorded that song first and I really think it was important and set the way for the rest of the album.' Gore had played the demo with an acoustic guitar which he'd expected to replace with a synth line, but after a few days of working on it, they decided to bring the acoustic guitar back in as the backbone of the track. 'It just sounded really good,' Gore said on the EPK, 'because it was just so different to everything else that was going on in the track.'

As on *Songs Of Faith And Devotion*, live performance would continue to be part of Depeche Mode's in-studio repertoire. After a gap of a few years, Depeche Mode tracks were once more picked up for use in television drama, with 'Dream On' featuring in the season finale of the third season of *Charmed* in May 2001, in a 2002 first-season episode of spy thriller *Alias* ('Masquerade'), and in the pilot episode of Fox crime drama *Fastlane* in 2002. Although the single topped the charts in Denmark, Germany, Italy and Spain, it stalled at number six in the UK, just failing to crack the Top 5. *NME* reacted to its 'spaghetti western atmosphere' describing the opening as 'unplugged and naked' before praising the 'stark electronics' and 'elemental passions' of the 'stripped down' sound.

'Shine' 5:32
Hard synth sounds and pervy lyrics: with 'Shine' Depeche Mode came home again. The deceptively gentle opening leads into a darker track, obvious from the opening lines: 'Put on your blindfold/and a dress that's tight', with the singer promising his companion a 'mystery night'. It burbles along pleasingly enough until the chorus crashes in. Pulsing synths and reverberating noises back the lyrics, demanding the subject of the song 'Shine for me'. This is about overcoming self-doubt, 'insecurities' and 'mediocrity'. Football crowd or acid house whistles see out the track, which devolves to a series of fading tones leading into 'The Sweetest Condition'.

'The Sweetest Condition' 3:42
While 'Shine' was never played live, 'The Sweetest Condition' was given a workout throughout the *Exciter* tour of 2001, heard on almost all dates. What exactly is 'The Sweetest Condition'? The clue is in the line: 'How I suffer the sweetest condition'. As always with Gore, sweetness is suffering or vice versa – they're interchangeable and connected emotions. As with so many Mode songs, it's about being enslaved by love (or obsession, if they can be differentiated): 'Bodily whole, but my head's in a mess/Fuelling obsession that borders psychosis'. The middle takes a melodic wander, but the verses are delivered with such power that the song performs above expectations.

'When The Body Speaks' 6:01
In a spirit of experimentation that pervades much of the underappreciated *Exciter*, the band built 'When The Body Speaks' differently. Gahan explained (to *Mean Streets* in May 2001) how the process differed:

> 'When The Body Speaks' was a demo where Martin added guitar. We recorded it with me just singing to guitar and we actually kept it that way – built the atmosphere around that and some strings. It's a highlight on the album for me... Usually for a Depeche Mode recording we build the atmosphere first and then my vocals on top of it. And the atmosphere would dictate the way I would go. This was totally opposite.

As had become habit since *Songs Of Faith And Devotion*, live strings made a return with 'When The Body Speaks'. In *Keyboard* magazine (May 2001), Gore explained he felt this was a more 'organic' track, based around guitar and vocals and that the addition of strings would bring added life to the sound. Like several other tracks on *Exciter*, Gore was going for a throwback sound:

A lot of the songs on this record have a kind of 1950s or 1960s influence, in a strange sort of way. They sound sort of current, but there are definitely references to the 1950s and 1960s in there. ['When The Body Speaks'] reminds me of the Righteous Brothers playing next door to a rave, because it's got that incessant beat – the bass and the drums going through it. But the actual solo on the top reminds me of the Righteous Brothers.

It's an expansive sound, with an almost 'heartbeat' rhythm building through the opening sounds, before Gahan's gently delivered lyrics slide in. The lyrics are harsh, but the music is not, a mismatch that gives the song unusual life. As always, there's a girl: 'I'm just a slave here/At the mercy/Of a girl'! Gore's lyrics, backed by those tender strings, explore the need for softness in relationships, for tenderness, touch, for fulfilment of 'the soul's desires'. It's a nice break before the darker elements of the next track change the tone entirely.

'The Dead Of Night' 4:50
It appears that 'The Dead Of Night' is Gore's take on some of Gahan's more disreputable activities during his five years as a heroin addict. While that's the broader context for a song where the title describes the denizens of a nightmarish after-hours world of addiction, the direct inspiration came from a particular VIP London nightclub, Browns. According to Gore (in the May 2001 *Flaunt*):

It was a really sad scene, the Red Room. Everyone was taking so many drugs because it was commonly known that it was perfectly cool to take drugs there. So the Red Room for me was the 'Zombie Room', because everyone in there was always talking way too fast, saying nothing and just staring. While you're there, all these people in the room are your best mates in the world. But the next day, if you bump into one of them on the street, you won't even know their name.

Producer Mark Bell (talking to Mode biographer Jonathan Miller) recalled it was a tricky track to put together, given the layers of sound involved. 'We used loads of different synths on 'The Dead Of Night', messing about with the envelopes and pitch controls. We just went completely silly and it became a jam session. Then, once we found something that worked, we made it into a sort of performance that really suited the song.'

On the *Exciter* EPK, Gore dubbed the track (and much of Mode's other output), 'weird pop': 'This is a great example of that. I think it won't fit in anywhere, but we never have, so that's not particularly a worry.' The opening builds up sounds like its leading to 'Barrel Of A Gun', and that's perhaps the nearest comparison. It's a dark, grinding track, with all sorts of electronic sounds buried in a sparkling mix, a chaotic sound that clears up for the chorus, before plunging into darkness again on 'We are the dead of night/We're in the zombie room/We're twilight's parasites/With self-inflicted wounds'.

'Lovetheme' 2:02
Another gear shift, as two minutes of instrumental noodling, sets the tone for the rest of the album, which veers dangerously close to Depeche Mode doing lounge music.

'Freelove' 6:10
Released on 5 November 2001 – which was also the final day of the Exciter Tour, which wrapped up in Mannheim, Germany – 'Freelove' was the third single from the album. It's a groovy track, one of the last completed. A belated release, it only spent three weeks in the UK Singles Chart, entering at number 19. However, like 'I Feel Loved' before it, 'Freelove' topped the US Dance Chart, hit number two on the UK Indie Chart and reached various Top 10 positions across Europe: number five in Denmark, eight in Germany and three in Italy and Spain, to name a few. In an attempt to find a fresh look for their promotional music videos, Depeche Mode had turned to director John Hillcoat for several of the singles from *Exciter*, including 'I Feel Loved', fourth single 'Goodnight Lovers' and 'Freelove'. Filmed in New Orleans in 2001, while the band were on tour, the video features them playing on a travelling float, with various people jumping aboard to dance. The entire package, song and video, had a 'Will this do?' vibe to it – perfectly fine, nothing objectionable, but not much to stir the blood, either...

'Comatose' 3:24
The first of just two Gore vocals on *Exciter*, 'Comatose', lives up to its title, almost. It's an attempt to capture that edge-of-sleep feeling, or that blissed-out feeling as the drugs kick in: 'Slipping in/Sliding out/Of conscious feeling'. There's also a suggestion of a dream state, and the unlikely claim that 'Dreams never deceive'. Even Gore recognised how odd this track was (in *Keyboard*, May 2001):

['Comatose'] was one of the weirdest tracks on the record. There's not really a bass going on in that one. There's a lot of really loud hi-hat. The majority of the rest of that backing track was actually a sampled organ that we filtered down until it ended up sounding like a steamboat or something. It works, in a strange kind of way.

According to Fletcher, 'Comatose' had a more 'traditional' and fuller Depeche Mode sound at one point, before the band and Mark Bell decided to go minimal with it. Although the Gore demo had a stronger edge to it, all involved felt it didn't quite work, so it was stripped back to basics and given a more sleepy/dreamy atmosphere in keeping with the lyrics and vocal.

'I Feel Loved' 4:20

Having asked 'Can you feel a little love' on the first single from *Exciter*, 'Dream On', Depeche Mode answered their own question with the second single, 'I Feel Loved', released on 30 July 2001. With a pumping rhythm, the track gets down to business right out of the gate. Gore was going for a dance track, starting out at 109 beats per minute (BPM) on the demo only to up the final version to a pacier 128BPM. The synth sounds on top, described by Gore as an 'aggressive, growly sound' (there is something of Mode's metal-bashing days buried in here), came from Mark Bell, using a Mercury virtual synth. There's not much lyrically going on, beyond the bouncy chorus, except to remember that in the depths of despair, someone out there loves you. According to *NME*, this was a 'pop trifle'! Depeche Mode featured once again on the soundtrack of witchcraft drama *Charmed*, with 'I Feel Loved' heard during the opening episode of the fourth season ('Charmed Again, Part 1') in October 2001: must've been a fan among the show's music supervisors! The track reached number 12 in the UK Singles Chart, hitting the Top 10 in Belgium, Canada, Denmark, Germany, Ireland, Italy and Spain. In the US *Billboard* 100, 'I Feel Loved' reached number four, hitting the top spot in the US Dance Chart – just as Gore clearly intended.

'Breathe' 5:17

The second Gore vocal on *Exciter*, 'Breathe' harks back to 'The Things You Said' from 1987's *Music For The Masses*. Like that song, it's about rumours or bad news. In 'The Things You Said' (another Gore vocal), the gossip was heard from 'friends' and was met with disappointment. Second time around, Gore draws inspiration from the Bible for the names of the gossipers involved: Peter, Paul, Mary and Ruth 'Who swore on the Bible/She's telling the truth'. That's followed by the addition of the likes of Simon, Sarah, Joseph and John. It's not the first time (and certainly wouldn't be the last) that Gore turned to his religious upbringing and once sincerely held beliefs of his youth as inspiration for his songwriting. The character names and the litany of the days of the week form a strong structure, with Gore's lively vocals laid against a backing of guitar and drum sounds, giving priority to the vocals over the music.

'Easy Tiger' 2:05

An instrumental bridging track used as the opening introductory music on the Exciter Tour leading into 'Dream On' live. It was also released as 'Easy Tiger (Full Version)' as an additional track on the 'Dream On' single release. Again, like 'Lovetheme', this is Mode verging on lounge jazz.

'I Am You' 5:10

To quote the Spice Girls, '2Become1' in Depeche Mode's take on co-dependency, 'I Am You'. Gahan's slow vocal is kicked back in the mix, an almost whispered echo, as Mark Bell's electronic sounds pulse along. While the music tends towards easy listening electronica, Gore's lyrical concerns are as dark as ever, making reference to 'Dark obsession in the name of love', pleasure that feels like sin and pain, and addiction that 'Keeps us craving endlessly'. They might be a little late to the acid house game, but Depeche Mode give the chorus of 'I Am You' a solid 1990s makeover, before a more classical sound appears about four minutes in. It's a really strange mix, as if the band and Bell couldn't decide on what approach to take, so simply threw everything they had at it. Bell, talking to Jonathan Miller, said of 'I Am You' and much of *Exciter* in general:

> Most of the percussion you hear is electronic stuff I did myself... I just got loads of silly noises from the analog stuff and then made layers in the sampler so the sound would change depending on velocity. It sounds more organic that way, though it's definitely electronic.

'Goodnight Lovers' 3:48

Originally titled 'Born a Lover', 'Goodnight Lovers' performed a double function as the closing track to *Exciter*, and the fourth and final single released (on 11 February 2002, just in time for Valentine's Day). In a strange quirk, the single didn't actually qualify to be counted for the UK Singles Chart due to some arcane rule that indicated that the four-track CD had one more track than the rules allowed. It did, however, enter the Budget Albums Chart straight at number one, the first Depeche Mode single to ever reach the top spot in any official UK chart outside of the UK Indie Chart. 'Goodnight Lovers' wasn't even released in the US. It reached the regular Top 10 in Denmark (7) and Spain (4). Reviewing the album in *NME*, Stephen Dalton said of 'Goodnight Lovers': 'Better still is beatific closing number "Goodnight Lovers", where Dave purrs and whispers over a gliding ambient lullaby to "all soul sisters and all soul brothers". This is the one to soften even hardened Mode haters, a gorgeous moment of sensual healing.' In describing the track as a 'lullaby', Dalton was spot on, as that was how producer Mark Bell (interviewed by Depeche Mode biographer Jonathan Miller) suggested that Gahan should approach the vocal performance:

> Dave's got a seven-month-old baby daughter now [Stella Rose, with actress Jennifer Sklias], so I suggested he sing the closing track 'Goodnight Lovers' as though he was really singing it to her, like a lullaby. I think that comes across. It's not role-playing, but something he could really feel.

Related Tracks

'Dirt' 4:59

This is that rare thing, a Depeche Mode cover version of a song by someone else. In this case, it's a cover of The Stooges' song 'Dirt' (from the 1970 album

Fun House), put out as an additional track/B-side to the single release of 'I Feel Loved'. It shouldn't come as a surprise that the Mode boys were fans of Iggy Pop, and the lyrics of this particular track are right on Gore's wavelength (although The Stooges' song is far simpler than most Mode tracks). Talking on the *101* concert film DVD, Gore revealed his love of Iggy Pop:

> I didn't discover Iggy Pop until about 1977, with *The Idiot* and *Lust For Life*. I went back and rediscovered some of his older stuff from The Stooges. Over the years, we haven't really covered too many songs. I just think that he always had a sense of humour and this darkness to his music at the same time, which is a hard thing to marry, and I think he has always done that really well.

NME called the Mode take 'a slo-mo gothcore stomp', and for some fans, the 'Mode do Iggy Pop' track was much more Mode sounding than the A-side, 'I Feel Loved'. Behind Gahan's growling vocals is a 1960s space-age electronica sound, the kind of thing Joe Meek ('Telstar') and 1960s children's fantasy television theme tunes used to deliver, and something Depeche Mode would gravitate more towards with 2009's *Sounds Of The Universe*.

'Zenstation' 6:26
Released as an additional track/B-side to single release 'Freelove', instrumental 'Zenstation' is accompanied by harmony vocalisations from Gore. It makes for nice background music, but it doesn't demand anyone's attention.

Playing the Angel (2005)

Personnel:

Dave Gahan: lead vocals, except on 'Macro' and 'Damaged People', backing vocals on 'Macro'

Martin Gore: guitar, bass guitar on 'Suffer Well', keyboards, slide guitar on 'The Darkest Star', backing vocals, lead vocals on 'Macro'

Andy Fletcher: keyboards, bass guitar

Recorded at Sound Design, Santa Barbara; Stratosphere Sound, New York City; Whitfield Street, London, January–July 2005

Producer: Ben Hillier

All tracks written by Martin Gore, except 'Suffer Well', 'I Want It All' and 'Nothing's Impossible' which were written by Dave Gahan, Christian Eigner and Andrew Phillpott

Released: 17 October 2005. Label: Mute

Running time: 52:16

Highest chart placings: UK: 6; US: 7; Australia: 45; Austria: 1; Belgium: 1; Canada: 3; Finland: 1; France: 1; Germany: 1; Italy: 1; Japan: 104; Spain: 2; Sweden: 1; Switzerland: 1.

Now firmly re-established as a trio with the relatively laid-back *Exciter*, the various members of Depeche Mode felt secure enough to explore new creative avenues while pondering their next move. In 2003, Martin Gore released his second solo project, *Counterfeit²* – a full 14 years on from the 1999 original. The result was a series of synth-driven cover songs produced in Gore's home studio in Santa Barbara. Tracks he tackled included Brian Eno's 'By This River', David Essex's 'Stardust', John Lennon's 'Oh My Love' and the jazz standard 'In My Time of Dying'.

Just six weeks later, Dave Gahan released his first solo record, *Paper Monsters*, on 2 June 2003. Gahan had first considered a solo project following the 2001 release of *Exciter*. He'd long wanted to write his own songs, but with Depeche Mode boasting such songwriting and production talent as Clarke, Gore and Wilder, he'd felt intimidated. Working in New York with musician friend Knox Chandler, Gahan co-wrote the ten songs on *Paper Monsters*, with the album spawning a trio of singles: 'Dirty Sticky Floors', 'I Need You' and double A-side 'Bottle Living'/'Hold On'. Gahan's album made the UK Top 40 Album Chart (at number 36), while cracking the Top 10 in several European markets (Germany, Sweden and Switzerland). The first single made the UK Top 20 (number 18), with the others faring less well, reaching numbers 27 and 36 respectively.

Critically, Gahan's solo effort received mixed-to-positive reviews, with a consensus welcoming his approach as a type of blues-driven electronica. Although surely influenced by Gahan's lengthy Depeche Mode history, *Paper Monsters* did enough to distinguish his solo work from that of the collective. Gahan set out on a solo tour, with his Paris gig recorded for the concert DVD *Live Monsters*. As the *Independent* noted of these developments: 'When

109

Depeche [Mode] reunite, the balance of power will not be the same.'

Having spent years shying away from an inevitable creative confrontation, Gahan – now suitably sober – was willing to take on the elephant that had long been lingering in the various recording studios used by Depeche Mode. During the press tour for *Paper Monsters*, Gahan described *Exciter* as 'Martin's album with my voice on it' in *Rolling Stone*, which actually summed up most of Depeche Mode's history. Gahan was blunt about his take on the future: 'Unless Martin is open to both me and him coming into the studio with a bunch of songs and supporting each other, I don't see that there's any point in going on and making another Depeche Mode record...'

It took a while for Gore and Gahan to get together to actually thrash out the future of their joint endeavour (with the ever-present but enigmatic Fletcher). By the end of 2004, the pair were overcoming any issues (Gore had reportedly been stung by Gahan's statements) and agreed to work together on their respective songs for the next Mode outing. Ever the peacemaker between the two Mode mercurial talents, Fletcher found himself acting as the referee. He told *Q* that 'Dave's songs are really good, now. Some of them will earn their place on the album.' Gahan initially wanted more than that, demanding the right to contribute a full half of the songs, but he was realistic enough to settle for just three tracks: 'Suffer Well', 'I Want It All' and 'Nothing's Impossible'. It was a breakthrough that signalled a positive future for a band that had been around for over two decades and which had weathered various creative and personnel crises.

The power imbalance between Gore and Gahan was perhaps unconsciously recognised in the fact that the band first reconvened to record the first material for what would become *Playing The Angel* in Gore's home town of Santa Barbara, rather than in Gahan's now-native New York. Early in 2005, Gore, Gahan and Fletcher gathered at Sound Design Studios to work with new producer Ben Hillier. He'd worked with Blur, Elbow and Doves, and recognised the need for Depeche Mode to rediscover their edge following the mellow vibes of *Exciter*. The band agreed that a return to the more focused live-in-studio performance approach that had made *Songs Of Faith And Devotion* stand out was the way to go, while not neglecting the synth-driven nature of the core Depeche Mode project (although Hillier would revert to the by-now 'old-fashioned' analogue synths that Mode had first set out with, rather than newer digital synths). Hillier saw *Exciter*, for all its relaxed nature, as being too programmatic, and he wanted a return to 'a live, performance element. I like to see a bit of humanism in the music... that was missing from the last record.'

Hillier found himself joining Fletcher in between the two creative powerhouses of Gore and Gahan. From an initial fear that their unstated competition might derail the project, Hillier quickly came to realise that he could use the undercurrent of rivalry to drive both of them to produce better work than ever before. Gore and Gahan could function as each other's worst critics, so spurring them on individually to produce the best material they could. 'It could have been disastrous,' Hillier told Steve Malins in *Depeche Mode: The Biography*. 'There is a competitive streak between Dave and Martin, no doubt about that, but it forced Martin into writing better songs.' Balance was restored in the recording process, with a further session in Gahan's New York base at Stratosphere Sound, and a wrap-up in London (where Fletcher still lived) at the Whitfield Street studio.

Playing The Angel – the album that resulted from this new spirit of co-operation – was a synthesis of much that had come before, combining Gahan's fresh songwriting approach with Gore's tried-and-tested technique, with both being driven to deliver the goods like never before. It combined the raw, edgy sounds of *Songs Of Faith And Devotion* with the clean, sharp electronica of *Violator*, producing a 'best of both worlds' approach to new soundscapes that generated some of Depeche Mode's best reviews in a long time. Scoring higher chart positions in the UK and US than *Exciter*, *Playing The Angel* was welcomed as 'the best thing they've released in a long time' (*Pitchfork*), 'their most self-assured and accessible release in a decade' (*Entertainment Weekly*), and 'so sure and committed it could be the work of a new band' (*Q*). The Depeche Mode train, after almost a quarter of a century, was firmly back on the tracks.

'A Pain That I'm Used To' 4:11

Opening track 'A Pain That I'm Used To' (with the return of the trademark distorted noise, this time a 'siren' sound) was the second single released (on 12 December 2005, following the album by two months). It took a while to come together to everyone's satisfaction, as Fletcher (who actually played a real bass guitar on this) recalled in the November 2005 issue of *Keyboard* magazine:

That song did start in Santa Barbara. It went through lots of stages. We were settled on the basic arrangement – the 'siren' intro, then pulsating bass, then Dave comes in with the opening line – [but] the rhythm just never seemed to groove properly.

Producer Ben Hillier also told the website Depeche-mode.com:

Getting the verses right was really difficult. The choruses always worked very well, and the riff sections always worked very well. We had all sorts of things going on in the verse. We probably did six or seven different versions of that before we settled on the final one.

It was worth the effort, as 'A Pain That I'm Used To' is a banger of an opener and an effective mission statement for the entire album. *Stylus* described the track as 'thrashing with fire and noise amid crunching vocal hooks, symbolising the start of something special', while *Mixmag* called the album's 'opening triple salvo of "A Pain That I'm Used To", "John The Revelator" and "Suffer Well"... a musical call-to-arms not heard since *Violator*.' High praise, indeed.

Uwe Flade directed the video, in which the band perform against a backdrop of violent stock car racing, featuring female drivers (and Gahan's cohort Christian Eigner on drums). The single peaked at number 15 in the UK and made the Top 5 in Belgium (three), Denmark (three), Hungary (one), Italy (two) and Spain (one). Only released digitally in the US, the single climbed to number five on the Hot Dance Music/Club Play Chart in January 2006. As with several other Mode songs, 'A Pain That I'm Used To' proved popular with film and television producers, with a slightly remixed instrumental version featuring on the trailer for the 2010 Disney/Nicolas Cage movie *The Sorcerer's Apprentice*, a 2006 episode of *Bones* ('Two Bodies in the Lab'), a 2015 episode of *Pretty Little Liars* ('The Melody Lingers On'), and a 2020 episode of *Brassic* ('Stealing a Wedding').

'John The Revelator' 3:42
Second track, 'John The Revelator', is the sandwich filling in the powerful trio of songs that open *Playing The Angel*. Although not a cover version, it is based upon traditional gospel songs with the nearest to the Mode update being the Son House track from the 1930s (which Gore owned as an 'old Shellac single'). The Mode song is Gore's, but the rhythm and construction comes from the original. Gore outlined the background to *La Libre* newspaper in 2005:

> ['John The Revelator'] is inspired by a traditional tune. It talks about faith in God, no matter what. It also denounces the belief in a God who punishes and damns. In the [Bible] Book of Revelation, John describes his visions of these seven angels descending, blowing into their seven trumpets and causing plagues, epidemics and floods that gradually exterminate a large part of humanity. Only the true believers remain. I do not believe in all that.

Heavily reinterpreted from the traditional song, 'John The Revelator' does not boast as clear a gospel sound as 'Condemnation'. Instead, it is an electronic-driven track that gives Gahan a vocal workout. The *Observer* noted: 'Depeche Mode's most satisfying songs have usually been their most direct. Those ranks are swelled by the murky gothic swing of "John The Revelator". It's not a straight cover of the country-blues standard, but it lets rip in a way little else does.' The *Manchester Evening News* applauded Depeche Mode's 'trademark brand of electronic rock that we've all come to expect from these electro stalwarts. There's a few bips here and a smattering of plips there to fuel the digitised feel of everything and it scores fairly highly for Gahan's vocal performance alone...'. Another Top 20 UK hit, with little promotion (the band were busy Touring The Angel), the single release reached number 18, while hitting the usual Top 5 spots across Europe. It was a double A-side with

'Lilian'. The promotional video by Anton Corbijn features live footage from the tour, enhanced by animated touches that bring his video projection graphics to life on stage (the angel figure that stalks Gahan, Gore's angel wings). The track was used in the UK motoring magazine show *Top Gear* and turned up in the 2006 Robin Williams-starring movie *Man of the Year*.

'Suffer Well' 3:49

The first Depeche Mode single (the third from *Playing The Angel*, on 27 March 2006) to feature lyrics written by lead singer Dave Gahan, 'Suffer Well' was a marker of things to come. Gahan had collaborated with Christian Eigner (who, with Peter Gordeno, formed vital musical support for the core Depeche Mode members on tour) and Andrew Phillpott (who wrote the music with Eigner). It was the first single from the band since 1981's 'Just Can't Get Enough' not written by Martin Gore. Some speculated that Gahan's lyrics were a response to the lack of support he'd felt from his bandmates during his period of drug addiction. The opening couplet – 'Where were you when I fell from grace/A frozen heart, an empty space' – could certainly be taken that way. In Ian Gittins' *Depeche Mode: Faith and Devotion*, Gahan said:

> It was definitely a little dig at them. I didn't write it like that, but when I sang it, I did picture Martin. It was, 'Why didn't you understand that I needed you the most then?' When I was crawling across the floor of that apartment in Santa Monica, inside I was screaming, 'Where the fuck are you?'

Gahan lifted the lid further on his Mode songwriting debut in *The Wave* in 2005:

> It was a much slower song and we just decided to go in a really pop way with it. Which is a contrast to what it's saying lyrically, which is: Suffer well, because whatever it is you're suffering, if you suffer well enough, you won't have to suffer any more. It's something that was said to me a long time ago, which I did not understand. Suffer well, and if you suffer well enough, you can move on.

Gahan had definitely moved on from his drug experiences, but he was happy to draw upon that dark time in his life for inspiration. Gahan's original demo was a slower take, with producer Ben Hillier speeding things up considerably and adding what he called the 'drum groove'. Singing his own material was not a new experience for Gahan (he'd already released his solo debut album, *Paper Monsters*), but it was a first for him when it came to Depeche Mode. 'Dave kept working on the vocals up to the last minute to get them just right,' recalled Hillier in a 2017 Facebook Q&A.

Gahan's song saw Anton Corbijn return to directing music videos for Depeche Mode, his first non-concert projection film since 1997's 'Useless'. The video features a handful of in-jokes: the limo driver is band manager

Jonathan Kessler, while Gahan's wife Jennifer Sklias is both the angel and the woman at the end. There is also the unforgettable sight of Gore and Fletcher as unlikely bride and groom mannequins. 'Suffer Well' reached number 12 in the UK Singles Chart, but was the band's seventh single to top the American Hot Dance Music/Club Play Chart. The *Irish Times* wrote: 'Dave Gahan's voice is as deep and murky as the title – and sounds better than ever.' The critic for *Q* warmed to Gahan's lyrical contribution: '[Gahan's] "Suffer Well" sums up the album's subtext of hard-won optimism. "I found treasure not where I thought/ Peace of mind can't be bought/I still believe", he croons, and you believe that the reformed rock-pig means it.' The *Guardian* suggested the song 'swirls into life with old-school analogue action and maintains a breathless pace.'

'The Sinner In Me' 4:56
A change of pace arrives with 'The Sinner In Me', along with a return to Gore's long-held lyrical concern with sin, suffering and darkness (not for nothing did the band subtitle *Playing The Angel* as 'Pain and suffering in various tempos'). Lyrically, it could be seen as Gore's response to Gahan's 'Suffer Well'. Lines like 'I'm still recovering/Getting over all the suffering' have a distinctive meaning when sung by Gahan. It's experimental, featuring the usual Mode electronic blips and bleeps over an insistent rhythm that fills in between the chorus. Gore can't help infuse the track with optimism, with the section that runs: 'But you're always around/You can always be found/To pick me up/When I'm on the ground'. 'The Sinner In Me' suffers the most spectacular musical breakdown, reflecting the mental condition of the singer. The instrumental break takes a detour from the more melody-driven song it's plonked into the middle of, only slowly returning to the subject at hand shortly before the conclusion, when the breakdown consumes the whole in finality.

'Precious' 4:10
In writing material for *Playing The Angel*, it seems that both Gore and Gahan dug deep into their own personal circumstances. This had always been a source of inspiration for Gore (almost the entirety of *A Broken Frame* was the younger Gore's 'break-up' album), but more than ever before the first single release from *Playing The Angel*, 'Precious' (released on 3 October 2005), captured a moment in Gore's life. After 16 years of marriage and a trio of children, Gore and his wife Suzanne Boisvert were divorcing. It was a difficult time, but Gore felt especially guilty about the effect on his children. He poured this into 'Precious', especially in the heartfelt opening refrain: 'Precious and fragile things/Need special handling/My God, what have we done to you?'
Talking to *Mojo*, Gore laid bare his inspiration:

I feel like I've failed in my marriage. I feel guilt... because of the children. Maybe the marriage was partly a charade for a while anyway. I felt guilty about that for... many years.

Gore expounded further in an interview with the German website netzeitung.de:

> My private life is pretty crappy. I'm about to divorce my wife, the situation
> has been going on for 16 months. My life is certainly not a walk in the park. I
> also have three children. 'Precious', the single, is a song that describes exactly
> this situation. There are other divorce songs on *Playing The Angel*. 'Precious'
> is about how my children cope with the divorce – which isn't very well. But
> the song ends with the verse 'I know you learned to trust/Keep faith in both
> of us'. All of our songs, even the most depressive ones, contain hope.

Gore's mining of his private life and emotional anguish drove 'Precious' to
number four on the UK Singles Chart, matching their previous highest single
chart position reached by both 1984's 'People Are People' and 1997's 'Barrel Of
A Gun', meaning the band had achieved a Top 5 single in each decade they'd
been in existence (to that point). The single reached the top spot in Denmark,
Sweden, Italy and Spain, as well as in the US Dance Singles Chart, and was a
Top 5 hit in Austria, Canada, Norway, Finland and Germany. The music video
(by Uwe Flade) sees the band perform upon a computer-generated cruise ship.
The bangs and clangs of the synth-driven music play well with Gahan's soulful
delivery of Gore's heartfelt lyrics, resulting in a near-perfect, mature Depeche
Mode track that found resonance with music fans worldwide.

'Macro' 4:03
A dense sonic soup, 'Macro' continues the experimentation of *Playing The
Angel* with a song that explores the cosmic through sex and devotion. Gore's
vocals power this emotionally complex track, dealing with enlightenment
through God-like nature. It's a vision of universal experience captured by
Gore's innate optimism where he hails 'One creation' to be the sum of all
things. He'd come a long way since 'See You'. Oddly – and largely as a result
of this song – Depeche Mode were revealed by the *Daily Mirror* to 'have the
most sophisticated lyrics' of all the UK's best-selling bands. In a data mining
exercise, the lyrics of various pop artists were examined using methods
usually applied to school textbooks. The results suggested that to understand
the average Depeche Mode song, the listener would have to have had over a
decade of formal education, suggesting a lower age of 15. As the paper noted,
the sophistication of Depeche Mode's lyrics outpaced that of such artists
as The Beatles, David Bowie and Queen! According to the *Mirror*: 'One of
Depeche Mode's most sophisticated songs was "Macro".'

'I Want It All' 6:09
The second track on *Playing The Angel* with lyrics from singer Gahan, 'I
Want It All', is not as strong as either 'Suffer Well' or the following 'Nothing's
Impossible'. It did feature on *Under the Radar*'s list of '10 Killer Depeche Mode
Songs Nobody's Listening To', suggesting it's an underrated entry in the band's

canon, alongside 'Lie To Me' from *Some Great Reward*, 'Halo' from *Violator* and 'Shine' from *Exciter*, among others. It's a slow burn that might have shone on *Exciter*, but gets somewhat lost amid the thumping trio of openers on *Playing The Angel* and the more experimental tracks around it. 'I Want It All' is perfectly fine, if a little simplistic lyrically. After all, everyone can have off days – Martin Gore rhymed 'revelator' with 'elevator' on 'John The Revelator'! There's a dreamy abstractness to the chorus, but it's not enough to stop it from drifting out of the listener's memory the minute it finishes.

'Nothing's Impossible' 4:21
The third of the Gahan-written songs on *Playing The Angel*, 'Nothing's Impossible', is slightly better than 'Suffer Well'. There's a dark drive that is very Mode, while Gahan's treated vocals give it an eerie touch. The disjunctive noises that follow the first verse could throw the listener off, just before the verse reclaims some melodic sense. Atmospheric, 'Nothing's Impossible' began with a very different sound before being filtered through Hillier. While the sound is dark and doomy, it's actually very positive, lyrically speaking: 'I still believe in love at first sight/Nothing's impossible'. The original demo is lighter, with a more whispered vocal. In the April 2009 edition of Germany's *Rolling Stone*, Gahan said:

> I think my songs are different [from Gore's], a different character, wilder. 'Nothing's Impossible' went into another direction than what I had as a demo. You can hear it in the [*Sounds Of The Universe*] boxset, it's great. This was my idea in the first place, but I had to give it up.

'Introspectre' 1:42
An inoffensive instrumental that, according to Gore (in *Gaywired*), is 'a nice atmospheric piece of music that leads really nicely into "Damaged People".'

'Damaged People' 3:29
The second of Gore's vocals, 'Damaged People' is emblematic of the dark territory he often trades in, but with an uplifting melodic treatment that is ultimately undercut by his inability to resist the temptation to stick a twist in the tale: 'I forget to sense I'm dying'! Otherwise, it's trademark Gore with 'Disturbed souls' and 'Depraved souls' vying for dominance, while love (or is it lust?) ultimately conquers all, no matter how twisted: 'When your lips touch mine/And I lose control'. It's fine, but something of a filler that was never going to enjoy an existence beyond its place between an instrumental and 'Lilian'.

'Lilian' 4:49
Released as a double A-side single with 'John The Revelator', this is one of those rare Depeche Mode songs titled after someone's name (other featured given names in song titles being 'Jesus', 'Judas', 'John', 'Jezebel' – sensing a

theme?). Which raises the question: 'Who is Lilian?' Gore was quick to offer a response at the netzeitung.de website: 'You really don't want to know who Lilian is!'

Someone is toying with a male suitor: 'You've stripped my heart/Ripped it apart/In the name of fun'. It's a throwback to Depeche Mode's earlier pop songs, which may explain its choice as a double A-side single (the combined release reached number 18 in the UK Singles Chart). Fletcher denied knowing who Lilian was (if there was a real-life version) and had an odd way of praising Gore's songwriting: 'I do not know [who Lilian is] either. But nevertheless the song is great for waking up at eight in the morning while heating up a plate of pasta.' Uh-huh?

'The Darkest Star' 6:55

This was the source for the album title *Playing The Angel*, only the third time a song lyric has resulted in an album title in Depeche Mode's history (the other two being *Construction Time Again* and *Black Celebration*). The song itself is an electronic prog epic, running to almost seven minutes, densely layered and deeply immersive. As a brooding closing track, it is well placed, summing up the experimental approach this album takes – a breath of fresh air after the more laid-back vibe of *Exciter*. Lyrically, it's about a dark romance, but some of Gore's lines could easily be describing the Depeche Mode fan base: 'Oh you dark one' and 'Eternal outsider' seem particularly applicable. 'The Darkest Star' noodles around, swinging from Gahan's drawn-out chorus vocals to dark throbs and thumps – there's something operatic about it, especially the 'Stay as you are' closing aria.

Related Tracks
'Free' 5:13

Released as the B-side to the single 'Precious', 'Free' is a fast-paced track that features many traditional (even old-fashioned) Depeche Mode sounds put together in a sonic soup that vibrates strongly but makes no particular impact. Ben Hillier deliberately took a throwback approach, as he told the DM News website in 2005: '"Free" is quite a driving, up-tempo track. It's got some great vintage synth sounds. It's a real analogue treat… a really good track.' Gore is at it again with his lyrics, with the singer in chains that bind him, torture him and blind him – no doubt chains of a romantic or sexual nature. There's 'heartache' and 'heartbreak' in quick succession, followed by a heavy dose of never being free. Naturally, this is all because he'll 'never recover/From this tenderness'. After all, doomy angst is 'what love brings'.

'Newborn' 5:34

Another B-side, this time to 'A Pain That I'm Used To', 'Newborn' could have easily slotted into *Playing The Angel*, except it lacks the experimentation that features in most of the final choices. It opens with a slow-burn build-up before Gahan's slight vocal kicks in. It feels for the first minute or so as if it would be more suited to an emotional Gore vocal, until 'Newborn' suddenly bursts into, er, new life. It's louder, with a more insistent vocal for the chorus, before flipping back for the verse. There's a draft of the sounds that would come to the fore on *Sounds Of The Universe* buried here, so this largely unsung track could be seen as a pointer to Depeche Mode's future direction.

'Better Days' 2:28

This B-side to single release 'Suffer Well' is a brief, but impactful doodle that again feels like a throwback rather than a forward move. It powers through with a solid, thumping rhythm and some *Black Celebration*-sounding 'found' sounds or twangs, before coming to a dead stop. The lyrics don't make much sense, but are delivered with gusto in an unfamiliar chanting style by Gahan.

Sounds of the Universe (2009)

Personnel:
Dave Gahan: lead vocals, except on 'Jezebel' and 'The Sun And The Moon And The Stars'
Martin Gore: guitar, bass guitar, keyboards, backing vocals, lead vocals on 'Jezebel' and 'The Sun And The Moon And The Stars'
Andy Fletcher: keyboards
Recorded at Sound Design, Santa Barbara; Chung King, New York City; May–December 2008
Producer: Ben Hillier
All tracks written by Martin Gore, except 'Hole To Feed', 'Come Back' and 'Miles Away/The Truth Is' written by Dave Gahan, Christian Eigner and Andrew Phillpott
Released: 20 April 2009. Label: Mute
Running time: 60:52
Highest chart placings: UK: 2; US: 3; Australia: 32; Austria: 1; Belgium: 2; Canada: 3; Finland: 1; France: 2; Germany: 1; Italy: 1; Japan: 31; Spain: 1; Sweden: 1; Switzerland: 1.

By the middle of the 2000s, Depeche Mode were firmly back on track. They'd recovered from the *Songs Of Faith And Devotion* era, with a trio of albums only one of which – *Exciter* – had failed to live up to its title. A trio once more, they'd recovered their touring mojo after the cautious Ultra Parties as well as the Singles Tour of 1998 and the 2001 Exciter Tour. The 2005–06 Touring The Angel gigs were, according to Dave Gahan, 'the most enjoyable live show we have ever done. The new material was just waiting to be played live. With the energy of the crowds, it just came to life.' It had been a remarkable recovery for a band barrelling towards its fourth decade of existence.

Between *Playing The Angel* and *Sounds Of The Universe*, Gahan had consolidated his songwriting with his second solo album, *Hourglass* (2007). Once again, he co-wrote the ten tracks with Eigner and Phillpott, who would also work on the trio of songs that Gahan contributed to *Sounds Of The Universe*: 'Hole To Feed', 'Come Back' and 'Miles Away/The Truth Is'.

Things had changed for their record label, Mute. Daniel Miller had sold the company to EMI for £23 million while continuing to run it as a separate concern and retaining an 'astonishing' degree of control. The two *Remixes* albums and *The Best of Depeche Mode Volume 1* (2006) had successfully exploited the band's back catalogue. A new single – the Gore-penned 'Martyr', recording during the *Playing The Angel* sessions – was released to promote the latest career retrospective that chronicled their 25-year musical journey.

Gahan, Gore and Fletcher reunited with *Playing The Angel* producer Ben Hillier in Santa Monica in May 2008 to begin *Sounds Of The Universe*, their 12th studio album. It was to be the most 'business-like' recording the band had ever engaged in, with Gore joining Gahan in sobriety. '[It's] one of the most disciplined records we've ever made,' Gahan told *The Quietus*. 'Martin and I just turned up every day to work, both of us very focused. He's written some fantastic songs, and I've got a few on there myself... there was something different about this one.'

Critics broadly welcomed the album, with *Entertainment Weekly* noting the band 'still sound genuinely inspired', while the *Daily Telegraph* pointed out their latest release 'shows up the imaginative constraints of most guitar-based rock'. *Rolling Stone* felt *Sounds Of The Universe* was a backwards step: 'The result sounds like a time machine back to the Eighties' adding that 'Depeche Mode should be poised for a comeback, but it is too soon to unpack those black turtlenecks'. *PopMatters* dismissed the second half of the album as 'a collection of tossed-off B-sides', while the *New York Times* claimed the album was 'an attempt at revisiting the past, admirable even as an act of defiant stubbornness or tenacious commitment', but 'even at its most imaginative, this is seamless Depeche Mode filler, music that could be made by any number of acolytes'.

Perhaps the band were just a little too sober? *Sounds Of The Universe*, while featuring a handful of modern Mode classics, was a slick and smooth album of seemingly self-satisfied electro pop with little of the edge that had featured so heavily on *Playing The Angel*. It's no *Exciter*, but it was a little too laid-back and created on autopilot compared to some of the band's past work produced under far more trying circumstances. Perhaps the creative tension and problematic inter-personal relationships of the past were necessary in the creation of truly great Depeche Mode music?

'In Chains' 6:53

Despite its discordant opening, the touchstone for 'In Chains' for Gahan and Gore was Marvin Gaye. Gahan saw it as a 'classic soul song', while Gore claimed 'there's something Marvin Gaye about it'. The opening tones are the electro equivalent of an orchestra tuning up, an idea that came to Gore in a dream, as he told *Keyboard* magazine:

I had a dream about the tuning up of the synths, as an orchestra tunes up. It so happened that 'In Chains' starts in the key of A minor. So we were able to start the album with the A440 tuning tone from the Minimoog, and just recorded, gradually tuning a load of synths to that. We thought that only real keyboard aficionados would recognize that initial, little click of the Minimoog [powering up], then the A440 going on.

In terms of lyrical content, 'In Chains' features the traditional Gore obsessions, with a romance described as akin to slavery, to being 'in chains'. Gahan chews down on the lyrics with gusto, delivering a great opening track that sweeps the listener into the rest of the album. It's got a nice structure, where the abstract synths are given substance by the rhymes delivered by Gahan.

'Hole To Feed' 3:59

Written by Gahan (and released as a double A-side with 'Fragile Tension'), 'Hole To Feed' became the subject of a long-running disparaging joke as being the worst Depeche Mode song of all time at fan blog Almost Predictable Almost. Despite that, some reviewers were well-disposed towards Gahan and company's effort. *Pitchfork* called 'Hole To Feed', 'busy yet spare, bounding along a sci-fi take on the Bo Diddley beat' while *The Quietus* hailed its 'minimal acid blues' with the song concerning 'the singer's addictive nature, and its minimalism is emphasised by the use of old equipment and a prominent, primitive rock guitar'. Gahan, talking to the *Guardian* in 2009, described the track as 'a very cynical song about wanting to fill a gaping hole but not knowing what to fill it with. About sometimes the idea [of] having a hole to feed all being a figment of my imagination when I'm actually fine'. It clearly came from his history of addiction, the need to feed the habit, even when it is doing nothing but harm. A decade on from his own near-death, Gahan was addressing his plight more directly in his songs than Gore ever did, with his more oblique or shaded takes on life, love and lust. The development of the song was 'a collective effort,' Gahan told Polish site interia.pl. '[It] ended up becoming something more rhythmic and lyrically cynical. Once we had developed the rhythmic structure, Martin played the guitar with some great parts, and the transition gave the song a completely different atmosphere.' The opening pounding rhythm and bubbling sounds set the scene, but Gahan's declarative delivery brings things to life.

'Wrong' 3:13

Released on 6 April 2009 as the first single from *Sounds Of The Universe*, 'Wrong' had an important role. According to Martin Gore, talking to Germany's *Rolling Stone* in April 2009:

> We decided to go with 'Wrong' because it's quite different from what we've done in the past. I heard the description 'future retro sound', which I liked a lot. A lot of the new songs have a Sixties-Space-Age-Pop-Sound. I always say I'm a traditional songwriter, in the way that I use melodies, chords and lyrics. Only the instrumental part is a unanimous Depeche Mode decision. But for me, electro and emotions work together, there is no contradiction.

The Space-Age-Pop-Sound would be the defining feature of *Sounds Of The Universe*, and while 'Wrong' was chosen to signify that shift in the band's sound, it is not quite as in alignment with that sonic approach as some of the other tracks. It's up there with 'Personal Jesus', 'Just Can't Get Enough', or 'Everything Counts' and 'Enjoy The Silence' as a loud crowd-pleaser that plays well live. It was helped along by a spectacular music video directed by Patrick Daughters (known for his work with The Kings of Leon). The video depicts a (seemingly) driverless Ford Crown Victoria creating merry mayhem on the streets of downtown Los Angeles. Like an extract from a movie, it becomes clear there is a bound-and-gagged occupant, hinting at a larger plot that has led up to this moment. At one point, the band are seen watching the car rush past, as it smashes through dustbins, traffic cones and pedestrians before crashing into a pick-up truck. The video made *Time*'s list of 'The Five Best Videos of 2009'. For Gahan, talking on the *Sounds Of The Universe* promotional EPK, there could have been no other choice for lead single:

> It's sort of an unconventional pop song. It's almost more of a rap or rant and its groove is a little different too. We didn't choose it because we felt it was the best song [from the album], we chose it because we felt that it was striking and a good song for the next chapter of what it is we're doing...

It proved to be a wise choice. While 'Wrong' only reached number 24 in the UK Singles Chart (the band's last Top 40 until 2023's 'Ghosts Again'), it scored much higher elsewhere, hitting the top spot in Scotland, *Billboard*'s Dance Club Songs Chart, Italy and number two in Germany. There's nothing wrong about that ...

'Fragile Tension' 4:09
The third single from *Sounds Of The Universe* (released on 7 December 2009, which might have been a better time to release 'Peace') was a double A-side of 'Fragile Tension' and 'Hole To Feed'. This marked the changes that had happened to the way music was released since the 1980s. CDs had effectively killed the notion of 'B-sides', with additional tracks and remixes making up the additional content, while the internet had made copying and distributing music much easier. 'Fragile Tension' suffered from being leaked early on the internet ahead of the album, and the track was not appreciated by Depeche Mode fans. The video accompanying the eventual official release was co-directed by Rob Chandler and Barney Steel, and went one better than 'Hole To Feed' by actually featuring the band. *The Quietus* noted the track 'harkened back to the band's synthier days without losing the layer of grunge it's carefully cultivated post-*Violator*'. Like much of *Sounds Of The Universe*, 'Fragile Tension' works well enough as part of the flow of the album, but out of context on its own, it simply doesn't stand up, a fact reflected in its failure to chart in the UK (due to the lack of a 7" released). It only reached number 27 in France and number 39 in the usually loyal Germany.

'Little Soul' 3:31
Written back to back with 'Peace', 'Little Soul' was part of a deliberate 'soulful' approach by Gore to several tracks that gave *Sounds Of The Universe* its overall theme and tone. 'I wrote ["Little Soul" and "Peace"] back to back,' Gore told *Billboard* magazine, 'and the flow of the album started to make more sense. I really felt they had a spirituality to them. That somehow

set a cornerstone for the rest of the writing.' Originally titled 'Footprint', 'Little Soul' fits nicely with the 'cosmic pop' feel of *Sounds Of The Universe*, with more space-age bubbling sounds in the mix. There's a yearning to Gahan's vocal delivery here that fits nicely, swallowing Gore's obsessions with infinity, singularity and 'channelling the universe'. A chugging guitar sound wraps things up.

'In Sympathy' 4:54
Perhaps lost in the flow, 'In Sympathy' tends to be overlooked and so is underrated. Musically, it's less 'spacey' than some of the others, and more readily identified as a Depeche Mode track. A driving rhythm and pounding synth lines back Gahan's rolling delivery, parsing out the chorus lines in a stop-start format dividing 'sympathy' almost into two words. Exploring the world of false compliments and hidden feelings, Gore's lyrics seem to present a character forever complimented on her looks, but who knows deep down, there's more to her than that, yet few seem to see it (except for the singer). It's an interlude on the album, clearing the way for 'Peace' to follow.

'Peace' 4:29
Written in conjunction with 'Little Soul', 'Peace' – released as the second single from the album on 15 June 2009 – is a heartfelt, if naive, meditation not on 'world peace' but on finding some form of inner peace or contentment. Perhaps unknown to Gore, he was exploring the aftermath of the turmoil of the mid-1990s over a decade later, when the various members of Depeche Mode found themselves in a new place. Relationships had come and gone (with Fletcher being the most contented and consistent), and each of them had matured, dealing better now with the vicissitudes of life than they had done in their rather wild thirties. Gore told *Mojo* in 2009 that 'Peace' was one of 'the most spiritual songs I've ever written. Peace will come to me. Inner peace. I don't want to come across as a born-again Christian or some New Age hippy, but maybe it is about feeling more connected to the universe'. For all its 'spiritual' nature, 'Peace' is an electronic heavy song that immediately struck a chord with a more reflective Gahan. 'When Martin played it to me for the first time, I turned around and said, "I think that's one of the best songs you've ever written,"' he told *Under the Radar*. 'Even in demo form, it was apparent that it was so full of melody, I thought it was just beautiful. Sometimes I don't know where he comes up with this stuff, to be honest.' The single, however, failed to perform, only reaching number 57 in the UK Singles Chart, a disappointing outcome that oddly matched their debut single in 1981, 'Dreaming Of Me'.

'Come Back' 5:15
Released as a B-side to 'Peace', this Gahan-written track was one of the singer's personal favourites on *Sounds Of The Universe*, partly due to the way

it had evolved far beyond the initial demo. He gave credit, in *Rolling Stone*'s April 2009 German edition, to Gore. 'Martin helped a lot [with my songs], he invested a lot of time, trying a lot. Sometimes I had to pressure him a little bit, but he had this idea with the backing vocals in "Come. Back", which is wonderful.' Originally more gospel in style, this was reworked to sound more like Elvis Presley given the Phil Spector 'wall of sound' treatment. The clanking, fuzzy guitar and distorted sounds provide a solid background to Gahan's vocal dance as he pleads for the return of ... what? A partner, a lover or a feeling, perhaps the drug highs he would like to feel once more without the attendant risk and lifestyle downsides.

'Spacewalker' 1:53
A plodding, time-filling instrumental; atmospheric but no great shakes.

'Perfect' 4:33
'Perfect' is the erm, perfect example of the sci-fi cosmic spin that Gore was exploring on *Sounds Of The Universe* (an approach that was not appreciated by much of the Depeche Mode fan base at the time). Exploring alternate history and divergent timelines – the kind of thing that featured heavily in the Marvel movies of the 2020s, but that was relegated to the sci-fi cognoscenti in the past – 'Perfect' hits on a neat storytelling device. That old lyrical favourite of Gore's, where an accused stands before a (metaphorical or real) judge and jury, returns after being missing for many years and it's the ideal line to get across the high concept of the song: 'The jury reached a different verdict/Before the judge dismissed the case'. In different worlds and parallel universes, the relationship between two people could have completely different outcomes. Things might not be great in the here and now, but somewhere out in the great multiverse, the stars are aligned and 'everything is almost perfect'. It's a prime example of Gore's inherent optimism and idealism given shape in a song that may have better suited a solo Gore release than a Depeche Mode album.

'Miles Away/The Truth Is' 4:14
This Gahan-penned song suffered a last-minute title alteration when Gore pointed out to the songwriter that there was already a Madonna song entitled 'Miles Away'. Talking to the *Guardian* in 2009, Gahan confessed: 'Martin does [change song titles]. He's very particular about his song titles. At the last minute, he'll change the title and he worries if there's another song with the same name.' Unlike Gore, Gahan was not so reticent about explaining his songs, so told Polish website interia.pl what was on his mind when writing the lyrics for 'Miles Away/The Truth Is':

This song is about someone whose thoughts are somewhere far away, about someone who hides behind a facade or a mask. [It] is about a friend: I knew that when I was with him and said something to him, he was actually mentally absent, even though he tried to convince me that he was not. 'Miles Away/The Truth Is' is not entirely about drugs, but they are always present somewhere in my songs. All my life, I [have] tried to escape from myself. Often with drugs, until it finally became clear to me that it was not bad to be myself.

'Jezebel' 4:41
Following Jesus, Judas, John and Lilian, it's back to the Bible for 'Jezebel'. It was a repeating theme that Gore had to admit to when talking to Swedish magazine *Zero* in 2009:

Betrayal, longing, suffering, religion, and sex, all in one song. What can I say? Maybe I've finally written the ultimate Depeche Mode lyric? Jokes aside, you don't have to put too much weight on the Biblical reference. The song is more about the importance of not believing everything you hear. To think for yourself.

All the greatest Gore hits are here: Hell, sin, sexy outfits ('They call you Jezebel/For what you like to wear'), moral failings ('morally unwell'), beauty and longing. *Pitchfork* reckoned the approach on 'Jezebel' was 'synth-lounge' (recalling *Exciter*), while *The Quietus* dubbed it an 'almost cabaret number... dedicated to a young woman who (presumably) has a bracing line in the kind of clothing that wouldn't go down too well in Saudi Arabia'.

'Corrupt' 5:02 (8:59 including silent gap and 'Interlude#5', starting at 8:16, which runs for 42 seconds)
Almost a return to *Violator*, 'Corrupt' is a fierce album closer that – lyrically at least – could be a throwback to *Black Celebration*. Originally titled 'Corruption', it is the most obviously Mode-like track on the entire album. It immediately sounds like Depeche Mode from the opening seconds, pumping synths behind Gahan's lizard-like creepy vocal. It's one of the few songs, alongside 'Wrong', that obviously lends itself to live performance – in later tours, it got fans up and dancing, even singing along to Gore's dark lyrics. The dirty, sleazy vibe lends itself to the patented Mode stadium electro-rock. It grinds along, mining Gore's darkness for all it is worth, as Gahan taunts and temps the target of his will to corruption. Going out on the once traditional, but seemingly recently forgotten, Depeche Mode raunchiness was an inspired move... if it hadn't been for 'Interlude #5' which follows 'Corrupt' and turns out to be a 42-second instrumental noodle based on 'Wrong'. 'Corrupt' was used in the final trailer for the second season of HBO's horror series *True Blood*.

Related Tracks
'Martyr' 3:23
Released on 30 October 2006 to promote *The Best of Depeche Mode Volume 1* (there hasn't to date been a Volume 2), 'Martyr' was a non-album single that

fell between *Playing The Angel* and *Sounds Of The Universe*. As such, it is something of a transitional track, capturing the period when Depeche Mode's production became a little too efficient and streamlined, resulting in perfectly fine music that lacked their previous edge. Originally titled 'Martyr for Love' – which better reflects the full lyric – this was the band's 45th single in a near 30-year career. It topped the charts in Europe (in Italy and Spain) while reaching a respectable number 13 on the UK Singles Chart, at a time when single sales were in decline. Deemed to have too 'poppy' a sound, the song didn't find a place on the more experimental *Playing The Angel* even though it was considered as a possible lead single. Seemingly 'homeless', 'Martyr' finally found its place as a promotional device that nonetheless performed well in sales terms. Musically and lyrically, 'Martyr' was actually a decent scene-setter for the first single from *Sounds Of The Universe*, 'Wrong'.

'Oh Well' 5:59

Sounds Of The Universe was the longest Depeche Mode album up to and including *Memento Mori*, clocking in at just over an hour across its 13 tracks. While some may question the quality of some of the tracks, and perhaps accuse the band of going for quantity over quality, there can be little doubt that the recording process proved especially fertile. As a result, there was a surfeit of extra tracks that didn't make the cut, with five of them ultimately released as part of the *Sounds Of The Universe* 'deluxe box set'. The first of these, 'Oh Well', proved to also be the first formal songwriting collaboration between Gore and Gahan (it wouldn't be the last). First released as the B-side to 'Wrong', 'Oh Well' began life as an instrumental that, according to Gore, 'Dave liked so much that he put some lyrics to it.' In the *Sounds Of The Universe* documentary, Gahan recalled:

> I went back to my room in Santa Barbara, and suddenly I [had] these ideas, and this melody, and some words, coming into my head. I put vocals on it, and vocal melodies. We recorded it... the first collaboration between us, which was done in completely different places, in completely different parts of America, and at completely different times. But nonetheless, it's a collaboration.

'Oh Well' is disco-tastique pulsing along through Gahan's lyrics and vocals. On its own, it would have been a better instrumental than 'Spacewalker', but Gahan added a new layer to Gore's tune making it into a proper song that sits quite nicely as a Depeche Mode track but would not have suited the overall trajectory of *Sounds Of The Universe*. Ideal B-side material, then...

'Light' 4:44

The title 'Light' is an adequate descriptor of this more poppy outing that – like 'Oh Well' – didn't fit comfortably among the other tracks on *Sounds Of*

The Universe. The touch might be light, but the lyrics once more express Gore's favourites – the duty of love, as in: 'You know we have to make a case for love/It's more of a duty/It's clear we have a mission from above/A mission of beauty'.

'The Sun And The Moon And The Stars' 4:41

One for the record books, as 'The Sun And The Moon And The Stars' is the longest Depeche Mode song title at 34 characters, ahead of *Spirit*'s 'No More (This Is The Last Time)' at 31 characters. It's a ballad, written and sung by Gore, that was out of step with the rest of *Sounds Of The Universe*. It doesn't quite work, with the heavy chorus drowning out Gore's vocal. There's a bit of religion in Gore's allegory for helpless love, with mentions of God and prayer. He contrasts the fleeting nature of love at first sight to such solid perennials as the sun, the moon, the stars, the wind and the waves – which ultimately will outlast us all and outlast all love affairs.

'Ghost' 6:26

A lost classic. While 'Ghost' may not have fitted neatly on *Sounds Of The Universe*, it deserved to find a place somewhere as a mainstream release; it is that strong a track. It opens with more 'tuning up' noises, like 'In Chains', but quickly settles into a haunting, twangy rhythm that perfectly complements Gahan's spooky rendition of Gore's lyrics. It's nicely constructed, almost a counterpart to 'Corrupt' in its chronicling of an absence, a presence that once dominated someone's (love) life, but is now missing, nothing but a 'Ghost' in their life. It's a shame the band didn't hold on to it, as it might have found a home on the subsequent album, *Delta Machine*. As it is, it's condemned to 'extra' status on a box set that appealed to dedicated collectors only. A shame.

'Esque' 2:17

A short BBC Radiophonic Workshop-style instrumental, but of little consequence.

Delta Machine (2013)

Personnel:
Dave Gahan: lead vocals, except on 'The Child Inside' and 'Always'
Martin Gore: guitar, bass guitar, keyboards, backing vocals, lead vocals on 'The Child Inside' and 'Always'
Andy Fletcher: keyboards
Recorded at Sound Design, Santa Barbara; Jungle City Studios, New York City; March–October 2012
Producer: Ben Hillier
All tracks written by Martin Gore, except 'Secret To The End', 'Broken' and 'Should Be Higher' written by Dave Gahan and Kurt Uenala
Released: 25 March 2013. Label: Mute
Running time: 57:55
Highest chart placings: UK: 2; US: 6; Australia: 16; Austria: 1; Belgium: 2; Canada: 2; Finland: 3; France: 2; Germany: 1; Italy: 1; Japan: 51; Spain: 3; Sweden: 1; Switzerland: 1.

Into their fourth decade as a successful band, Depeche Mode faced an uncertain future. Album sales were still strong, with recent releases easily reaching the UK Album Chart Top 10 (*Ultra* 1; *The Singles 86>98*, 5; *Exciter*, 9; *Playing The Angel*, 6; *Sounds Of The Universe*, 2), but the staying power was absent. The records fell rapidly out of the charts in the weeks immediately after release, suggesting they were being snapped up by eager fans but failing to reach the wider pop music audience they'd once commanded (with the likes of *Music For The Masses*, *Violator* and *Songs Of Faith And Devotion*). The same was true for their singles: long gone were the days of UK Singles Chart Top 10 hits like 'Just Can't Get Enough' (8), 'See You' (6), 'Everything Counts' (6), 'People Are People' (4), 'Master And Servant' (9), 'Enjoy The Silence' (6), 'I Feel You' (8), 'Condemnation' (9), 'In Your Room' (8), 'Barrel Of A Gun' (4), 'It's No Good' (5), 'Dream On' (6) and 'Precious' (4). It was a huge spread of solid hits, from 1981 to 2005, 14 Top 10 singles (including 2004's 'Enjoy The Silence 04' [7]), across almost three decades. The material from *Playing The Angel* was still reaching the Top 20. However, from *Sounds Of The Universe*, there was a steep fall off in chart positions for Depeche Mode singles, with 'Peace' reaching a dismal 57! The three singles from 2013's *Delta Machine* fared even worse – 'Heaven', 60; 'Soothe My Soul', 88; and 'Should Be Higher', 81. The singles released from the next album, *Spirit* failed to chart at all. So what had gone 'wrong' (to quote another relatively poorly performing single)?

The original fan base from the 1980s was ageing, as were the band themselves, and the sales of singles suggested they were not gathering more 'devotees' as they had throughout the 1990s. Perhaps the musical core of the band – Gore and Gahan – had taken their eye off the ball in pursuing their own solo projects. Gahan recorded *The Light The Dead See* (2012) with UK duo Soulsavers, while – in an unexpected move – Gore reunited with original Mode man Vince Clarke in VCMG's collection of instrumentals, *Ssss* (2012). While album sales were solid and singles fell off a cliff, touring continued to be hugely lucrative – there was every incentive for the band to release new material every four or five years to allow for a highly remunerative world tour (the Delta Machine Tour would gross close to £200 million, playing to two million people across ten months).

That sense of 'business as usual' applied to the creation of *Delta Machine*, which followed the by now well-established production process organised by producer Ben Hillier, with recording in Gore's backyard (Santa Barbara) and Gahan's new 'home town' (New York). Lyrically, Gore admitted the songs explored aspects of his and Gahan's lives now that they'd sobered up and settled down. Perhaps the chaos and tensions that were a feature of several of Depeche Mode's best albums were essential to the creation of good music? There was nothing bad about anything on *Playing The Angel*, *Sounds Of The Universe* or *Delta Machine* (a trilogy shepherded by Hillier), but perhaps the passion had gone. The band were now mature individuals doing a job of work – Depeche Mode were an efficient music-making machine, but they seemed to have lost their souls.

Pitchfork leapt upon that aspect of Depeche Mode's most recent release: 'People who make machines use the term "delta" to mean "change",' wrote Douglas Wolk. 'Depeche Mode aren't so keen on that any more... The partnership of singer Gahan and songwriter Gore can't escape the machine they've become, or the holding pattern they're stuck in... What made Depeche Mode work... was their constant pushing forward of their sound – expanding the vocabulary of what electronics could do in pop songs. But they stopped pushing forward long ago, and now they don't even bother pretending technology has opened up new possibilities for recorded sound in the past 20 years... There is not a single moment of shock or freshness on *Delta Machine*, and it's enormously frustrating to hear what was once a band of futurists so deeply mired in resisting change.'

That might have been a bit harsh – after all, *Delta Machine* reached number two in the UK Album Charts (as well as hitting the top spot in five European countries), a better performance than either the laid-back (or, to some, dull) *Exciter* and the experimental *Playing The Angel* – but there was nonetheless a kernel of truth in the point *Pitchfork* was making. Clearly, fans were being well served, but the band's wider appeal had diminished since 2005. They no longer 'crossed over' to become part of the wider pop music cultural conversation. Every group has their ups and downs, but Depeche Mode had risen from being initially dismissed by the British music press as simple 'plinky plonky' teen idols to become a stadium-dominating, worldwide-selling behemoth. They'd had three decades of solid hits, so perhaps it was time for something different in their fourth decade. Could they shake things up again, the way they had done with the hugely contrasting *Violator* and *Songs*

Of Faith And Devotion, and recapture the experimental nature of *Ultra* and *Playing The Angel*? Could Depeche Mode leave complacency behind and rediscover their... *Spirit*?

'Welcome To My World' 4:56

The ideal album opener, 'Welcome To My World' is instantly recognisable as being from Depeche Mode. It also became the opening salvo in the 2013–14 Delta Machine Tour, preceded by a two-minute instrumental introduction lifted from the middle of the song. 'Welcome To My World' is a sometimes uneasy mix between the upbeat and the positive with the dark and degraded. It was written (and sung) by a band that was in a happier place – although there had been disagreements about whether Depeche Mode had a future in advance of the recording of *Delta Machine*. As Gore told French website *20 Minutes*: 'It is true that [we] are more calm now than ever before. But this song is written from a much more personal point of view. I feel more at peace in my life and much better physically. Simply a happier person.' Any fear that such happiness might tame the darker turn that Gore's lyrics often took would quickly be removed. As the song turns almost operatic, it also threatens the singer will 'ride your broken wings', which – on balance – doesn't seem that upbeat after all...

'Angel' 3:57

The sonic disruptions of 'Welcome To My World' (that were somewhat lost in live performance, where a more 'straight' rock version was delivered) continue directly into 'Angel', a track that sometimes feels as if it fell off the back of *Playing The Angel* (which it may well have done). As with the previous song, it delivers a similar mix of optimism and darkness, with the declaration 'I've found the peace I've been searching for' (which reflected the band's individual members at this time) being immediately disrupted by the eruption of machine noise (echoing sounds from *Violator*) and an increase in the tempo. It's brilliantly constructed, with an aggression and drive entirely missing from much of *Sounds Of The Universe*. This was first unveiled during a press conference in Paris on 23 October 2012, where Depeche Mode announced a new album and tour. It accompanied a black-and-white video montage of the band at work in the New York studio, which visually played up their camaraderie and work ethic. The line about finding 'peace' returns at the end of 'Angel', this time free of the earlier sonic disruption, so perhaps, for once, peace triumphs.

'Heaven' 4:03

Lead single from *Delta Machine*, 'Heaven' – released on 31 January 2013 as the band's 50th single – was indicative of Depeche Mode's selling power in different countries. While the single only managed a poor number 60 on the UK Singles Chart, it hit number one in Hungary and on the *Billboard*

US Dance Club Songs chart (it reached number two on the *Billboard* US Hot Single Sales Chart). Although it only reached number 19 in Italy, it was designated 'gold' for digital downloads exceeding 15,000 units there. Elsewhere in Europe, 'Heaven' was a Top 15 hit, including in Belgium (12), Germany (2) and Spain (11). The changes in format releases, from 7" singles to a combination of digital downloads, CD releases and 12" singles was part of it, but it also seemed that – beyond the dedicated fan base that drove *Delta Machine* to number two in the UK Album Chart – Depeche Mode had fallen out of favour in the UK as a 'pop' band. Perhaps, at this late stage in their career, they were returning to their status as a 'cult band', as they were in the days before *Music For The Masses*. Gahan revealed his feelings about 'Heaven' in the electronic press kit (EPK) that accompanied the album:

> Of all the incredible songs that Martin has written over the years that I have been lucky enough to sing and perform, once in a while, a song comes along – hopefully, I'll write one of those myself one day – that's something I have to sing. It feels like I'm putting on a pair of boots that I've worn for years, that I love. It fits. As soon as I heard that song – he had played me the demo – I knew exactly what I wanted to do with it. There's no other song like it on the record. That was one song from this record that I knew... was gonna be the linchpin to this session. Everything has got to be as good as this. To me, 'Heaven' is one of the reasons why I still make music.

'Heaven' is a slower track that fits nicely in its position on the album, but may have been seen as a surprise choice for lead single as it is less representative of the album as a whole. There is undeniably something of The Beatles in Gore's song, and that may have been why Gahan found it so pleasing to his ear. *Louder than War* noted: 'Depeche chose a ballad as their comeback single. "Heaven" broods in its downright patronising braveness and displays that even the 80s stalwarts can produce a ballad of rather magical quality. Again, the mix is so sparsely put together that every click, beat, and tap can be heard.' *The Quietus* felt 'Heaven' was 'too focused at the mainstream American radio market', but it was welcomed by *Billboard* (reinforcing the point made by *The Quietus*): 'The most personal and coincidentally beautiful vocal of *Delta Machine* comes on "Heaven", the official lead single. It's a synth-rock slow jam that goes very alt-rock on the chorus, with some ripping vocal harmonies.'

'Secret To The End' 5:12

Of the various misfortunes to befall Gahan during the Tour Of The Universe in 2009–10 – among them an attack of gastroenteritis just before taking the stage in Athens, which saw eight shows cancelled; tearing a calf muscle during on-stage exertions in Spain; and a medically mandated 'vocal rest' during the California dates – the worst, clearly, was his diagnosis of cancer following the discovery of a malignant tumour in his bladder, which was successfully removed. It is little wonder that such an experience would find expression through his songwriting. Talking to *Q* in March 2013, Gahan said:

> [That diagnosis] certainly did affect what I wrote. 'Secret To The End' for *Delta Machine*, every verse ending with, 'Is this the end? Should this be the end?' It was seeing myself for the first time. The wondering, 'Why, why, why? What's it all about?' I'm going to do something useful with it, try to be the best father and husband I can be ... and the best musician. I wrote myself back into life.

There was an irony, given all he had been through in the 1990s – much of it self-inflicted – that Gahan should continue to suffer health-related issues as he entered his fifties. However, the repeated breathy refrain of 'Could this be the end?' and 'We've come to the end' no doubt struck some Depeche Mode fans as a possible signal that *Delta Machine* might be the band's final outing, especially given the further line: 'The final chapter in the contract expires soon'. Actually, it wasn't to be the end, as at least two more albums would follow, but it did suggest that not everything lasts for ever and as Depeche Mode headed towards their fifth decade, the end was far closer than the beginning.

'My Little Universe' 4:24

The one chart that Depeche Mode seemed guaranteed to succeed on in the 2010s was *Billboard*'s US Dance Club Songs (where 'Heaven' hit the top spot, despite only reaching number 60 in the UK Singles Chart). Except, Depeche Mode were not a 'dance' band, they didn't make 'dance' music. Well, 'My Little Universe' – despite its slow start – stands out on *Delta Machine* as a deliberately constructed techno dance tune, one that doesn't fit smoothly with the rest, as Gore admitted to Santa Monica radio station KCRW: 'Out of all of my songs on [*Delta Machine*], that's the one that changed dramatically. For ages, we'd think that it wasn't gonna go on the album. It was too fiddly, it had chord changes that it didn't need. So we stripped it right back.' Gahan's breathy delivery floats over techno bops, infiltrated by additional twangs. Talking to Canadian website *Exclaim!*, Andy Fletcher expounded further on just how 'My Little Universe' was deconstructed to its final form:

> [It's] a very techno track. It's out there, that one. It's a little jewel, that track. It sort of breaks up the more built-up tracks and where it is on the album – track five – it's really a nice position... It was just a normal pop track and we layered and layered and layered stuff on it... it wasn't sounding right, so in the end we just completely stripped it down to how it is now, and now it sounds great.

'Slow' 3:45

A complete change of pace (and genre) from 'My Little Universe', 'Slow' is immediately clearly a riff on Depeche Mode's frequent electro-blues excursions. As speculated about 'Angel', 'Slow' was in actual fact, a song from years back that Gore revived and retooled for *Delta Machine*. It was originally a demo from the *Songs Of Faith And Devotion* era, and it is easy to imagine it given that rock treatment. Instead, the blues elements are played up, augmented by electro backing and suitably slow vocal treatment. Of 'Slow' Gahan told German station Radio Eins: 'It fits really well with everything we're doing now, because of its blues influence, and I think Martin pulled from that school a lot more on this record.'

As to the song's subject, for once (in the same interview) Gore was not coy about his subject: '[It's about] sex! Let's call it like it is. "Slow" is a sensitive, erotic song about the joy of sex. Sometimes, things are very simple!'

'Broken' 3:58

The obvious single from *Delta Machine*, 'Broken' – co-written by Gahan and Kurt Uenala – was bizarrely not released as a stand-alone. Lyrically, it's core Depeche Mode, with Gahan echoing years of working with Gore by using such terms as 'pain', 'suffer', 'tears' and – of course – 'broken'. Musically, it's nicely structured and provides an easy-to-listen groove that might have won it radio play. Alas, that was not to be, although someone seems to have liked the song because a live studio session from the recording of 'Broken' was published on the official Depeche Mode YouTube channel on 27 April 2013 – which could easily have been a proto-music video.

'The Child Inside' 4:16

Is this the most Gore-style track ever written and performed by Martin Gore? It might just be. 'The Child Inside' is the quietest track on *Delta Machine*, but the lyrics make a lot of noise, much of it a culmination of Gore's lyrical concerns since back in the 1980s. The sequence of opening lines that run 'There is darkness and death in your eyes/What have you got buried inside/ The shallow grave in your soul/The ghosts there have taken control' may be the single darkest and gloomiest series of lines that Gore ever strung together. The thing that makes all this bearable is Gore's lightness of touch in his vocals, and the spare burblings in the background. It's odd, more suited to a B-side or bonus release rather than as part of a sequence on an album. The lyrics and construction are stranger than usual for Gore, so much so that it feels like something he might have put together as part of his solo work rather than a track suited to Depeche Mode. This couplet is sure to appeal to those 1980s goth fans of Depeche Mode, however: 'Why were you always inside/On days when the weather was fine'. It ends on the line 'The child inside you died', which is not at all cheerful.

'Soft Touch/Raw Nerve' 3:26

Disliked by many ('a B-side at best' opined fan site Almost Predictable
Almost), the oddly titled 'Soft Touch/Raw Nerve' is the ideal antidote to the
self-indulgence of 'The Child Inside'. It's a loud, percussive, driving track that
doesn't let up (until that false ending). It's crying out to be performed live,
which is why it is such a shame that it has seen fewer than ten live outings
in total. Structured around the repetition of the chorus lines twice each time,
the song might not make immediate sense lyrically, but it throbs along, lifting
to new heights when Gore's backing vocals and some thumping echoes kick
in. Just when you think it's all over, it revives and bangs on for another 20
seconds. Guaranteed to wake you up if you dozed off during 'The Child Inside'.

'Should Be Higher' 5:04

Released on 11 October 2013, 'Should Be Higher' was the third single from *Delta
Machine* and the third Depeche Mode single co-written by Gahan, following
'Suffer Well' and 'Hole To Feed'. Common to several songs on *Delta Machine*
are questions of addiction, or – more specifically – the plight of a former
addict who must constantly resist whatever poison they initially fell for. Gahan
admitted as much when talking to *Mojo* in March 2013: 'I was out Christmas
Eve, a nice restaurant, everyone drinking. I thought, "Why can't I just have a
glass of wine?" But I don't any more, because even one glass opens a whole
Pandora's box. My mind immediately thinks, I can go much higher. That's what
"Should Be Higher" is about – that line, "The lies are more attractive than the
truth". I still draw on that stuff when I'm singing and performing, to dig my way
out of trouble.' *Pitchfork* agreed: 'As for Gahan's own songs – this time, their
music is by Kurt Uenala – they're generally a reasonably convincing imitation of
middling Gore. His "Should Be Higher" is yet another on the pile of ex-junkie
lyrics...' *DIY* magazine recognised the 'waltzing, brooding sway... an effortless
and sombre build-up to a swirling and hypnotic pay-off. Gore lends his backing
vocals perfectly, creating beautiful contrasts with Gahan, as well as stunning
harmonies.' The accompanying video was made up of concert footage shot by
Anton Corbijn. As a result, 'Should Be Higher' got no higher in the UK Singles
Chart than number 81, but that was seven positions better than 'Soothe My
Soul'. The highest chart position the song achieved anywhere was number 19, in
Germany. The chart positions of single releases would suggest that the bottom
had fallen out of the Depeche Mode market, but that was clearly not so as *Delta
Machine* itself reached number two in the UK Album Chart and the following
2013–14 Delta Machine Tour was a huge artistic and financial success. It's a
strange position for the band to find themselves in: none of the three tracks
released from subsequent album *Spirit* made any dent in the charts at all ...

'Alone' 4:29

A thumping throwback to old Mode, 'Alone' throbs along foregrounding synth
sounds along with Gahan's heartfelt performance as 'your father, your son,

and your Holy Ghost and priest'. There's a lovely instrumental sweep between verses, and a cascade of 'plinks' and 'plonks' that go back beyond the *Black Celebration* era in their sound – a very welcome blast from the past that merges well with all the modern Mode sounds explored here. Despite that, 'Alone' goes a bit weird in the middle with the odd vocal effects on the lines 'Now it's too late/Too late for/Words that should have been said/Long ago' and trails off a bit inconclusively, all of which serves to indicate that even at this late stage in their musical adventures, Depeche Mode were not afraid to go out on a limb and explore something new while still incorporating the best of the past. Still, it's easily one of the best tracks on *Delta Machine*.

'Soothe My Soul' 5:22

The second single from *Delta Machine* continued the poor UK Singles Chart performance. Released on 6 May 2013, the single reached a high in the UK of number 88! Across Europe, it performed better, hitting the top spot in Hungary and number nine in Belgium, however, even in long-loyal countries like France (45) and Germany (22) the band's chart placings took a tumble. 'Soothe My Soul' did well in the US, albeit well away from the mainstream *Billboard* chart, reaching number seven on the US Dance Club Songs Chart and number 27 on the US Alternative Play Chart. There's something reminiscent of 'Personal Jesus' in the song's call-and-response structure, perhaps as the original had been 'in the air' thanks to the single release of 'Personal Jesus 2011', which reached number five in Hungary. *The Quietus* certainly recognised the track's lineage: 'Another upbeat, techno-pop number... a bollock-busting stomper of a chorus... All credit is due to leaving the new "Personal Jesus" right to the penultimate track of the album. A classic, classic Depeche Mode track, this, they've really pulled it off here.' *Clash Music* dubbed the track 'an improbable sequel to "Personal Jesus"', while *Music OHM* described it as '"Personal Jesus" on Viagra, pairing echoey verses with a frenetic industrial beat and cascading deluges of synthesizer'. As with 'Heaven', Warren Fu's restricted square aspect ratio black-and-white video was another band performance, interspersed with images of a writhing naked woman and a snake (imagery perhaps better suited to 'Lilian' or 'Jezebel').

'Goodbye' 5:03

A fitting title for the closing track – and one that caused much fretting among the fan base that (to slightly misquote 'Secret To The End') this could be the end. Opening with a 'Personal Jesus' style blues riff, there's more than a whiff of *Violator* here. This could have been the final statement from a band for whom 'Now misery is strange'. The general good vibes and happiness that seemed to infuse the lives of Gahan and Gore during this period are reflected in the lines 'Now I'm pure, now I'm clean/I feel cured and serene'. Gore felt there was something of The Beatles about 'Goodbye', and it is certainly there in the chanting of 'Goodbye' throughout the song, but this is much more a spin-off from 'Personal Jesus' if it is anything at all.

Related Tracks
'Long Time Lie' 4:25
'Long Time Lie' – a collaboration between Gore and Gahan – began life as a Gore instrumental, during which he'd asked Gahan for his opinion. It was producer Ben Hillier who clued Gahan into the notion that this casual approach might have been Gore's way of inviting Gahan to come up with some lyrics. Talking to the German *Sonic Seducer* magazine, Gore declared: 'This time it really felt like a proper collaboration... I first wrote a slower instrumental track, but Ben [Hillier] thought that it would be a good idea if Dave were to add lyrics and melodies to it. So that's what he did, and during a recording session, I took it with me and reconstructed the instrumental part around it. It feels more as though we have created the song together.' It's a spare track, and it's easy to see why it didn't make the cut on the album. However, the collaboration points to a possible way forward for Depeche Mode, creating a more harmonious feeling between the band's principal contributors.

'Happens All The Time' 4:20
A Gahan co-written track that sounds more like a solo Gahan song than a Depeche Mode production, it's easy (again) to see why this was relegated to 'extra' status. It plods along, with melodic atmospheres and electro-stabs backing Gore's wistful vocals, but it never really gets anywhere significant. Whatever it is that makes Depeche Mode special, it's gone AWOL here.

'Always' 5:07
Written and performed by Gore, this should have replaced the oddball 'The Child Inside' on *Delta Machine*. As it is, 'Always' was relegated to 'extra' status along with the Gahan offcuts, so Gore must've been dissatisfied with something about it – perhaps the distorted vocals? As with several tracks on *Delta Machine*, there are echoes of Gore's collaboration with Vince Clarke as VCMG, with the electronic sounds, while the overall approach echoes some of the youthful experiments of The The frontman Matt Johnson from the early 1980s, oddly. Whatever, it's an approach that doesn't suit Gore: vocally, he should probably stick to what he does best – heartfelt and higher-pitched, rather than opting for a rock approach. Leave that stuff to Gahan, it suits him better.

'All That's Mine' 3:23
Released as a B- side to the first single from *Delta Machine*, 'Heaven', 'All That's Mine' was given a showcase not often afforded Gahan-written tracks. Pulsing and percussive, this is much more the Mode sound than 'Happens

All The Time', so its choice as a B-side makes sense. Ploughing a sailing metaphor in which the singer is lost like a ship at sea, there's a gentle pop sound to 'All That's Mine' that Depeche Mode rarely explore these days.

Spirit (2017)

Personnel:
Dave Gahan: lead vocals, except on 'Eternal' and 'Fail'
Martin Gore: guitars, keyboards, synthesisers, backing vocals, lead vocals on 'Eternal' and 'Fail'
Andy Fletcher: keyboards, synthesisers, backing vocals
Recorded at Sound Design, Santa Barbara; Jungle City, New York City; April–August 2016
Producer: James Ford
All tracks written by Martin Gore, except 'You Move', 'Cover Me', 'Poison Heart' and 'No More (This Is The Last Time)'; 'You Move' written by Gore and Dave Gahan, 'Cover Me' and 'Poison Heart' written by Dave Gahan, Peter Gordeno and Christian Eigner, and 'No More (This Is The Last Time)' written by Dave Gahan and Kurt Uenala
Released: 17 March 2017. Label: Columbia/Mute
Running time: 49:23
Highest chart placings: UK: 5; US: 5; Australia: 14; Austria: 1; Belgium: 1; Canada: 4; Finland: 5; France: 1; Germany: 1; Italy: 1; Japan: 62; Spain: 2; Sweden: 3; Switzerland: 1.

Contrary to some fans' and music writers' impressions, Depeche Mode have always been a political band. Their first two albums – *Speak & Spell* and *A Broken Frame* – were light electro-pop (a reputation it took them years to shake off), but their third outing, *Construction Time Again*, tackled a variety of 1980s political topics. The songs 'Pipeline', 'Everything Counts', 'Two Minute Warning' and 'The Landscape Is Changing' all engaged with topics from social and economic inequality to climate change and nuclear war. While most of their subsequent albums focused on inter-personal relationships, sex, shame and guilt, they did occasionally explore contemporary politics, as in the media focus of *Black Celebration*'s 'New Dress'. In that light, the lyrical content and political focus of *Spirit* should have come as no surprise.

Perhaps it was the settled home lives of the three core members that saw their attention turn to wider world issues. Gahan was living in New York with his wife Jennifer Sklias and their daughter. Fletcher was the group's long-term family man, married to Gráinne Mullan for over two decades, with two children. Gore, divorced from Suzanne Boisvert in 2006, married Kerrilee Kaski in June 2014. They now have two daughters. While Fletcher still enjoyed the occasional pint, both Gore and Gahan – after years of substance abuse – were both clean living, focused on their families. This awareness of their own happiness and contentment contributed to the growing disenchantment all three Mode members began to feel with the world around them in 2015.

In an interview with *Vevo* in May 2017, Gahan stated:

You can't help but be influenced [by events]. When you are making any kind of art, I would hope you would be influenced by what's going on around you. We're really kind of upset at what's going on in the world. We've always touched on things [like this] and our albums over the years have had themes running through them, some more obvious than others.

The emergence of a new breed of populist leaders and a dramatic swing to the right among the world's so-called liberal democracies – which affected both the United States and the United Kingdom – was the background against which Gore began writing new material that would form Depeche Mode's 14th studio album in 37 years. The failure of the Scottish Independence referendum in 2014, the unexpected success of the Brexit referendum in 2016, and the looming figure of Donald Trump in the run-up to the 2016 American presidential election were inescapable. The Brexit vote to leave the European Union after over 45 years hit Gore and Gahan hard, even though neither had lived in the UK for years. Gahan admitted to being 'shocked' by the Leave campaign victory, while Gore said: 'We were all depressed by the outcome of the referendum.'

By April 2016 – with Trump looking set to win the White House – the trio gathered in Santa Barbara. After three records with Ben Hillier, they opted for fresh input, bringing in James Ford who'd worked with the Arctic Monkeys. A four-month process ensued, taking in New York's Jungle Studios. As Gore confirmed at the October 2016 press conference in Milan launching the album, called *Spirit*, and the subsequent world tour, contemporary events informed many of the songs. 'The world is in a big mess at the moment,' said Gore. 'It is very difficult, I think, to make an album and not acknowledge that. [We can't] brush it all aside and pretend it's not happening.'

Where reaction to the Ben Hillier-produced albums had been mixed and a feeling had begun to grow that Depeche Mode were coasting on past glories, the critical response to *Spirit* was largely positive, welcoming the group's refreshed political engagement. *Pitchfork* noted that *Spirit* 'is so convincing in spite of its radical shift in tenor... for both the band and the audience, that shift couldn't have come at a better time'. The *Guardian* dubbed the album 'an hour-long howl of outrage and horror... Depeche Mode sound raw and alive and rigidly opposed to merely going through the motions.' *Rolling Stone* admitted, 'It's easy to get swept away in their gospel', while *Classic Rock* concluded that with *Spirit* 'Depeche Mode are growing old angrily, and it suits them.'

Ageing had been on the minds of the Mode members for some time. During the Tour Of The Universe in 2009–10, Gahan had contemplated turning 50 and wondered how much longer – given his health and injury issues – he could realistically keep up his on-stage performance. Now, during the 2017–18 Global Spirit Tour – the longest they'd ever played, running almost 15 months across 130 shows in front of over 2.5 million people – Gahan saw 60 ahead (in 2022). Gore and Fletcher would reach 60 one year earlier. Although there was the model of 1960s groups like the Rolling Stones, who were still active after 60 years having begun in 1962, to follow, Depeche Mode had a tough decision to make in the wake of the epic Global Spirit Tour whether they could face it again.

Since their start in 1981, Depeche Mode had been the recipients of many awards, some of which they had openly disdained. 'Enjoy The Silence' had won the Brit Award for Best British Single in 1991, and the band had been repeatedly nominated for awards from the *Billboard* Music Awards. They'd won the MTV Europe Music Awards Best Group accolade as recently as 2006. *Songs Of Faith And Devotion, Ultra, Exciter* and *Playing The Angel* had all been nominated for Best Album at the MTV Awards (*Ultra* had won in 1997). The biggest career accolade – one they could not ignore – finally came in November 2020 when Depeche Mode were inducted into the Rock and Roll Hall of Fame. Dubbed 'Rock's highest honour', the award goes to 'the people who shaped the history of rock and roll'. By 2022, there had been just over 350 inductees since the Hall's beginning in 1986 (a good five years after Depeche Mode had begun their career). The ceremony was conducted virtually due to the worldwide Covid-19 pandemic. Gore, Gahan and Fletcher (all of whom appeared to be delighted) participated, while the contributions of Vince Clarke and Alan Wilder were acknowledged. 'I think music really brings people together, and God knows we need that more today than it seems any other time,' said Gahan, continuing to channel the message of *Spirit*. Daniel Miller and Anton Corbijn were also singled out for their contributions, as were 'the new boys' (according to Gahan) Peter Gordeno and Christian Eigner – who'd been performing live with the band for the better part of two decades! 'Growing up, listening to music on the radio and having music, it really kind of helped us to feel normal, feel part of something,' said Gahan. 'That's what music does for people and I think that's what Depeche Mode has done for many people.'

Just at the time when Depeche Mode might have been regrouping to create new music, and 41 years after the band had started in 1981, Gore and Gahan and Depeche Mode fans worldwide were shocked by the unexpected death of co-founding member Andy Fletcher on 26 May 2022, at the age of just 60. Fletch died at home, as a result of a rare aortic dissection which impedes the flow of blood to the heart. In a statement, Gahan and Gore spoke of their loss: 'We are shocked and filled with overwhelming sadness with the untimely passing of our dear friend, family member and bandmate Andy "Fletch" Fletcher. Fletch had a true heart of gold and was always there when you needed support, a lively conversation, a good laugh or a cold pint.' Alan Wilder said Fletch's unexpected death was 'a real bolt from the blue'. Many musicians and bands, including members of The Cure, Pet Shop Boys, Gary Numan, Alison Moyet and Vince Clarke, expressed their condolences to Fletch's family.

For many, Fletch's death signalled the end for Depeche Mode, even if he was no longer a vital contributor to the band musically. However, on 15 August 2022, about six weeks later, the official Depeche Mode Facebook page posted an image of Gahan and Gore apparently together in Gore's Santa Barbara home studio, seemingly working on new music. After over 40 years, and with just two of the original members remaining, it appeared that the Depeche Mode story had not yet come to an end...

'Going Backwards' 5:43

Album opener 'Going Backwards' sets the tone for the tracks that follow, and as the second single released (on 23 June 2017), it was the ideal follow-up to the dramatic 'Where's the Revolution'. *Clash Music* welcomed the song's scene-setting role as the curtain-raiser for *Spirit*. 'From the off, with the edgy, slow-building opener 'Going Backwards' – with its trademark bass-heavy rhythms and edgy, nagging melody befitting of a classic Depeche Mode set piece – it's clear that *Spirit* is going to be a challenging listen...', while *Mixmag* reckoned it was 'among the most anthemic things Depeche Mode have done this century, apocalyptic both in sound and lyrics, and perfect for these dark times'. For Gore, this along with 'Where's the Revolution' had been among the earliest compositions for *Spirit*, suggesting a direction he'd not consciously set out to follow. '[I went] down the road of social commentary/ political route,' he told *Classic Pop* in 2017, 'which I felt was a dangerous route to go down.' Gore explained this further to Amazon Music Germany: 'An album starts taking shape, for me, really, when you have about four songs together, and we had gone down a cynical path. And I thought, "Okay, well, maybe I just gotta go with this..." I think that from an early point we all deep down knew that it would be the first track on the album, so it was an important track. Even though we never regarded it as a single or anything like that, it was more of a statement.' The track – as with 'Welcome To My World' from *Delta Machine* – became the opening song for the Global Spirit Tour. The video, directed by Timothy Saccenti, was lifted from the Highline Sessions (that also featured the band's cover version of Bowie's 'Heroes'; see below).

'Where's The Revolution' 4:59

The first single from *Spirit* was 'Where's The Revolution' on 3 February 2017. Despite a light-hearted humorous video directed by a returning Anton Corbijn, the single failed to chart in the UK (the first ever Depeche Mode single to do so). It made the Top 20 in various European charts, including in Belgium (13), Hungary (3), Italy (17) and Spain (18). The music video, reflecting the radical political revolutionary message of the song in a jokey way, saw the three members of Depeche Mode don huge Karl Marx beards and appear to be corralling the 'masses'. At certain points in the black-and-white video, Gahan's jacket, various flags and Gore's guitar are all depicted in a politically charged red. With lyrics addressing misinformation, religion, patriotism and terrorism, 'Where's The Revolution' was an advance taste of what was to come on *Spirit*, and served to shock some Depeche Mode fans out of their musical complacency (as the band no doubt intended). No less relevant in 2023 than it was in 2017, 'Where's The Revolution' remains a *cri de coeur* for people-driven change in the political system.

Gore recalled (to trackrecord.net) that it was one of the first songs he'd written back in 2015: 'There was a sense of things going wrong and the world wasn't in a great place then. That was pre-Brexit, but you know there were awful problems going on.' Gore cited such events as ongoing conflict in the Middle East, racial strife in the US and the growing threat from Russia. Gore told an Amazon Music Germany event that 'It's always good if you have a track that kind of sums up the album, and it's even better if that song is [anthemic], and it's kind of powerful. So, fortunately, this time around, we had "Where's The Revolution". We felt that was a great statement to make and should definitely be the first track to be released to bring us back with a statement.'

'The Worst Crime' 3:48
It may be hard to tell from the enigmatic lyrics – with references to compulsory attendance at a town lynching – but Gore claims 'The Worst Crime' is actually about the climate emergency. He told *Classic Pop*: 'Usually I don't talk about the songs too much, but I will about this one a little bit. It's metaphorical and about climate change and us destroying the world, and how we are all guilty... so the lynching is us, we are all being lynched.' He elaborated further at *The Quietus*: 'For me, it's a song about humanity hanging itself and the worst crime being the destruction of the planet, because there are so many crimes that we're committing on a daily basis, but this is the worst crime because we are not just doing it to ourselves, but we're also doing it to future generations.'

Where Fletch was a declared fan of 'Going Backwards', for Gahan, this was the one that caught his attention, although he put a different spin on the subject matter. 'Actually, this is one of my favourite songs on the album. It has a beautiful melody, but lyrically it's pretty slamming the way we divide each other, [the] racial divides...'

Whatever it's about, 'The Worst Crime' continued the pattern of lyrical and musical minimalism that was a hallmark of James Ford's production of *Spirit*. The sparseness of the musical construction allows the lyrical content to come through clearly, although interpretation is up to the individual. It's a dramatic change in approach from the likes of *Playing The Angel* or *Delta Machine*, but with this song and the others on the album, it's still uniquely Depeche Mode.

'Scum' 3:14
Easily one of the strangest tracks on *Spirit*, 'Scum' takes some getting used to. From Gahan's distorted vocals (which was based upon Gore's demo version)

to the song's lyrical rapping rant, it's an outlier in the Mode catalogue. Gore told German station Radio Eins in 2017: 'I like "Scum" particularly because it's very different for us. Quite aggressive, but it's also got a real kind of sleazy groove to it. There's something very unusual for us about that song.' The 'Pull the trigger' refrain is quite catchy, even if the overall message seems nihilistic, focusing on how a selfish, self-interested person might waste their life's potential. The 'What have you ever done for anyone' and 'What will you do when judgement time has come' suggest as much while harking back to Gore's often ploughed lyrical obsession with facing judgement.

'You Move' 3:50
This Gore/Gahan collaboration is a welcome move away from the political and social focus of *Spirit*'s first four tracks and a return to the avowedly personal. Following *Delta Machine*, both Gore and Gahan continued to pursue solo projects, with Gore producing his instrumentals collection *MG* (2015) and Gahan hooking up with Soulsavers for the 2015 album *Angels & Ghosts*. Gore's album included such magnificent song titles as 'Plinking', 'Hum' and 'Creeper', which could all be used to describe various Mode sounds. After the album was completed, Gore had some unfinished tracks left over. At a loss as to what to do with one, he sent it to Gahan. In the casual and uncertain way that their songwriting collaborations seem to come about ('You Move' was the first track they deliberately co-wrote for inclusion on a Depeche Mode album, as opposed to being something included as an extra on a 'deluxe' release), Gahan wasn't sure what Gore wanted him to do with the track. Talking to Amazon Music Germany, Gahan explained:

Martin had sent me this rhythm track that was really odd, and he said, 'I don't know what to do with this, maybe you can have a go at doing something to it.' So I was baffled at first, but it almost felt like he had sent me an incredible challenge, because it has such a weird time signature and weird sounds. And there wasn't a lot of chord structure to it that I could really latch on to. So I let it just simmer... I went into my studio and I formulated my idea into a melody and this lyric came out.

'You Move' is an iconic Depeche Mode relationship song, the kind of track the band usually focus heavily on but which was on the back burner when it came to *Spirit*. It's a grower that has a tendency to become lost among the political tumult that dominates the album.

'Cover Me' 4:52
The third and final single from *Spirit* was 'Cover Me' (released on 6 October 2017), co-written by Gahan with Depeche Mode's touring musicians Peter Gordeno and Christian Eigner. Gahan seems to have picked up the thematic concerns of Gore's 'The Worst Crime' but cleverly balances a song that could

be about a personal relationship with its potential wider meaning. Talking to UK radio DJ Phil Marriott in 2017, Gahan explained: 'I wanted ["Cover Me"] to be very cinematic, and I had this idea of us finally destroying this beautiful planet that we live on. Hence the northern lights: it's just one in many millions of beautiful things... the oceans, things that we take for granted.'

It's undoubtedly one of Gahan and company's best efforts, and its instrumental second half is up there with any of Gore's middle-period Mode instrumentals – although Gore claims at least some of the credit for that. 'In the studio, we really took it on and made it into something that was even better,' he told Amazon Music Germany. 'The bit at the end, that really long instrumental piece, did not exist before. So I think that has made that song into something that was much better than [Gahan's] demo.' For the *Guardian*, Gahan's effort was 'a lone crack of light amid the otherwise consuming darkness' of *Spirit*. For *Clash Music*, it was 'one of those redemptive songs that Depeche Mode are so good at, with that slow climb out of misery towards some kind of anguished optimism'. The video by Anton Corbijn was shot around Venice Beach in October 2016 and featured Gahan as a wandering astronaut.

'Eternal' 2:25

Gore wrote 'Eternal' as an address to his first daughter with new wife Kerrilee Kaski. Addressing the inclusion of lyrics like 'And when the black cloud/ Rises/And the radiation falls/I will look you in the eye/And kiss you', Gore told German syndicated news agency interviewpeople.com: 'Isn't it romantic! [laughs] Okay, let's just say it's my way of romance. I think that when you put a child into this era, you have to take the worst into account. There is this omnipresent danger of every kind, including atomic wars.' Lyrically, 'Eternal' is a call back to Alan Wilder's environmental and anti-nuclear songs from *Construction Time Again* like 'The Landscape Is Changing' and 'Two Minute Warning', but with a much more sophisticated musical and production approach. Gore told *Consequence of Sound*: 'It's quite dark and bleak, and it talks about a mushroom cloud rising and radiation falling. The instrumentation is really strange and quite experimental and really something unlike anything we've done for a while.'

'Poison Heart' 3:17

Written by the trio of Gahan, Gordeno and Eigner, 'Poison Heart' is a break-up song in the Gore mode (although it could be interpreted from a political standpoint). As with 'Secret To The End' on *Delta Machine* and on *Spirit*'s 'No More (This Is The Last Time)', the lyrics from 'Poison Heart' highlighting the fact that 'Now we're closer to the end' had fans worrying once more about the winding up of the Depeche Mode project. For Gahan, the obvious interpretation was not his intention, telling *Rolling Stone*: 'It's not intended to be a breakup song. I was watching the news... I was writing through my own inability to really relate to another human being. There must be something wrong with me, poison in my heart. It was fun to play with that imagery, and it became more worldly – greed and lust and wanting what you want when you want it and nothing else matters. So I was breaking up with myself, trying to evolve, trying to break up with old ideas that I think are [not] working for me...'

'So Much Love' 4:29

This was the last track Gore wrote for *Spirit*, although it doesn't occupy that slot on the album's rundown. The negativity of so many of the tracks, reflecting the way he and so many others felt about the world situation, had become overwhelming. 'I felt that I had to write something positive,' he told *Rolling Stone* France. 'I felt that I had to say that, with all this going [on], it doesn't matter what you do to me, there is still a lot of love in me.' With its clanging percussion and insistent vocal from Gahan, 'So Much Love' is a counter-intuitively aggressive song about love. Gahan confirmed that at one point, 'So Much Love' was intended as the final track for *Spirit*, to end on an up note, but that Gore wanted to go in a different direction. 'Martin felt that we should end the album in a different way,' Gahan told *Paradiso*, 'so I was pretty much outvoted.' Gore explained his choice to Amazon Music Germany: 'One of the suggestions was for us to finish on that song, but it didn't really work. It worked thematically: it would have been great. But it was the only really fast song we had. And to end on that, people would have to get through all the slow songs before getting to, you know, faster than, I don't know what it is, 110 [BPM] or something.' The song is actually faster than Gore imagined, at 140 BPM.

'Poorman' 4:26

There can be no denying that Depeche Mode has made rich men of Gahan, Gore and Fletcher. One of the criticisms laid at the door of *Spirit*, perhaps fairly, concerns their right to call out the 'one per cent' in their domination of the economic discourse while everyone else suffers when they are well on their way to joining that rich class themselves. Gore addressed the issue talking to *Drowned in Sound*: '[With] "Poorman" people could say, "OK, how could you say that [as a rich man]?" I agree [with] paying taxes and I would be quite happy to pay higher taxes. I think huge multi-national corporations should be paying tax and they should be paying large amounts of tax.' A direct critique of the so-called 'trickle down' theory of economic prosperity that has dominated American economics since Ronald Reagan when Depeche Mode first formed, 'Poorman' is a form of heavily electronic blues (less obviously so than a couple of the tracks from *Delta Machine*). The chorus lyrics are bald: 'Corporations get the breaks/Keeping almost everything they make/Tell us just how long it's going to take/For it to trickle down/When will it trickle down', making this a clear companion piece to both 'Where's The Revolution' and 'Going Backwards'. A modern take on the likes of 'Everything Counts' with all its 'grabbing hands', 'Poorman' has a bitter edge to it, with the

Mode men coming to the subject of economic inequality from the opposite end of the spectrum they once inhabited as youthful denizens of Basildon.

'No More (This Is The Last Time)' 3:13

Co-written by Gahan with Kurt Uenala, 'No More (This Is The Last Time)' is another of those relationship songs that also has a wider political edge. According to Fletcher (speaking to Kentucky station 91.9 WFPK): 'That is the more classic Mode track. It's one of Dave's songs. He came in with a few demos and that one has changed quite a lot from his original demo.' Another fast track at 160BPM, it's again somewhat spare in production terms, with 'This is the last time' lyrics once again troubling the more depressive Mode fans. It's a political song about separation (although written pre-Brexit, it has those echoes). Fletcher addressed this in his WFPK interview. 'We've done an album like this before [politically focused], our third album *Construction Time Again*, and we write songs in general about politics, but we usually use analogies like sex or religion to get the message across. This [one] is a lot more direct. We've always written songs about the world we live in.' Fletcher went on to claim that both Gahan and Gore had become even more politically concerned since living in the US. 'James [Ford] and myself were slightly worried in the beginning with the song content, the political aspects, but as we recorded the situation was evolving all the time. We swung around to thinking, "Yeah, this is the right way to go."'

'Fail' 5:07

Martin Gore's chosen track to end *Spirit* concludes with the depressing sentiments 'We're fucked' and 'We've failed'. Cheerful stuff. It's actually the first Mode track to contain what might be considered a swear word. Gore (who sings) addressed this when talking to the German outlet *Intro* magazine. 'It is indeed the first case that we use the f-word. I find it appropriate because in the last song, it once again underlines the dark mood on *Spirit*. When I began writing songs at the end of 2015 and early 2016, it felt to me as if the world was slowly getting doomed. I just had to make it a theme... No wonder I got a gloomy look at the world and concluded: "We're fucked"!' As so often in Depeche Mode's history, Gore had successfully merged a depressing subject matter with uplifting music, saving what could have been a downer of a finale from total failure. He told *Classic Pop*: 'The good thing about it is the lyrics might be depressing, but the music is so pretty. Once the lyrics stop, it ends on this nice lilting gentle piece of music. That's the little bit of hope.'

Related Tracks
'Heroes (Highline Session Version)' 6:30

Depeche Mode's take on David Bowie's 'Heroes' effectively brought their story full circle. It was the final track recorded by the trio of Gahan, Gore and

Fletcher prior to Fletcher's unexpected death. It was this song that Gahan was performing during a rehearsal at Woodlands School in Basildon that saw him recruited by Vince Clarke, Gore and Fletcher to front their band, then known as Composition of Sound. Shortly after Gahan joined, that band became Depeche Mode.

During the sessions recorded at New York's Highline Stages (filmed by Timothy Saccenti) on 3 August 2016, Depeche Mode included a heartfelt cover of 'Heroes' alongside four tracks from *Spirit*: 'Going Backwards', 'So Much Love', 'Poison Heart' and 'The Worst Crime'. Gahan told *Classic Pop:* 'When we started rehearsing [for the Global Spirit Tour], I brought up the idea of maybe doing a Bowie cover, especially after losing him [Bowie died in 2016, aged 69]. Martin and I were both huge fans, and still are. So it just seemed right, Martin was into it. It's got a real early Depeche flavour to it.' The video of 'Heroes' from the Highline Sessions was released online on 22 September 2017, while an audio-only version was included on the extravagant 18 CD MODE box set release from November 2019. If there was to be no more music from Depeche Mode following the death of Andy Fletcher, that would have been as suitable a point as any to end things – to many fans, the Depeche Mode 'Class of 81' will always be their heroes. Memento mori...

Memento Mori (2023)

Personnel:

Dave Gahan: lead vocals, except on 'Soul With Me'

Martin Gore: keyboards, guitar, melodica, percussion pads, backing vocals, lead vocals on 'Soul With Me'

James Ford: additional synths, programming, piano, guitar, bass guitar, pedal steel guitar

Recorded at Electric Ladyboy, Santa Barbara, California; Shangri La, Malibu, California; mixed at Studio Zona, London; July-October 2022

Producer: James Ford

Engineering, additional programming and production: Marta Salogni

All tracks written by Martin Gore, except 'Wagging Tongue' by Dave Gahan & Martin Gore; 'Ghosts Again', 'Don't Say You Love Me', 'My Favourite Stranger', and 'Caroline's Monkey' by Martin Gore & Richard Butler; 'Before We Drown' by Dave Gahan, Peter Gordeno & Christian Eiger; 'Speak To Me' by Dave Gahan, Marta Salogni, Christian Eiger & James Ford

Released: 24 March 2023

Label: Columbia/Mute

Running Time: 50:24

Highest Chart Placings: UK: 2, US: 14, Australia: 36, France: 1, Germany: 1, Italy: 1, Japan: 28, New Zealand: 38, Norway: 5, Scotland: 4, Spain: 2, Sweden: 1, Switzerland: 1

Not for the first time, Depeche Mode – now a duo – faced the prospect of creating new music in the absence of a core band member. In 1982, they'd produced *A Broken Frame* following the departure of songwriter Vince Clarke. That brought Martin Gore to the fore as a songwriter and proved the band could continue without one of its motivating forces. In the aftermath of the painful creation of 1993's *Songs Of Faith And Devotion* and the debauched Devotional Tour, all-round musician and production supremo Alan Wilder decided his days with the band were at an end. That left the core trio of Gahan, Gore, and Fletcher to once more prove they had the chops to carry on. The result was 1997's *Ultra*, an album many fans thought could never exist, given the circumstances (including Gahan's near-death experience). Now, after the tragic early death of Andy Fletcher, aged 60, Gahan and Gore faced the same challenge once more – could they, should they, carry on...?

   Work on *Memento Mori* had tentatively begun prior to Fletch's passing, so there was something for the remaining pair to work with – and working on new music was one way they coped with their loss. 'There was only one Fletch,' Gahan told *Consequence Of Sound*, 'Fletch had not heard any of the songs. In the studio, he did have a really powerful presence and everything to say about what we were doing. I know he would have loved a lot of the stuff and he also would have been the first to say, "Why do you have to have so many songs about death?"'

To realise *Memento Mori*, Gahan and Gore called in as much help as they felt they needed. Throughout the Covid-19 lockdowns, Gore had been writing. He'd also deepened his friendship with The Psychedelic Furs' Richard Butler and – in a move seen as controversial by some – the pair collaborated on several songs, a quartet of which featured on *Memento Mori*. On the production front, James Ford was called back, with a fresh input of production and mixing creativity from award-winning Italian producer Marta Salogni, known for her work with Björk and Goldfrapp.

'Martin and I did have a brief conversation,' confirmed Gahan, 'and we both came to the same conclusion pretty quickly that we were going to definitely continue. We were going to move forward, whatever that was going to look like without Fletch.' Although twelve songs made the final cut, at least sixteen were recorded and those may later be released as bonus tracks.

Recording *Memento Mori* was a smooth process as Gahan and Gore found a new way of relating, both personally and creatively, without the mediation of Fletch. The result was an appropriately moody production, full of ominous atmospheres, intense electronic textures, and ethereal lyrics open to multiple interpretations. Gahan explored the diversity in his voice as never before. Some fans greeted the album as 'non-political' following *Spirit*. However, the songwriters subtly mixed political concerns with the personal – a trick that Depeche Mode had long ago mastered.

With *Memento Mori*, Depeche Mode were having a 'moment' once again. 'Never Let Me Down Again' (the B-side on German promo 7" of 'Ghosts Again') became prominent thanks to its use in HBO's *The Last Of Us* – streaming tripled overnight – and in the BBC series *The Gold*. 'Policy of Truth' appeared in the rebooted *Quantum Leap*, 'Shake the Disease' popped up in *Welcome To Chippendales*, 'Enjoy the Silence' featured in *Freeridge*, and 'Just Can't Get Enough' was used prominently in *Cocaine Bear*. 'That was nuts,' said Gahan on *The Last Of Us*. 'We didn't expect that. It's like it's our time again. It's amusing because we're getting this weird recognition again.'

For *The Quietus*, *Memento Mori* was 'an absolute triumph... Universal themes of mortality, love, anxiety; a handful of pop gems and an economical stripping back of [their] stadium-ness, making it their best this side of the century'. *NME* agreed, saying: 'Depeche Mode have always turned turmoil, tension, and life's darker moments into magic... comfortably their best album this side of the millennium.' For *Pitchfork*, the album revealed that 'there are new ways yet for Gahan and Gore to... approach their old magic', while *Rolling Stone* claimed: '*Memento Mori* is their finest piece of work since 2005's *Playing The Angel*. Depeche Mode have ... gone back to what they do best – inviting us to explore the black chasm of our hearts, culminating in the finality of death itself.' For *Far Out Magazine*, Depeche Mode had given 'nuanced and considered treatment to their distinctive sound [and] introduced new depth to their morbid allusions, exhuming light from darkness and finding comfort in reality... a triumphant return.'

The band kicked off a major world tour in March 2023, beginning in the US, that would keep them on the road for most of 2023, and possibly beyond. The future beyond that? 'Who knows what we have in store for us?' Gahan told *NME*. '*Memento Mori* really sums that up: "Remember that you must die". What you do here today, you have to embrace. Today meaning, "being in Depeche Mode for the next couple of years!"' Gore had a subtly different take: 'If the tour goes as planned, it'll be 45 years when we're done. We're slowly approaching the half-century mark, and the closer we get, the better chance we'll have to reach it.' He seems to see that as a challenge.

Memento Mori served up a bleak celebration – a richly textured, dark yet positive album, full of songs introspective and expansive, dark and light. It's their strongest work in years, and exactly what has been expected from them since the early-1980s.

'My Cosmos Is Mine' 5:18

Ironically, *Memento Mori* opens with the last song Martin Gore composed. Different from many Mode album openers, 'My Cosmos Is Mine' launches a moody vibe that runs throughout. Gore said the song was about 'powerlessness' in the face of world events, such as the Russian invasion of Ukraine in February 2022, when he drafted the lyrics. Gore said it's about 'protecting your inner self from the attacks of the world [and] prefer[ing] to hide somewhere'. The Gore-sung chorus of 'No more, no war' reinforces that. Gore, however, recognised that such retreat is 'rather short-sighted, because we have to accept responsibility [for] our planet's well-being'. It's a slow opener, but a lush track, with deep sonic waves, scratches, and bursts under a heavy, industrial-style production. The insularity of the track echoes the insularity of the lyrics preaching retreat rather than confrontation, self-comfort rather than a difficult conversation. It was the second track heard from *Memento Mori*, released on YouTube exactly one month after lead single 'Ghosts Again'. Where that song was upbeat sonically yet lyrically downbeat, 'My Cosmos Is Mine' reflected the other tones on the album: a reduced tempo (83BPM), darker concerns, and Scott Walker-esque wall-of-sound production, concluding in some reversed Gore vocals, recalling 'Mercy In You'.

'Wagging Tongue' 3:25

Officially, Gore and Gahan have only collaborated directly (outside of extras like 'Long Time Lie' or 'Oh Well') on one Mode album before: 'You Move' from 2017's *Spirit*. 'Wagging Tongue' is their second credit. Heavily electronic, it's perhaps their most 'electro' sound since *Ultra*, channelling *Trans-Europe Express*-era Kraftwerk. Gahan adopts a very nasal delivery for this 1990s throwback. The opening lines suggest a meditation on 'cancel culture': 'You won't do well to silence me/With your words or wagging tongue.' That's reinforced further with the second verse opening: 'I won't be offended/ If I'm left across the great divide.' There's what initially seems a plodding quality here, a relentless one-note beat, but that actually adds to the tune's memorability. 'It's positive,' said Gore of the overall approach on 'Wagging Tongue', 'It's pop, but not too much pop.' This also features the first of three references to 'angels': 'Watch another angel die'. A slow grower.

'Ghosts Again' 3:58

Released on 9 February 2023, 'Ghosts Again' was the first single, offering an initial taste of the first music from the band since the death of Andy Fletcher. With obvious echoes of New Order and the Pet Shop Boys (yet still distinctly Mode-ish), 'Ghosts Again' initially appears simple but gets deeper on repeated listens. It's also the first of four tracks co-written by Gore and Richard Butler of The Psychedelic Furs (the others being 'Don't Say You Love Me', 'My Favourite Stranger', and 'Caroline's Monkey'). Along with the overall 'light' sound, built on soulful guitar and an understated melody, the lyrics, which may initially appear simplistic, and Gahan's upbeat delivery effectively wrap the morbid words in deeper meanings. Synths kick in heavily about two-thirds through, building to an emotional climax. The line 'Everybody says goodbye' particularly hits home, apparently written prior to Fletch's death. A fusion of melancholia and joy, 'Ghosts Again' was the ideal curtain raiser for *Memento Mori*.

Anton Corbijn returned to direct the video for 'Ghosts Again'. In black and white (naturally), the clip opens with Gahan and Gore clad in black hoodies playing chess on a New York rooftop, emulating the 1957 Bergman film *The Seventh Seal*. Corbijn then lays it on thick with Gahan crawling through an artificial graveyard. In the run-up to the release and the tour, the band staged live performances for European and US TV, with 60-year-old Gahan (embracing his greying hair) displaying an infectious enthusiasm. 'Ghosts Again' was the lead track, often paired with 'Wagging Tongue' and/or 'My Favourite Stranger', with 'greatest hits' like 'Personal Jesus' and 'Precious'.

On the UK Singles Chart for 17-23 February, 'Ghosts Again' was a new entry at 20, their highest single performance since 'Wrong' (24 in 2009) and a vast improvement over recent years. The following week, the song had fallen to 56, repeating the pattern of fans snapping up the single in the first week. After just two weeks in the Top 100, 'Ghosts Again' vanished (although it reached thirteen in the US *Billboard* Hot Dance/Electronic and Rock/ Alternative Airplay charts, two on the Adult Alternative Airplay chart – higher than 'Wrong', 'Precious', and 'Dream On' – and one on the Hot Trending Songs Powered by Twitter chart). The CD single release featured a Mode cover of 1974's Gordon Lightfoot song 'Sundown' as a B-side.

'Don't Say You Love Me' 3:44

Opening with some nicely arranged strings, 'Don't Say You Love Me' is another Gore and Butler collaboration that lyrically, and in Gahan's theatrical vocals, draws upon Jacques Brel, Kurt Weill, and Bertold Brecht.

Gahan told Zane Lowe: 'It's very Scott Walker. To me, it's this beautiful torch [song], but I love those kinds of songs. It's like a movie...' Depeche Mode have a long history of movie-inspired songs, whether the actual movie exists or not, and 'Don't Say You Love Me' is the latest of their trademark cinematic synth-blues tracks. It's a 'story' song, abstract enough for the listener to impose their own narrative, but featuring Gore's essential twist-in-the-tale in the clever final lines: 'You'll be the laughter/And I'll be the punchline, of course.' The mid-point instrumental break is an achingly beautiful respite from the despair inferred in the lyrics. Not for the last time on this album, there's something of the classic James Bond theme song here, added to by Gahan's magnificent vocals through the song's second half until the bitterly ironic final lines.

'My Favourite Stranger' 3:55

According to Gahan, 'My Favourite Stranger' is 'about having a shadow, someone who follows you around and tells you things. Do you listen to the lie or the truth?' That's one interpretation, but Gore and Butler's lyrics are open to much wider considerations. One is of split personality, with the 'favourite stranger' as an alternate self. Gore's final lyrical shocker suggests we're actually listening to a killer, a 'favourite stranger' who 'Leaves crime in my wake/And blood on my hands' – as if in being unable to admit to dark deeds, the singer is coming apart. Then again, it could be an alien invasion/body snatchers sci-fi narrative in which a 'perfect stranger' is 'my imitation'. There are intimations of a lack of self-knowledge, the death of the personality or the person you used to be, possibly even a metaphor for Alzheimers. Alternatively, when singing the line 'Puts words in my mouth/All broke and bitter', did it occur to Gahan that his 'perfect stranger' could be songwriter Martin Gore? All this is wrapped up in a plodding rhythm, synths, and static fuzzy guitar work that propels the track to a warped finish.

'Soul With Me' 4:15

Coming at the mid-point, 'Soul With Me' is Gore's big solo ballad: he wrote the track and performs the vaulting vocals. Here's yet more showstopping theatricality, mixed with 1960s pop pioneers, as identified by Gore (in the May 2023 *Uncut*):

> When I was writing it, I felt like it almost had a *Pet Sounds*-era Beach Boys sound mixed with some Kurt Weill chords, but then also a homage to gospel music with its soul-influenced chorus. It's musically a very interesting outlier.

Death is the subject that stalks *Memento Mori*, from that title through the absence of Fletcher and to the lyrics of several tracks. As with 'Ghosts Again', 'Soul With Me' greets that final curtain in an upbeat mode, accepting the inevitability of the end but facing it accompanied by a glam stomp. 'I'm heading for the ever after' declares Gore, followed by references to heading towards 'the light', going 'where the angels fly', being 'ready for the final pages', and 'kissing goodbye to my earthly cages'. At every stage of this evolution into the great beyond, Gore is at pains to point out he's 'taking my soul with me'. It's big and dramatic, an upbeat celebration of life in the face of death. Where 'Ghosts Again' promises a reunion in the afterlife, 'Soul With Me' suggests we'll journey heaven-ward intact, complete with our 'souls', whatever they (or we) may be made from. As *The Quietus* suggested, 'Soul With Me' is a Mode take on 'My Way' and is 'likely to be the new chosen soundtrack to many a Mode fan's cremation'.

'Caroline's Monkey' 4:17
When the *Memento Mori* track listing first appeared, many suspected it was a spoof. That was due to the more-Mode-than-Mode titles like 'People Are Good' and 'Never Let Me Go', riffs on old classics ('People Are People' and 'Never Let Me Down Again'). However, the biggest offender was 'Caroline's Monkey' – surely not a Depeche Mode song title! Well, the track listing turned out to be wholly accurate and 'Caroline's Monkey' joins the short list of Mode songs featuring a woman's name in the title, alongside 'Lilian' and 'Jezebel'. It's also the album's first overt 'drug song', as shown rather literally by the title (and confirmed by Gore: it's about 'a drug addict and addiction, yes'). Drug addiction offers 'no satisfaction' yet promises 'sweetness/Forgiveness, and everything', yet it 'drives like a demon' causing 'ice in her veins', while clawing 'at her back' and 'leaves chaos and ruin'. Overall, though, 'Caroline's Monkey' is ultimately disappointing perhaps due to its musical and lyrical familiarity: it's somehow lesser than the many varied parts it is built from. There are just too many elements that don't cohere, with a delightful chorus that nonetheless sounds like it's from a different song entirely. The chorus suggests each of the unsatisfactory 'better thans' ('fading/falling/folding/fixing') are 'sometimes' (now there's a Mode title) better than offering solutions ('failing/feeling/losing/healing'). An instrumental version might be a decent listen. Co-written between Gore and Butler, the song also functions as a follow-up to The Psychedelic Furs' 'Pretty In Pink', also starring Caroline.

'Before We Drown' 4:08
The propulsive opening of 'Before We Drown' marks the start of a suite of classic Mode songs, a run of four tracks that incorporate sounds of the past with the band's modern voice. Written by Gahan, with touring musicians Gordeno and Eiger, it's four minutes of classic Mode, so much so that *The Quietus* commented: '"Before We Drown" feels so imbued with Depeche Mode-ness that it's almost an AI interpretation of Depeche Mode.' (Notably, in 2003 musician/comic Liam Lynch released an album of 'fake' songs, including a spot-on 'Fake Depeche Mode Song'.) There's some truth there, but the

153

familiar 'Mode-ness' of the twangs and thrums is counterpointed with the soulfulness of Gahan's vocals. The lyrics capture a simple feeling of evolution, the need to learn from failure, and the ability to move forward: 'First, we stand up, then we fall down/We have to move forward, before we drown'. From a tentative start, Gahan developed the knack of writing songs that could have come from no other band. Perhaps he helps keep Martin Gore on his toes? After all, 'Before We Drown' was, according to *Rolling Stone*, 'another stand-out track'.

'People Are Good' 4:24
The delightfully cynical 'People Are Good' plays like a 21st-century response to 1984's 'People Are People', as Dave Gahan seemed to accept (speaking to Portuguese publication *Expresso*):

> In fact, in a way, they both say pretty much the same thing. Not much has changed over the past 40 years. Why is there all this hate and all this fear? The question is always the same. But this new song is a bit different, because we thought it was quite funny to say that 'people are good' and then add: 'keep fooling yourself'. This phrase, 'people are good', is repeated many times, and what we ask is: are people actually good?

Amid *Music For The Masses* soundscapes, *Computer World*-era Kraftwerk, and the scratchy, distorted tyre screech riff that recalls 'I Feel You', the answer seems to be 'No, not really'. The switch from the earlier 'Keep reminding myself/That people are good' to the later 'Keep fooling yourself/People are good' turns the question around on the listener. 'People Are Good' – pure, distilled Gore – features the return of the personal politics, the focus on relationships between people, and questions about their motivations that have driven so much of the Mode back catalogue.

'Always You' 4:19
With 'Always You', Depeche Mode remastered the mix of the personal and the political, merging the latter with the overwhelming importance of the escape into personal relationships. The political content is obvious, if less starkly presented than on *Spirit*: 'The world's upside down... no solid ground... there are no more facts... reality's cracked' and 'there are no more words... life's too absurd... I could not explain... why insanity reigns'. This is wrapped up in a sonic blanket of early Depeche Mode sounds and sweeping themes that, according to *Rolling Stone*, were 'reminiscent of their tumultuous 1993 long-player *Songs Of Faith And Devotion*'. These political concerns are anchored in a relationship, where one partner relies on the other to be 'The light that leads me from the darkness' – a classic Depeche Mode line if ever there was one. The song builds to an ecstatic finale, with Gahan's repeated cries of 'Always You' pushed to the limit of tolerance.

'Never Let Me Go' 4:04

A confident, aggressive banger seemingly designed for stadium play, 'Never Let Me Go' is the finest Depeche Mode track for a long time, and easily both the best and the most traditional on *Memento Mori*. Amid the splats and hisses, the opening distinctive guitar riff recalls Adrian Borland's highly-underrated early-1980s outfit The Sound. There are wider echoes of *Black Celebration* amid the noises here, with the distorted guitars recalling both *Songs Of Faith And Devotion* and *Ultra*. It's one of those songs sung by Dave where he's apparently in pursuit of another: 'I'm waiting for your love/I know you'll want me' and 'It was plain from the start/You've been running from me'. However, what comes through even stronger than that familiar lustful Mode territory is the sense of time as a precious resource that mustn't be squandered: 'There's only so much time/We have to play with/To waste it is a crime/We have so much to give'. This is a songwriter – Gore, the older of the pairing – coming to terms with his own mortality, and the idea that he might be in the final quarter of life. The battle between 'light' and 'dark' referenced on 'Always You' and another reference to angels ('The angels will praise us') – the third song to do so, alongside 'Wagging Tongue' and 'Soul With Me' – suggest conscious echoes of *Playing The Angel*.

'Speak To Me' 4:37

Album closer 'Speak To Me' is an all-hands-to-the-pump production. It began life as a song idea from Dave Gahan, which he co-wrote with Christian Eiger, before turning it over to Gore and producers James Ford and Marta Salogni, who developed it further:

> Initially, the idea sort of came to me, and the song was incredibly elevated by Martin, James, and Marta, into a different place, to another world, somewhere else. That's exactly where I wanted the song to go as well. It was beyond what I could have really put together myself... Marta is a genius with tape looping and using analogue tape to create these loops.

Gahan saw the track as the perfect bookend to opener 'My Cosmos Is Mine' in that it responds to current world events and specifically the absence of reasonable leadership. 'I'm actually not referring to any of the leaders that we have right now,' noted Gahan of his lyrics to Portugal's *Expresso*, 'I'm talking about something that is not a person, but our conscience. I believe that we always know what the right thing to do is, but we invariably end up making the wrong choices.' The song cries out for 'some kind of plan' to right the world, a 'drug of choice' that will 'turn it all around'. That also refers to 'the power of disappearing with a drug' (as Gahan told *Mojo*). Gahan dubbed his lyrics, especially his Gore-like conclusion ('I'm listening, I'm here now, I'm found'), as 'sarcastic', but that might be a shield for the exposure of wearing your heart on your sleeve. 'There's an absolute peace

155

and joy in the emptiness of the end... And we just came to the conclusion that it should just be the end.'

Like several previous Mode album cappers (primarily 'Goodbye' from *Delta Machine*), 'Speak To Me' builds (across a final minute-and-20-seconds) to 'A Day in the Life' Beatles-like climax. Although along the way it summons elements of *Songs Of Faith And Devotion*, there's something off about 'Speak To Me'. It's slow, majestic, and classical, with electronic bleeps (some notably familiar) zapping in at the halfway point, but it's somehow less than it should be. For *The Quietus*, death was once more everywhere on *Memento Mori*: 'Closer "Speak To Me"... pulses towards discordancy, reminding you that with the flip-side of bittersweetness comes the inevitable ends that we all must face'. Like a lot of tracks on *Memento Mori*, 'Speak To Me' will no doubt prove to be a grower. If nothing else, across the past four decades fans have learned that repeated listening gives almost any Depeche Mode track 'New Life'.

Bibliography

Baker, T., *Dave Gahan: Depeche Mode & The Second Coming* (Independent Music Press, 2009)

Baker, T., *Depeche Mode: The Early Years 1981–1993* (Independent Music Press, 2013)

Christopher, M., *Depeche Mode FAQ* (Backbeat, 2020)

Gittins, I., *Depeche Mode: Faith and Devotion* (Palazzo Editions, 2019)

Malins, S., *Depeche Mode: The Biography* (André Deutsch, 2013)

May, K. & McElroy, D., *Halo: The Story Behind Depeche Mode's Classic Album Violator* (Grosvenor House, 2022)

Miller, J., *Stripped: Depeche Mode* (Omnibus Press, 2008)

Spence, S., *Just Can't Get Enough: The Making of Depeche Mode* (Jawbone, 2011)

Works Consulted

Special Depeche Mode issues of *Record Collector*, *Classic Pop*, *Uncut* and *Q* magazines

Websites Consulted

Wikipedia, Almost Predictable Almost, DMLive Wiki, depmode.com, oldsite. recoil.co.uk, loudersound.com, imdb.com, tunefind.com, classicpopmag.com, youtube.com, vimeo.com, davegahandevotion.com, archivesdepechemode. com, thequietus.com, officialcharts.com, depeche-mode.com, dmremix.pro

Also available from Sonicbond

On Track series

Alan Parsons Project – Steve Swift
978-1-78952-154-2
Tori Amos – Lisa Torem 978-1-78952-142-9
Asia – Peter Braidis 978-1-78952-099-6
Badfinger – Robert Day-Webb
978-1-878952-176-4
Barclay James Harvest – Keith and Monica
Domone 978-1-78952-067-5
The Beatles – Andrew Wild 978-1-78952-009-5
The Beatles Solo 1969-1980 – Andrew Wild
978-1-78952-030-9
Blue Oyster Cult – Jacob Holm-Lupo
978-1-78952-007-1
Blur – Matt Bishop – 978-178952-164-1
Marc Bolan and T.Rex – Peter Gallagher
978-1-78952-124-5
Kate Bush – Bill Thomas 978-1-78952-097-2
Camel – Hamish Kuzminski 978-1-78952-040-8
Caravan – Andy Boot 978-1-78952-127-6
Cardiacs – Eric Benac 978-1-78952-131-3
Eric Clapton Solo – Andrew Wild
978-1-78952-141-2
The Clash – Nick Assirati 978-1-78952-077-4
Crosby, Stills and Nash – Andrew Wild
978-1-78952-039-2
The Damned – Morgan Brown
978-1-78952-136-8
Deep Purple and Rainbow 1968-79 –
Steve Pilkington 978-1-78952-002-6
Dire Straits – Andrew Wild 978-1-78952-044-6
The Doors – Tony Thompson
978-1-78952-137-5
Dream Theater – Jordan Blum
978-1-78952-050-7
Electric Light Orchestra – Barry Delve
978-1-78952-152-8
Elvis Costello and The Attractions –
Georg Purvis 978-1-78952-129-0
Emerson Lake and Palmer – Mike Goode
978-1-78952-000-2
Fairport Convention – Kevan Furbank
978-1-78952-051-4
Peter Gabriel – Graeme Scarfe
978-1-78952-138-2
Genesis – Stuart MacFarlane 978-1-78952-005-7
Gentle Giant – Gary Steel 978-1-78952-058-3
Gong – Kevan Furbank 978-1-78952-082-8
Hall and Oates – Ian Abrahams
978-1-78952-167-2
Hawkwind – Duncan Harris 978-1-78952-052-1
Peter Hammill – Richard Rees Jones
978-1-78952-163-4

Roy Harper – Opher Goodwin
978-1-78952-130-6
Jimi Hendrix – Emma Stott 978-1-78952-175-7
The Hollies – Andrew Darlington
978-1-78952-159-7
Iron Maiden – Steve Pilkington
978-1-78952-061-3
Jefferson Airplane – Richard Butterworth
978-1-78952-143-6
Jethro Tull – Jordan Blum 978-1-78952-016-3
Elton John in the 1970s – Peter Kearns
978-1-78952-034-7
The Incredible String Band – Tim Moon
978-1-78952-107-8
Iron Maiden – Steve Pilkington
978-1-78952-061-3
Judas Priest – John Tucker 978-1-78952-018-7
Kansas – Kevin Cummings 978-1-78952-057-6
The Kinks – Martin Hutchinson
978-1-78952-172-6
Korn – Matt Karpe 978-1-78952-153-5
Led Zeppelin – Steve Pilkington
978-1-78952-151-1
Level 42 – Matt Philips 978-1-78952-102-3
Little Feat – 978-1-78952-168-9
Aimee Mann – Jez Rowden 978-1-78952-036-1
Joni Mitchell – Peter Kearns 978-1-78952-081-1
The Moody Blues – Geoffrey Feakes
978-1-78952-042-2
Motorhead – Duncan Harris 978-1-78952-173-3
Mike Oldfield – Ryan Yard 978-1-78952-060-6
Opeth – Jordan Blum 978-1-78-952-166-5
Tom Petty – Richard James 978-1-78952-128-3
Porcupine Tree – Nick Holmes
978-1-78952-144-3
Queen – Andrew Wild 978-1-78952-003-3
Radiohead – William Allen 978-1-78952-149-8
Renaissance – David Detmer 978-1-78952-062-0
The Rolling Stones 1963-80 – Steve Pilkington
978-1-78952-017-0
The Smiths and Morrissey –
Tommy Gunnarsson 978-1-78952-140-5
Status Quo the Frantic Four Years –
Richard James 978-1-78952-160-3
Steely Dan – Jez Rowden 978-1-78952-043-9
Steve Hackett – Geoffrey Feakes
978-1-78952-098-9
Thin Lizzy – Graeme Stroud
978-1-78952-064-4
Toto – Jacob Holm-Lupo 978-1-78952-019-4
U2 – Eoghan Lyng 978-1-78952-078-1
UFO – Richard James 978-1-78952-073-6
The Who – Geoffrey Feakes 978-1-78952-076-7

Roy Wood and the Move – James R Turner
978-1-78952-008-8
Van Der Graaf Generator – Dan Coffey
978-1-78952-031-6
Yes – Stephen Lambe 978-1-78952-001-9
Frank Zappa 1966 to 1979 – Eric Benac
978-1-78952-033-0
Warren Zevon – Peter Gallagher
978-1-78952-170-2
10CC – Peter Kearns 978-1-78952-054-5

Decades Series
The Bee Gees in the 1960s –
Andrew Môn Hughes et al 978-1-78952-148-1
The Bee Gees in the 1970s –
Andrew Môn Hughes et al 978-1-78952-179-5
Black Sabbath in the 1970s – Chris Sutton
978-1-78952-171-9
Britpop – Peter Richard Adams and
Matt Pooler 978-1-78952-169-6
Alice Cooper in the 1970s – Chris Sutton
978-1-78952-104-7
Curved Air in the 1970s – Laura Shenton
978-1-78952-069-9
Bob Dylan in the 1980s – Don Klees
978-1-78952-157-3
Fleetwood Mac in the 1970s – Andrew Wild
978-1-78952-105-4
Focus in the 1970s – Stephen Lambe
978-1-78952-079-8
Free and Bad Company in the 1970s –
John Van der Kiste 978-1-78952-178-8
Genesis in the 1970s – Bill Thomas
978178952-146-7
George Harrison in the 1970s – Eoghan Lyng
978-1-78952-174-0
Marillion in the 1980s – Nathaniel Webb
978-1-78952-065-1
Mott the Hoople and Ian Hunter in the 1970s –
John Van der Kiste 978-1-78-952-162-7
Pink Floyd In The 1970s – Georg Purvis
978-1-78952-072-9
Tangerine Dream in the 1970s –
Stephen Palmer 978-1-78952-161-0
The Sweet in the 1970s – Darren Johnson from
Gary Cosby collection 978-1-78952-139-9
Uriah Heep in the 1970s – Steve Pilkington
978-1-78952-103-0
Yes in the 1980s – Stephen Lambe with
David Watkinson 978-1-78952-125-2

On Screen series
Carry On... – Stephen Lambe 978-1-78952-004-0

David Cronenberg – Patrick Chapman
978-1-78952-071-2
Doctor Who: The David Tennant Years –
Jamie Hailstone 978-1-78952-066-8
James Bond – Andrew Wild –
978-1-78952-010-1
Monty Python – Steve Pilkington
978-1-78952-047-7
Seinfeld Seasons 1 to 5 – Stephen Lambe
978-1-78952-012-5

Other Books
1967: A Year In Psychedelic Rock –
Kevan Furbank 978-1-78952-155-9
1970: A Year In Rock – John Van der Kiste
978-1-78952-147-4
1973: The Golden Year of Progressive Rock
978-1-78952-165-8
Babysitting A Band On The Rocks –
G.D. Praetorius 978-1-78952-106-1
Eric Clapton Sessions – Andrew Wild
978-1-78952-177-1
Derek Taylor: For Your Radioactive Children –
Andrew Darlington 978-1-78952-038-5
The Golden Road: The Recording History of
The Grateful Dead – John Kilbride
978-1-78952-156-6
Iggy and The Stooges On Stage 1967-1974 –
Per Nilsen 978-1-78952-101-6
Jon Anderson and the Warriors – the road to
Yes – David Watkinson 978-1-78952-059-0
Nu Metal: A Definitive Guide – Matt Karpe
978-1-78952-063-7
Tommy Bolin: In and Out of Deep Purple –
Laura Shenton 978-1-78952-070-5
Maximum Darkness – Deke Leonard
978-1-78952-048-4
Maybe I Should've Stayed In Bed –
Deke Leonard 978-1-78952-053-8
The Twang Dynasty – Deke Leonard
978-1-78952-049-1

and many more to come!

Would you like to write for Sonicbond Publishing?

At Sonicbond Publishing we are always on the look-out for authors, particularly for our two main series:

On Track. Mixing fact with in depth analysis, the On Track series examines the work of a particular musical artist or group. All genres are considered from easy listening and jazz to 60s soul to 90s pop, via rock and metal.

On Screen. This series looks at the world of film and television. Subjects considered include directors, actors and writers, as well as entire television and film series. As with the On Track series, we balance fact with analysis.

While professional writing experience would, of course, be an advantage the most important qualification is to have real enthusiasm and knowledge of your subject. First-time authors are welcomed, but the ability to write well in English is essential.

Sonicbond Publishing has distribution throughout Europe and North America, and all books are also published in E-book form. Authors will be paid a royalty based on sales of their book.

Further details are available from www.sonicbondpublishing.co.uk. To contact us, complete the contact form there or
email info@sonicbondpublishing.co.uk